# The Global Crisis in Foreign Aid

*Space, Place, and Society*
John Rennie Short, Series Editor

# The Global Crisis
# in Foreign Aid

*Edited by*
Richard Grant and Jan Nijman

*With a Foreword by*
John Rennie Short

Syracuse University Press

The paper used in this publication meets the minimum requirements of American
National Standard for Information Sciences—Permanence of Paper for Printed
Library Materials, ANSI Z39.48-1984.♾

LIBRARY OF CONGRESS CATALOGING-IN-PUBLICATION DATA

The global crisis in foreign aid / edited by Richard Grant and Jan Nijman. — 1st ed.
      p. cm. — (Space, place, and society)
      Includes bibliographical references and index.
      ISBN 0-8156-2771-8 (cloth : alk. paper).
      1. Economic assistance.  I. Grant, Richard.  II. Nijman, Jan.  III. Series.
   HC60.G534    1998
   338.91—dc21                                                        97-33567

Manufactured in the United States of America

*To the memory of Marcelo Méndez
and Elizabeth Sotelo de Méndez.*

# Contents

Part Five
*Conclusion*

# Tables

# Figures

# Maps

# Foreword

## John Rennie Short

At the end of the second millennium, foreign aid debates are mired in controversy. These debates go beyond foreign policy issues or budgetary concerns and address the fundamental question of the global nature of our existence. As global citizens, as citizens of individual countries, and as individuals, we are still highly divided by race, class, gender, and opportunities in global society. At the same time, we see ourselves as increasingly connected through our shared occupancy of the same planet. In order to capture these relationships, terms such as the global economy, global culture, global society, and regime change are widely employed by academics and commentators. "Global" has become an adjective, a goal, a source of change, a setting for a New World Order. In scholarly thinking about international development, Globalism has replaced Progress as the dominant metanarrative.

In this volume, Richard Grant and Jan Nijman bring together a set of deliberations that move beyond vague assertions about the workings of this global community in foreign aid. In examining aid policies, payments, and politics, they draw attention to an important link between different countries and different parts of the world. Foreign aid concerns not only a transfer of money, goods, and services: it is about the definition of development. Subsumed under the aid regime are obligations that reflect and embody power relations in the global community. The transfer of funds via foreign aid is an important redistribution mechanism in the creation and evolution of the global order. The two editors are to be congratulated for bringing together a wide range of contributors who look at both the evolution and likely trajectory of aid, the donors as well as the recipients of aid, and the changing role of aid in the New World Order. Their volume is global in scope and includes chapters on the donor aid policies and recipient experiences from all of the major world regions.

This timely work stands out in the scholarly literature on foreign aid because of the inclusion of contributors from eight policy representatives from a range of prominent donor and recipient countries (United States, Japan, Netherlands, Bolivia, Egypt, Bangladesh, El Salvador, and Poland). In this way, the book provides a view inside the foreign aid policy process, as well as concrete perspectives on the changing aid priorities of selected donors and recipients.

Ultimately, the crisis of foreign aid is a reflection of a broader crisis in our global society. Foreign aid is an important mechanism that links and divides, connects and separates diverse parts of the world. These connections have political, economic, and moral implications. This examination of the changing nature of the aid regime reveals the strains and conflicts in our evolving global community.

# Contributors

*J. Brian Atwood* is Administrator of the United States Agency for International Development, Washington D.C. He simultaneously holds positions as President Clinton's Coordinator for Disaster Assistance, as Under Secretary of State for Management, and as Chairman of the Overseas Private Investment Cooperation Board.

*Peter Boone* is Lecturer at the London School of Economics and Program Director for the Post Communist Reform Program at the Center for Economic Performance. He has written extensively on the topic of foreign aid.

*Youssef Boutros-Ghali* is Minister of State at the Council of Ministers for International Cooperation in Egypt. He was formerly Associate Professor of Economics at Cairo University and Economic Advisor to the Prime Minister and to the Governor of the Central Bank. His ministry oversees all development cooperation projects in Egypt.

*Anwarul Karim Chowdhury* is Executive Director of UNICEF in New York. He has served in a variety of executive functions on the staff of the United Nations and in the Ministry of Foreign Affairs of Bangladesh. From 1986 to 1990 he was Ambassador of Bangladesh to the United Nations.

*Ton Dietz* is Professor of Geography at the University of Amsterdam, with a specialization in development problems. His research interests are in pastoralism, semiarid lands, development assistance, and nongovernmental organizations.

*Alasdair Drysdale* is Professor of Geography at the University of New Hampshire. He has written extensively on the Middle East for American and European journals. His books include *The Middle East and North Africa: A Political Geography* (1985) and *Syria and the Middle East Process* (1991).

*Jean-Paul Faguet* studied public policy and economics at Princeton University and Harvard University. Formerly he worked at the World Bank's Bolivia Resident Mission, where he supervised developmental and environmental projects. He is currently a Ph.D. candidate at the Development Studies Institute of the London School of Economics.

*Richard Grant* is Associate Professor of Geography at the Maxwell School of Citizenship and Public Affairs, Syracuse University. His research interests include the geography of foreign aid, international trade, and economic globalization. He is a former Pew Faculty Fellow at Harvard University and the recipient of the Daniel Patrick Moynihan Award for 1996–97.

*Sven Holdar* is former Director of Yale University's Civic Education Project in Kiev. He specializes in geopolitics, regime theory, and the politics of foreign aid. His recent publications focus on the political and economic transitions in East Europe and the Soviet Union. He is the author of *The Evolution of Foreign Aid Regimes* (1998).

*John Houtkamp,* University of Amsterdam, is Research Associate at the African Studies Center in Leiden, The Netherlands. His research interests are in the political geography of Africa, the political economy of tropical produce, and human rights issues.

*Marnix Krop* is Director of the Strategic Policy Orientation Unit of the Ministry of Foreign Affairs in The Netherlands. He formerly held high-level positions in the policy planning staffs of the Ministry of Defense and the Ministry of Foreign Affairs. He is a key advisor to the Ministers of Development Cooperation and Foreign Affairs on Dutch foreign aid policy.

*William M. LeoGrande* is Professor of Government in the School of Public Affairs at American University in Washington, D.C. He writes on Latin American politics and U.S.–Latin American relations. He is coauthor of *Confronting Revolution* (1986) and *Political Parties and Democracy in Central America* (1990).

*Mirna Liévano de Marques* is Director of the Escuela Superior de Economíca y Negocios in San Salvador and former President of the Social Investment Fund of the Salvadoran Government. She has held many prominent positions in the Ministry of Economics and the Ministry of Planning as well as in public institutions involved in economic and social development.

*Marcelo Méndez Ferry* was Deputy Secretary of the Directorate of Public Investment and External Finance of the Ministry of Economics in Bolivia. Mr. Méndez and his wife died tragically in an accident before publication of this book. This work is dedicated to them.

*Wieslaw Michalak* is Associate Professor of Geography at Ryerson Polytechnic University in Canada. He studied geography and philosophy in Poland, England, and France and formerly held positions at universities in Australia and England. His main research interests are in philosophy, industrial society, and the transformations in East Europe. His recent publications focus on regional economic integration and liberalization policies in East Europe.

*Krzysztof J. Ners* is Professor of Development Economics at the Warsaw School of Economics and Director of the Policy Education Centre on Assistance to Transition, Warsaw. He specializes in the transformation from centrally planned economies to free markets and in the role of foreign assistance. Most recently, he wrote *Assistance to Transition 1995 Survey*.

*Jan Nijman* is Professor of Geography at the University of Miami. His research includes geopolitics, foreign policy, world cities, and the process of globalization. He is the author of *The Geopolitics of Power and Conflict* (1993) and *The Global Moment in Urban Evolution* (1996).

*Leo van Grunsven* is Assistant Professor of Geography at the University of Utrecht, The Netherlands. From 1985 to 1990 he was professor at the National University of Singapore. He is also the former editor of the *Journal for Economic and Social Geography*. His interests are in development and regional economics in Asia. He is the editor of *Regional Change in the Asian Pacific Rim* (1998).

*August van Westen* is Assistant Professor of Geography at the University of Utrecht, The Netherlands. Previously, he worked as an advisor in several United Nations Development Programme (UNDP) projects in Malaysia and at the UN headquarters in New York. His research focuses on industrial restructuring and trade in the Asian Pacific region. He is the editor of *Manufacturing Mosaics: Regional Industrialization Patterns in Developing Countries* (1999).

*Hiroyuki Yanagitsubo* is Executive Director of the Association for Promotion of International Cooperation, which is part of Japan's Ministry of Foreign Affairs. He previously held positions with the Asian Development Bank.

# Abbreviations

| | |
|---|---|
| ACP | Africa, the Caribbean, and the Pacific |
| APEC | Asia Pacific Economic Cooperation |
| *ARB* | *Africa Research Bulletin* |
| ASEAN | Association of South East Asian Nations |
| CEE | Central and Eastern Europe |
| CFA | Communauté Financière Africaine |
| CMEA | Council for Mutual Economic Assistance |
| CPR | Component plus residual |
| DAC | Development Assistance Committee |
| EBRD | European Bank for Reconstruction and Development |
| EC | European Community |
| ECU | European Currency Unit |
| EDF | European Development Fund |
| EIB | European Investment Bank |
| EPA | Economic Planning Agency |
| EPU | European Political Union |
| ESF | Economic Support Fund |
| EU | European Union |
| FAA | Foreign Assistance Act |
| FDI | Foreign Direct Investment |
| FMLN | Frente Farabundo Martí para la Liberacíon Nacional |
| FMS | Foreign military sales |
| FSA | Freedom Support Act |
| G-7 | Group of 7 |
| G-24 | Group of 24 |
| GAO | General Accounting Office |
| GATT | General Agreement on Tariffs and Trade |
| GDI | Gross domestic investment |
| GDP | Gross domestic product |
| GNI | Gross national income |
| GNP | Gross national product |

| | |
|---|---|
| GSP | Generalized System of Preferences |
| IBRD | International Bank for Reconstruction and Development (World Bank) |
| ICORC | International Conference on the Reconstruction of Cambodia |
| IDA | International Development Association |
| IDB | Inter-American Development Bank |
| IFC | International Finance Corporation |
| IMF | International Monetary Fund |
| JICA | Japan International Cooperation Agency |
| LDCs | Least-developed countries |
| LICs | Lowest-income countries |
| MITI | Ministry of International Trade and Industry |
| MOF | Ministry of Finance |
| MOFA | Ministry of Foreign Affairs |
| NAFTA | North American Free Trade Agreement |
| NGO | Nongovernmental organization |
| NICs | Newly industrializing countries |
| NIE | Newly industrializing economy |
| NIS | Newly independent states |
| OAPEC | Organization of Arab Petroleum Exporting Countries |
| ODA | Official development assistance |
| OECD | Organization for Economic Cooperation and Development |
| PHARE | Poland and Hungary: Assistance for Reconstructing Economies |
| PPDA | Peace, Prosperity, and Democracy Act |
| PRK | People's Republic of Kampuchea |
| SAI | Special Assistance Initiatives |
| SAL | Structural adjustment loan |
| SAP | Structural adjustment program |
| SEED | Support for East European Democracies |
| SLORC | State Law and Order Restoration Council |
| TACIS | Technical Assistance for the Commonwealth of Independent States |
| UNCED | United Nations Conference on Environment and Development |
| UNCTAD | United Nations Commission for Trade and Development |
| UNDP | United Nations Development Programme |
| UNECE | United Nations Economic Commission for Europe |
| UNHCR | United Nations High Commission on Refugees |
| UNO | United Nicaraguan Opposition |
| USAID | United States Agency for International Development |

# Part One

## *The Nature of the Crisis in Foreign Aid*

# The Foreign Aid Regime in Flux
## *Crisis or Transition?*

### Richard Grant and Jan Nijman

SINCE THE SECOND WORLD WAR, foreign aid has become an insti-
tutionalized part of international relations. Beginning with the
Marshall Plan in the late forties, aid has become a common foreign policy instrument of donors and has accounted for an important source of
income for many developing countries. By 1990 foreign aid flows to developing countries accounted for $72 billion, their highest levels ever
(World Bank 1995, 3). Virtually all countries have received aid at one
time or another. Even the current largest bilateral donor, Japan, received
aid after World War II to help finance the construction of the bullet train
project.

Throughout the postwar period foreign aid as a policy tool has
evolved in the ways it is provided, and the importance of various donors
and recipients has shifted. The present era of change, however, is unprecedented. Beginning in the late 1980s and early 1990s, domestic debates in donor countries coincided with watershed changes in the global
geopolitical environment. Consequently, donors faced a whole new set of
demands for aid giving. For instance, public and parliamentary support
for aid waned as electorates became preoccupied with domestic issues
such as urban decay, crime, and drugs. Some aid agencies struggled to
justify their expenditures, and aid budgets became increasingly diluted
by new demands, such as the environment, refugees, drug trafficking
prevention, and the promotion of democracy.

On the recipient side there has been a significant turnover in potential candidates for aid, mostly from former Cold War allies to additional claimants in the newly democratic states. As a result, recipients are now concerned that their aid programs are being squeezed by too many competing donor interests and commitments. Also, the continued economic stagnation and aid addictions of a number of recipients have raised serious questions about the effects of prolonged assistance. Academic research on foreign aid has, in addition, unveiled many incidents of failures, development disasters, and misappropriated funds (e.g., Lappé, Collins, and Kinley 1981).

In this book we discuss the changing role of foreign aid in the context of the transforming global order. The term *aid* is used in accordance with the Organization for Economic Cooperation and Development (OECD) definition: those flows to countries and multilateral institutions provided by official agencies and governments. Each international transaction must satisfy two conditions. First, aid must be administered so that its main objectives are the promotion of economic development and the welfare of the recipient. Second, aid must be concessional in character (typically with interest rates below the market rate) and contain a grant element of at least 25 percent of the total aid package. Recently a newer objective of assisting transitions to liberal democracy has been added. In terms of foreign assistance, aid usually refers to medium-term development assistance (five- to ten-year projects).

Part 1 reviews the nature of the crisis in foreign aid. Part 2 concentrates on the reorientation of foreign aid policies of major global donors, and part 3 examines the changing role of foreign aid in regions. The donor accounts of foreign aid are based on both quantitative analyses of foreign aid data and qualitative analyses of official publications; they also refer to domestic debates. The concentration is on bilateral aid, whose volume is much larger than that of multilateral aid: on average, around 70 percent of OECD aid is bilateral.

In the recipient chapters, all major forms of aid—including multilateral assistance—from all sources are considered. Multilateral assistance includes donations channeled through multilateral development agencies, such as the World Bank and regional development banks (e.g., the African, Asian, and Inter-American Development Banks). These chapters examine the changing volumes, types, and emphases of aid and the various aid destinations and sources within regions.

Part 4 presents the views of foreign aid practitioners representing different official points of view across the world. It should be noted that these writings represent individual views and may not necessarily reflect the official views of the agencies that employ the practitioners. Part 5, the conclusion, provides assessments of the character and foci of the new foreign aid regime and of the new emerging order.

By combining two levels of analysis (donor and recipient) in this book as well as the views from academic researchers and aid practitioners, we offer a synthesis of views on foreign aid that we hope will be a significant contribution to contemporary knowledge on foreign assistance.

## The Foreign Aid Regime

In the foreign aid process, we can observe principles, norms, rules, and decision-making procedures around which donors and recipients' expectations revolve and can explain their occurrence by the existence of an international aid regime (Holdar 1993a, 455). Because of the loose character of the rules and organization and the varying coherence, this regime is more flexible than its counterpart in trade and monetary relations.

States adhere to the regime's norms and principles even though such adherence confines their independent decision-making powers. Participants of the regime act under constraints of bounded rationality: the regime does not substitute for continuous calculations of self-interest but instead makes for rules of thumb to which governments comply (Holdar 1993a). The existence of a hegemony (one state dominating the international system politically, economically, and culturally) is also important for the creation and maintenance of the regime, but the regime can outlast a hegemonic order (Holdar 1993a). Subsumed in the aid regime is an elite ideology of economics and politics such that an establishment consensus, typically held by OECD leaders, the World Bank, the International Monetary Fund (IMF), and other influential international organizations, frames that regime. Currently, the development policy consensus favors market forces, export-led growth, and good governance.

The foreign aid regime originated during the ideological confrontation between the United States and the Soviet Union. The Western aid system began formally in 1961 with the establishment of the Development Assistance Committee (DAC) of the OECD. Using aid to encourage recipients to align themselves with the Western camp, OECD donors

Greece
Turkey
1947.

also hoped to deter any experiments with socialism. In addition, OECD donors employed aid to respond to the disintegration of European empires and the formation of newly independent states. In general, they disbursed aid for recipients to pursue a capitalist development model and (re)create their economies as a simulacrum of the Western model.

Foreign aid is a useful policy instrument because it is relatively benign, flexible, and multipurpose. In the past, donors accepted to varying degrees the modernist paradigm of development, which was imbued with a belief in growth, progress, and social engineering. Donors additionally were motivated by a combination of concerns: geopolitical or geostrategic (Lebovic 1988; Orr 1990), economic (Hook 1995), special relationship and regional clustering (McKinlay and Little 1978; Holdar 1993b), and humanitarian (Lumsdaine 1993). Political motives were always present in aid giving because they realized public relations effects; placated domestic constituencies (politically liberal and immigrant); generally improved relations with recipients, fellow donors, and multilateral organizations; and served as a diplomatic tool to exert diplomatic pressure. Moreover, large donations improved the donors' national prestige and helped cultivate great power status (Orr 1990).

The old foreign aid regime has withered, and there is as yet no new and stable set of prevailing rules to guide foreign aid policies for either donors or recipients. Of course, in some important ways foreign aid policies are only part of the wider problem of redefining a state's foreign policy and "geopolitical codes." In our view, as long as many states have not redefined their general foreign policy interests in the aftermath of the Cold War, it is unlikely that donors can present purposeful foreign aid policies. For both donors and recipients, the question is whether they value foreign aid and, if so, how to apply it to further their interests. The foreign aid regime is entering a crisis as well as a transition. Most recipient countries have failed to develop in the modernist sense (i.e., they were unable to replicate the same Western stages of growth or development experiences). The foreign aid crisis may be symptomatic of a larger paradigm shift in how we conceptualize the world and global development.

In chapter 2, Boone and Faguet examine multilateral aid and the role of foreign aid in reducing poverty. They suggest that even though multilateral aid was not used very successfully during the Cold War, many lessons have been learned. Accordingly, they offer ways in which multilateral aid (short-, medium-, and long-term) may be used more effectively to reduce poverty in the future.

## Adjusting for the New Aid Regime

Both donors and recipients are adjusting to the geopolitical transition in unique ways. Part 2 of the book looks at donors. In chapter 3, Nijman examines the evolution and development of United States foreign aid policy. The tone and emphasis of Washington's assistance is undergoing some important changes from its Cold War underpinnings toward facilitating the New World Order and the United States' role in it. Domestic pressures such as aid fatigue, budgetary strains, and a Republican-dominated Congress also complicate aid reorientation.

In chapter 4, Grant looks at the spectacular transition of Japan from postwar aid recipient to the largest bilateral foreign aid donor by late 1980s. Japan stands alone among bilateral aid donors in favoring increased aid contributions for the twenty-first century. In contrast to others, high levels of domestic support for foreign assistance are evident there, and the government views aid as multipurposeful in addressing Japan's global concerns.

Holdar in chapter 5 examines the evolution and development of European Union (EU) aid policies and their responses to recent geopolitical change. More complicated than other donors' foreign aid policies, EU foreign assistance reflects individual aid preferences and emphases as well as Community-wide policy emphases. EU foreign aid (re)orientation takes into consideration how fifteen individual donors coordinate at the EU level as well as legitimize their individual foreign aid programs. Accordingly, EU foreign aid policies reflect both major developments internal to the Union and changes in geopolitical order.

Part 3 of the book looks at the recipient side and the reordering of the lineup of potential aid beneficiaries there. Middle Eastern recipients are examined in detail by Drysdale in chapter 6. Not only have these recipients been affected by the geopolitical transition, but events such as oil crises and the Gulf War also have a unique impact on the region and the role of individual countries, both regionally and internationally.

African recipients too have been affected by the change in global order. As Dietz and Houtkampf note in chapter 7, some have been abandoned as Cold War orphans (notably Zaire and Somalia), and others risk being forsaken for their failure to foster development and for their aid addictions (notably Mozambique and Angola). Foreign aid appears to be contributing to institutional inertia inside African governments and to have removed incentives for progressive change.

In chapter 8, LeoGrande addresses aid to Central American recipients. Aid was traditionally viewed by recipients as essential to bolstering stability amid regional economic and former military crises in Nicaragua and El Salvador. The geopolitical transition has encouraged reductions of United States assistance to the region, and the size of EU and Japanese aid programs now rival Washington's.

The end of the Cold War had fundamental consequences for the roles of Eastern Europe and the former Soviet Union, which switched from being aid donors to aid recipients. As Michalak discusses in chapter 9, a complete reversal of Western attitudes and policies to the region transpired. Most aid to the region is now designated for a new category of foreign assistance—to assist transitions to market and liberal democracies.

Van Grunsven and van Westen, in their examination of foreign aid to the Asia-Pacific Rim in chapter 10, note that some former recipients of the region (notably Japan and South Korea) have graduated to donor status and are beginning to advocate an Asian development model for global development. These authors also discuss the unevenness of development in the region and the significance of aid to Asian development.

Part 4 of the book presents views on foreign aid by national practitioners. Each of the contributors views foreign assistance from a unique vantage point as a high-ranking member of a particular aid establishment. In contrast to detailed academic analyses presented elsewhere in the book, this part provides policy statements from inside the policy process, putting forth the views and priorities of respective governments in terms of foreign aid. A wide variety of national perspectives from the largest aid donors (e.g., United States and Japan) and an array of recipients' viewpoints including newer (e.g., Poland), fluctuating (e.g., El Salvador) and a traditional large recipient (e.g., Egypt) is offered.

In part 5, Grant and Nijman evaluate the crises for foreign aid among intellectuals seeking a paradigm for development and policymakers looking for more aid effectiveness. They reflect on the emerging transnational liberal order, the crisis of modernity, and the impact of these developments on foreign aid for the twenty-first century.

In sum, this volume exposes important differences among donors and recipients in terms of the role of foreign aid in their policy environments, their economic well-being, and their international policy agendas. However, taken together, these writings also reveal some striking general changes in the overall foreign aid regime. New challenges and opportunities for donors and recipients that constitute the present global crisis in foreign aid may be summarized as follows. For aid donors, the challenges are to:

1. reallocate aid in the post–Cold War era;
2. revamp development aid after its past failures, especially in Africa;
3. legitimatize current and future foreign aid budgets to national taxpayers;
4. decide on the role of foreign aid in addressing global concerns such as refugee flows, environmental degradation, and drug trafficking;
5. determine priority among a rapidly growing list of eligible recipient countries;
6. coordinate aid among an increasing number of bilateral and multilateral organizations;
7. reassess the value of foreign aid in relation to the increased emphasis on free markets and the role of the private sector; and
8. determine the role of foreign aid in new vital foreign policy areas such as peacekeeping missions and trade relations.

The aid recipients' challenges in many ways mirror those of the donors. Recipients are compelled to:

1. adjust to the abrupt termination of geopolitically motivated financial flows, especially for the so-called Cold War orphans;
2. adjust to new conditions for development aid such as "good governance" and economic liberalization;
3. stand out from the crowd of eligible recipients by shaping a new image as an emerging market, a transitional country, a government committed to sustainable development, a government eliminating corruption, or a government combating drug trafficking;
4. acquire and maintain representation in an increasingly dense network of bilateral and multilateral agencies;
5. weigh the disadvantages of aid in terms of dependency and "addiction"; and
6. weigh the new costs of aid conditionality against the benefits of enforcing a true transnational liberal regime that would allow poor countries access to the economic markets in rich countries.

Shifting our lens away from the policy process, the most salient theoretical concerns of the volume relate the changing foreign aid regime to a number of key debates in international affairs. The foreign aid crisis is linked to:

1. fundamental shifts in world politics in the era of globalization;

2. the tenuous relationship between state and market;

3. competition among one single global aid regime and multiple coexisting, regionally based foreign aid regimes;

4. the emergence of a new aid regime as a vindication of modernism or, in contrast, as an illustration of the postmodern crisis;

5. the renewed politicization of foreign aid, both in terms of its institutional organization (e.g., the reorganization of USAID in the U.S. Department of State) and in terms of the increased role of aid in military operations and economic policy; and

6. the use of foreign aid as a continued expression of hegemonic ideologies in the political world-system.

These questions, essential to understanding the present crisis and the possible emergence of one or more new foreign aid regimes, are the subject of discussion in the final chapter of the volume.

## 2

# Multilateral Aid, Politics, and Poverty
## *Past Failures and Future Challenges*

### Peter Boone and Jean-Paul Faguet

AFTER FIFTY YEARS of foreign aid and investment, little has been achieved to reduce deprivation in most parts of the world. Most of Africa and much of Asia is still mired in chronic poverty. The scale of global inequality remains vast: several dozen of the poorest countries register a yearly GNP per capita (World Bank 1994a) barely equal to a few days' pay in the richest countries. More than twenty countries have primary-school gross enrollment ratios below 75 percent (World Bank 1994a), and in forty-two countries more than 10 percent of the children die before age five. Only a handful of countries, such as Sri Lanka, Costa Rica, and China, have made some progress toward poverty reduction. If present trends continue, thirty years from now the global situation will be little better in relative terms and much worse in absolute terms as population growth in the poorest countries multiplies the number of poor.

In this chapter we focus on the role of foreign aid in reducing poverty. Clearly, foreign aid is also used as a foreign policy tool, with objectives that are not always consistent with poverty reduction. But with the end of the Cold War, the role of aid as a tool in foreign policy will probably be reduced, and the emphasis of aid programs may once again turn to poverty reduction. We present an overview of empirical evidence on the successes and failures of aid programs with the aim of recommending a future role for multilateral aid agencies.

In this chapter we first outline early arguments for and against aid, showing the theoretical ambiguity surrounding the question of the potential impact of aid. Second, we summarize evidence from previous research on the impact of foreign aid on growth, investment, and human development indicators. Third, we examine the effectiveness of public infrastructure programs and relate these to the debt crisis in Sub-Saharan Africa, arguing that the major legacy of large aid flows in the 1960s and 1970s is not higher income but rather a large debt burden. Fourth, we discuss several examples of short-term aid programs that have been successful. We conclude with a discussion of the future role for development assistance.

## Early Arguments For and Against Aid

Despite the rapid growth in aid, there are not compelling theoretical underpinnings or empirical evidence that foreign aid programs work. John Maynard Keynes took the view that capital shortages were a primary cause of poverty. The World Bank was created, in part, because of his assessment that developing countries needed financing for major public and private investment projects. Aid proponents argued that developing countries have low savings because of their absolute poverty. Because they cannot afford to save and world capital markets are imperfect, they need a jump start with foreign aid to take off (Rostow 1990).

Capital, however, may have been more widely available than aid proponents suggested. During the late nineteenth century and in the inter-war period, world capital markets functioned quite well. Britain was a major exporter of capital to the New World, where both private and public investments, most notably railways, were financed by bond issues. And in the twentieth century, Korea financed substantial investments through foreign borrowing beginning in the early 1960s.

In addition, the argument that poor countries have low savings because households cannot afford to save is also more complicated. Today the richest 20 percent of the population earn 50 percent of total income in low-income countries, and it is the high-income elite that determine investment and savings levels and patterns. Therefore, why some high-income elite save and invest while others do not needs to be considered.

Other critics of foreign aid programs (e.g., Bauer 1971 and Friedman 1958) argue that the root cause of poverty is not capital shortage but rather government failure. Low investment in many cases is due to government corruption and distortionary economic policies. Aid giving may not alleviate these problems and lead to higher investment or growth. Growth can be achieved only by removing the distortions to development.

## The Cross-Country Impact of Aid

We begin our examination of the empirical effects of aid by looking at the impact of the largest component of aid flows: funds that include all nonmilitary aid with at least a 25 percent grant component. The empirical results presented here summarize previous research of the impact of foreign aid on economic and human development indicators using cross-country regressions (table 2.1). Our simple graphs that summarize the relation between aid and improvements in human development indicators are based on regression results from approximately one hundred developing countries.

There are difficulties with measuring the impact of aid in cross-country regressions. First, there is the potential simultaneity bias: it takes a certain time before the impact of aid is visible, but most studies measure aid and its effects at the same moment in time. Because aid is given to relatively poor countries, a simple regression of infant mortality on aid would erroneously predict that higher aid leads to higher infant mortality (Papanek 1973). To get around this problem, we note that much of the variance in aid flows is a result of political determinants. For example, former French colonies receive substantially more aid than their equally poor neighbors. Therefore we need to address whether the additional aid that former French colonies receive, compared to other similar countries, results in positive effects on growth and human development indicators.

The second problem is that aid encompasses many expenditure categories; thus, pooling different types of aid may bias our results (Cassen and Associates 1994; Killick 1990). Even when donors prioritize particular expenditures, the final aid allocation is quite flexible. Only a small fraction of aid is tied to the purchase of goods and services from the donor (30 percent). When aid is targeted (usually based on the prevailing rationale of the donor), donors and recipients initially negotiate over how to allocate aid, after which recipients can dispose of project receipts and benefits over long periods of time. Pack and Pack (1993) found that governments were able to fully redirect aid for alternative uses ex post

*Table 2.1* General Characteristics of Aid *(in Sample of 97 Countries)*

| | |
|---|---|
| Average aid/GNP ratio | |
| 81–90: range 0.00–0.54, sdev 0.112 | 0.086 |
| 71–80: range 0.00–0.35, sdev 0.035 | 0.056 |
| In base sample | |
| 81–90: range 0.00–0.144, sdev 0.039 | 0.042 |
| 71–80: range 0.00–0.146, sdev 0.045 | 0.046 |
| Grant component (1980) | 0.93 |

| *Restrictions on Procurement of Aid* | |
|---|---|
| *Category of Procurement* | *Total aid (%)* |
| Untied | 70 |
| Partially tied | 5 |
| Tied | 25 |

| *Uses of Aid* | |
|---|---|
| *Type* | *Total aid (%)* |
| Emergency aid | 5 |
| Food aid | 13 |
| Social and admin. infrastructure | 20 |
| Program aid | 6 |
| Economic infrastructure | 32 |
| Other | 24 |

| *Sources of Aid* | |
|---|---|
| *Type* | *Total aid (%)* |
| Multilateral | 25 |
| Bilateral | |
| France | 10 |
| Japan | 11 |
| OPEC | 5 |
| United Kingdom | 3 |
| United States | 14 |
| Other | 32 |

| Aid as a Percentage of GDP from Donor Countries (Members of DAC) | |
|---|---|
| 1970 | 34 |
| 1980 | 35 |
| 1990 | 34 |

Source: OECD(a) (1992).

Note: The term *social and administrative infrastructure* applies to health care, education, technical assistance to governments, etc. *Economic infrastructure* includes highways, electricity, irrigation, and other large public investment projects. Program aid is balance of payments support.

facto. Therefore, aid is highly fungible. The one exception is when small countries receive very large amounts of aid. In such cases, one investment project can be 50 percent of GNP, meaning that aid is no longer fungible. In 96 countries, most aid goes to consumption, and there is no significant impact on investment (figs. 2.1 and 2.2). The CPR (component plus residual) plots in the figures show the residuals from regression equations after controlling for other factors that are potentially correlated with aid and the dependent variable.

Given that most aid goes to consumption, it is not surprising that it has no significant impact on growth (fig. 2.3). The point estimate from this regression is insignificant, but it implies that a 10 percent increase in the annual aid/GNP ratio causes a 0.4 percent rise in the average growth rate over the full ten years. These results imply that the factors causing high investment and growth in developing countries neither correlate with foreign aid receipts nor are engendered by them. This is strong evidence that capital shortage is not the major cause of poverty in developing countries.

The poor do not benefit when a country receives higher aid flows. Higher aid flows do not have a significant impact on improvements in

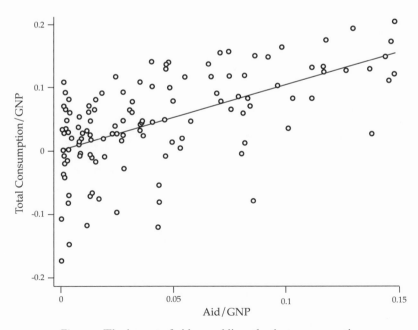

*Fig. 2.1.* The impact of aid on public and private consumption

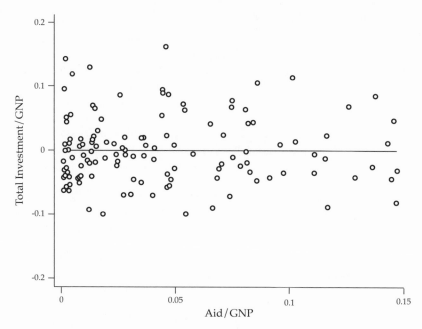

*Fig. 2.2.* The impact of aid on public and private investment

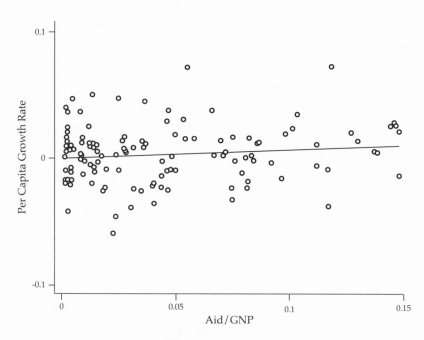

*Fig. 2.3.* The impact of aid on growth

life expectancy (fig. 2.5), and aid does not correlate with improvements in primary-school enrollment ratios (fig. 2.6). Infant mortality is highly related to nutritional standards, sanitation, provision of basic health services, housing conditions, and maternal education (fig. 2.4). Evidence from countries (e.g., Chile, China, and Sri Lanka) shows that infant mortality improves quickly when these basic factors improve; thus infant mortality can be considered a "flash" indicator of the conditions of the poorest groups in the population.

The coefficient estimates in figure 2.4 imply that countries that received 10 percent higher aid as a fraction of GNP had a 2 percent greater improvement in infant mortality than countries that received no aid. This extremely small impact indicates that the poorest fraction of the population do not receive much of the benefits of aid programs. But there is no question that aid funds are spent. It seems likely that long-term aid receipts are actually used to increase the size of government and the civil service or perhaps to make transfers to relatively wealthy members of the political elite.

These results are consistent with the negative predictions of Bauer (1971) and Friedman (1958), but it is still possible that certain political

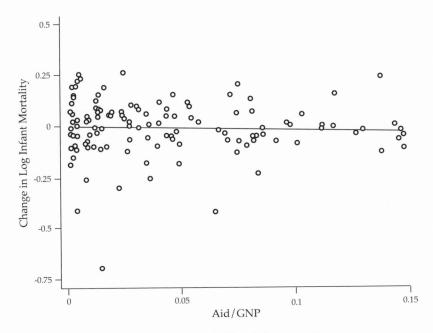

*Fig. 2.4.* The impact of aid on infant mortality

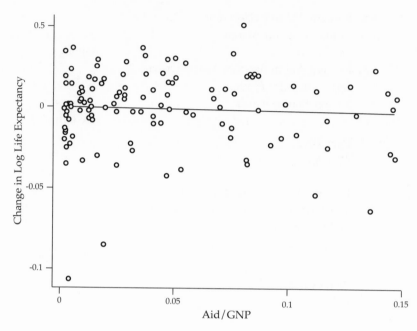

*Fig. 2.5.* The impact of aid on life expectancy

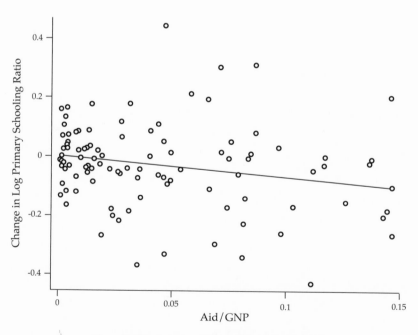

*Fig. 2.6.* The impact of aid on primary schooling

regimes use aid more effectively than others. It is often claimed, for example, that liberal and democratic political regimes use aid more effectively because they are more representative of the poor. Boone (1995) found, however, that liberal democracies do not use aid more effectively than other regimes. Even in democracies the poor are relatively weak actors in the political process precisely because they lack education and good health. When governments receive additional funds, it is only natural that they allocate them to their strongest political supporters.

Lack of improvement in human development indicators and the continued high levels of infant mortality in aid recipient countries are clear signs that poverty reflects government failure. Caldwell (1986) and Dreze and Sen (1992) showed that countries can radically improve basic human development indicators when they choose to. Examples from Cuba, Sri Lanka, China, and the Indian state of Kerala demonstrate that concerted government efforts to introduce good public health programs lead to dramatic improvements in infant mortality and life expectancy. These programs are not costly. The World Bank (1993) estimated that a health program costing 3.1 percent of GNP in low-income countries would be sufficient to bring life expectancy and infant mortality indicators close to OECD standards.

## Is Public Infrastructure Oversold?

Public infrastructure investment, accounting for 20 percent of aid allocations, is the basis of multilateral aid programs. The International Bank for Reconstruction and Development (IBRD; i.e., the World Bank) and International Development Association (IDA) provided $13.6 billion for infrastructure investment in 1991. Has this been successful? Was it really needed?

There are two arguments for donor provision of public infrastructure investment. First, capital shortage may be the cause of poverty. Second, cash-strapped governments cannot afford public spending, and poor infrastructure can be a bottleneck in development.

The World Bank provides direct measures of the efficiency of the projects it finances. The Bank's estimated returns on these projects range from 8 to 21 percent (table 2.2). Returns vary systematically across regions, with Sub-Saharan African projects earning the lowest returns. These figures suggest that individual projects earn lower rates of return than one would expect. But these numbers probably do not accurately represent the overall impact of aid on macroeconomic performance.

*Table 2.2*  Reestimated Rates of Return on World Bank Infrastructure
Projects for Evaluated Projects by Region *(Unweighted Averages)*

|                                          | *1974–75* | *1985* |
| ---------------------------------------- | --------- | ------ |
| Eastern Africa                           | 15.0      | 9.5    |
| Western Africa                           | 27.0      | 8.4    |
| East Asia and Pacific                    | 20.6      | 20.6   |
| Europe, Mediterranean, and North America | 11.5      | 14.7   |
| Latin America                            | 16.2      | 14.8   |

Source: World Bank 1988, 9.

First, World Bank estimated returns are generally overestimated at the
time of project approval. More important though, the satisfactory performance of individual projects may not reflect the broad macroeconomic impact of aid. Recipient governments can use foreign aid to reduce
their own public investment programs.

## Can Centralized Allocation of Infrastructure Be Efficient?

Although the overall effectiveness of infrastructure programs is unclear, there is still the important question of how best to allocate assistance for infrastructure investment. Is centralized allocation of funds
through large development institutions the best means to select infrastructure projects? Internal investment criteria and discipline in the
World Bank can never be expected to mimic market conditions. Mosley
(1991) reported that bank staff are encouraged to disburse loans as part
of the bank's internal incentive structure. Moreover, recipient countries
are required to pledge that the World Bank is senior to all other creditors; the International Monetary Fund (IMF) and regional development
banks have similar clauses. The result is that governments service multilateral debt before attending to other creditors. Furthermore, politicians,
motivated by the possibility of private or political gain and the reality of
electoral cycles or political instability, are willing to enter into projects
even when the social returns are low or negative. Such a lending system
can provide a mechanism for an explosion of debt and inefficient public
infrastructure investment in developing countries because of easy access
to multilateral credit facilities.

## The Dangers of Inefficient Investment

The Sub-Saharan African debt buildup is the most striking example of the failure of international development programs. It was already apparent by the late 1950s that aid projects were not generating sufficient government revenues to allow recipients to repay their loans. This led to the creation of the IDA, sister agency to the IBRD, which was made responsible for providing long-term lending to developing countries, with a ten-year grace period and concessional interest rates.

This failure of foreign aid to cause growth is generally consistent with the findings and arguments made by previous researchers (Mosley 1991). A large part of aid was probably used for consumption, most likely by permitting governments to increase budget transfers and/or the size of government. Further, despite a probable upward bias, the World Bank's estimated returns on investment projects in Sub-Saharan African countries were generally low (table 2.3). This finding puts into question the ability of donors to screen projects with adequate rigor and leads us to conclude that nonguidance of market mechanisms in the process is an important reason why lending to Africa got out of hand.

## When Does Aid Succeed?

There are, of course, numerous examples of successful aid programs. Famine relief and immunization drives are prime examples of inexpensive programs where relatively small amounts of assistance have been decisive. Sachs (1994) presented a clear case in favor of aid to assist countries attempting financial stabilization or entering into large-scale liberalization programs. His research demonstrated that during the last century virtually every country that successfully stabilized received foreign assistance.

Such short-term aid also has clear theoretical backing for its potential usefulness. During high inflation the government needs to muster the political strength to make tough budget decisions and raise credibility so that households and enterprises will once again trust the domestic currency. Here foreign assistance provides bridge financing while budget measures take hold and governments gain political strength. Additionally, international support usually raises a government's credibility.

Foreign assistance has also played a key role in encouraging shifts in economic policies and political structures. For instance, U.S. aid to Tai-

*Table 2.3* Regressions Showing the Impact of Aid on Consumption, Investment, Infant Mortality, Life Expectancy, and Schooling *(Panel Data Using Base Sample with Decade-averaged Data, 1971–80, 1981–90)*

| | Dependent Variable | | | | |
|---|---|---|---|---|---|
| | I | II | III | IV | V |
| RHS variable | Public & Private Cons. GNP | Investment GNP | Δ log Infant Mortality | Δ log Life Expectancy | Δ log Primary Schooling |
| AID/GNP | 1.016 | 0.030 | −0.202 | −0.024 | −0.688 |
| | (4.83) | (0.17) | (0.42) | (0.29) | (1.30) |
| LGNPCAP[a] | −0.098 | 0.035 | 0.034 | −0.005 | −0.212 |
| | (2.54) | (1.06) | (0.32) | (0.31) | (2.17) |
| LGNPCAP$^2$ | −0.007 | −0.002 | 0.018 | −0.004 | −0.041 |
| | (1.17) | (0.44) | (1.04) | (1.28) | (2.40) |
| Per capita GNP growth rate | −0.076 | 0.873 | −0.563 | 0.076 | 1.254 |
| | (3.03) | (4.12) | (0.97) | (0.76) | (1.90) |
| Population growth rate | −1.931 | 1.988 | 4.449 | −0.072 | 0.667 |
| | (2.17) | (2.66) | (2.00) | (0.18) | (0.30) |
| Terms of Trade[b] | 0.105 | −0.168 | 0.200 | 0.089 | 4.198 |
| | (0.27) | (0.53) | (0.23) | (0.59) | (4.28) |
| Debt Rescheduling[c] | −0.008 | 0.003 | 0.040 | −0.005 | −0.014 |
| | (0.48) | (0.26) | (1.02) | (0.78) | (0.34) |
| Sub-Saharan Africa | −0.033 | −0.007 | 0.062 | −0.028 | 0.062 |
| | (1.74) | (0.44) | (1.44) | (3.40) | (1.31) |
| Asia | −0.061 | 0.021 | −0.010 | 0.002 | 0.047 |
| | (2.91) | (1.17) | (0.20) | (0.30) | (0.90) |
| Latin America | 0.017 | −0.040 | 0.015 | 0.002 | 0.034 |
| | (0.99) | (2.86) | (0.38) | (0.24) | (0.84) |
| log (dependent variable at start of period) | | | 1.001 | 1.101 | 0.865 |
| | | | (11.1) | (6.38) | (7.53) |
| Level of dependent variable at start of period | | | 0.000 | −0.006 | −0.003 |
| | | | (0.13) | (1.78) | (1.68) |

*(table continues)*

*Table 2.3* (continued)

| RHS variable | Dependent Variable | | | | |
|---|---|---|---|---|---|
| | I | II | III | IV | V |
| | Public & Private Cons. GNP | Investment GNP | Δ log Infant Mortality | Δ log Life Expectancy | Δ log Primary Schooling |
| Time | −0.021 (1.38) | 0.012 (0.95) | −0.016 (0.45) | 0.004 (0.67) | −0.005 (0.12) |
| Constant | 0.670 (12.5) | 0.296 (6.56) | −0.487 (2.10) | 0.007 (0.01) | 0.693 (1.99) |
| R2 | 0.615 | 0.463 | 0.963 | 0.980 | 0.869 |
| SEE | 0.063 | 0.053 | 0.145 | 0.025 | 0.148 |
| N | 123 | 123 | 123 | 123 | 105 |

Note: Ols estimates, t-statistics in parentheses, standard errors are adjusted for a random individual specific component.

The regression results reported here are fully described in Boone (1994, 1995). The main findings reported there are shown to be robust when we directly measure aid using regression techniques. The data on foreign aid were provided by the OECD, and all remaining data are from the World Bank.

a. LGNPCAP is the log of GNP relative to OECD countries.

b. Terms of trade is the cumulative loss of income measured as a proportion of GNP over the decade. The terms of trade loss/gain is calculated by the World Bank (1993).

c. Debt rescheduling is a dummy variable set to one between 1981 and 1990 for countries that entered into Paris Club negotiations during that period.

wan played a decisive role in ensuring the success of nationwide land reform in the early 1950s (Cheng 1961). Washington's commitment to reduce aid to Korea provided the political impetus for the government to stabilize its macroeconomic policies, open the economy, and promote exports.

World Bank conditional aid programs do not have clear positive or long-lasting impacts. Mosley (1991) summarized results from several case studies. It is not evident that World Bank conditionality is strongly enforced—or that it is even enforceable, given the range of commitments made. Bank conditionality generally involves several dozen specific conditions, but in practice countries can implement only a fraction of these and still not risk loan suspension. The reason behind this discrepancy may reflect the incentive structure of the bank: if it measures its own performance by success in approving and disbursing loans, then it is not really in the interest of bank staff to suspend loans because of noncompliance in conditionality.

The lesson here is that foreign aid programs can be successful during and after periods of significant political change. These are times when (new) interest groups are still forming and the role of government is being redefined. Very often the government has a mandate to carry out rapid reform or is in a position where a few key reformers can introduce changes that eventually become self-sustaining. But once interest groups are entrenched and governments settle into more stable political patterns, the potential for major reforms is greatly diminished. In these cases even conditional foreign aid is a weak instrument to provoke changes in economic policies.

## Whither Multilateral Institutions? Whither Foreign Aid?

The evidence from the last fifty years points to three broad conclusions. First, poverty and the lack of economic development are not driven by capital shortages. Although aid programs have transferred large capital flows to developing countries, investment has not risen significantly in response and consumption has increased instead; this condition suggests that a lack of investment opportunities may be the main reason for low investment and savings. Poor investment possibilities could, in turn, be driven by such factors as the absence of clear property rights as well as by political instability, poor economic policies, and the government's lack of credibility.

Second, we must attribute to government failure the lack of improvement in human development indicators in many countries. This failure may be caused by political deadlock or by decisions to spend resources on uses other than the provision of basic services to the poor. A small number of the poorest nations have shown that concerted efforts by governments can lead to sharp improvements in human development indicators.

Finally, both examples and sound theoretical reasons support the position that short-term aid can be effective during revolutionary periods when governments have the opportunity and/or mandate to carry out major reforms. During these periods aid can strengthen governments that choose to introduce major liberalization programs or enfranchise the poor in the political system. And reforms that lead to better education and health for the poor may well result in their political voice being strengthened to the point that they become self-sustaining.

These lessons and the end of the Cold War have already caused some changes in the aid industry. There are more efforts now to ensure that countries introduce structural adjustment programs agreed upon with the IMF before they are eligible for substantial foreign assistance, and aid agencies are shifting expenditures away from large infrastructure projects and toward health care and education.

Amid such changes, what role is left for multilateral institutions? Economists have changed their views toward the role of the public sector in the economy: throughout the world governments are privatizing activities that used to be considered well within the public domain. The private sector is held to be generally more efficient and does not face the incentive problems that both governments and aid agencies face. This narrowing of the public domain should be applied to aid programs. In recent years there has been a spectacular rise in foreign investment for public infrastructure in developing countries. Today, foreign investors can travel easily and communicate instantaneously with most regions of the world, and their resources have followed. Examples include toll roads in Mexico, dams in Argentina, telecommunications facilities in Mongolia, and energy and power plants in China. Poor countries can and should seek to harness these financial flows by adjusting their macroeconomic policies to promote investment.

Multilaterals should phase out their major infrastructure programs and instead promote the rapid growth of private investment flows, both foreign and domestic, by helping countries to design policies and legal reforms that improve their access to funds. They could also piggyback on these projects, providing partial financing or guarantees against political instability, nationalization, and other such noneconomic risks that international agencies may be better equipped to take on.

Market discipline will then be the guiding factor that determines the choice of investment projects, leaving multilaterals in a passive role in the project selection process. This discipline will pressure governments to maintain an economic climate conducive to investment in the long term, thus providing a more credible, clear, and binding conditionality than the current programs of the World Bank and other donors. It will also reduce, though certainly not eliminate, the possibility of another major debt crisis in these countries.

Several of the multilateral agencies have built up considerable technical and research expertise. They have every reason to continue to take advantage of this expertise. But technical assistance should also be subject to more competition and openness. The World Bank could sharply reduce its size and instead move to a system where it contracts more services from private consulting firms or experts.

Finally, research on aid programs suggests that long-term aid can be sharply reduced and possibly replaced by short- and medium-term programs more directed at poverty reduction. The clearest examples of the successful use of foreign aid have been during periods of revolution and crisis. Aid, such as famine relief, can be helpful during stabilization; it can also provide the political support new governments and reformers often need when they push through major economic and political reforms.

To improve the aid process, we should bring much greater competition into the aid allocation process. We should target aid to countries that introduce major poverty eradication campaigns and that take measures to liberalize their economies. This aid should be highly conditional, and we should be prepared to stop foreign aid if reforms slow or are reversed. When government failure is a major cause of poverty, aid must be used as a tool to change government incentives. In this way we can support reformist factions within existing governments and give greater incentives for all governments to embark on programs to help the poor.

# Part Two

## *Changing Donor Policies*

# 3

# United States Foreign Aid
## *Crisis? What Crisis?*

### Jan Nijman

I N 1992, Senator Patrick Leahy characterized the U.S. foreign aid program as "exhausted intellectually, conceptually, and politically. It has no widely understood and agreed set of goals, it lacks coherence and vision, and there is a very real question whether parts of it actually serve broadly accepted United States national interests any longer" (quoted in White Paper 1992, 5). The lack of a widely agreed purpose made foreign assistance programs an easy target for federal budget cuts.

In the late 1980s, debates about the reorientation of U.S. foreign aid gathered momentum in policymaking circles in Washington and among scholars (e.g., Sewell 1991; Clad and Stone 1993; Preeg 1993). Pressures for change came mainly from three directions. First, for years there had been mounting criticism of the United States Agency for International Development (USAID) for its poor strategic management of aid programs. Second, waning public support for foreign aid—and foreign affairs in general—demanded new aid justifications. Finally, watershed changes such as the ending of the Cold War made many aid programs obsolete.

In this chapter I analyze U.S. foreign aid by focusing on the domestic policy environment and the reformulation of its aid objectives, while complementing the discussion with an examination of changes in the implementation of foreign aid programs and the geography of aid. My analysis is based on USAID data, 1966–96.

## The Forms and Purposes of United States Foreign Aid

U.S. aid has taken many different forms, including economic and military aid. Economic aid entails development aid managed by the USAID, food aid, the Peace Corps, credits for exports, disaster assistance, and the so-called Economic Support Fund (ESF). Military aid includes grants for the purchase of military equipment, credit financing of military sales, and military education and training. This official categorization is based on the form in which aid is provided: all assistance that involves military equipment or training is designated "military aid," whereas the rest is termed "economic aid." This is an important distinction because the form of aid is easily confused with the purpose of aid.

The form of assistance is not always a reliable indicator of the donor's aid motivation. Most military aid serves U.S. geopolitical interests by strengthening American allies around the world and may additionally serve the donor's commercial interests. In comparison, economic aid is much more ambiguous: aid can promote development in the recipient country, the economic well-being of the donor, or the security interests of the donor. Economic assistance has often served geostrategic aims. For example, the ESF was used to finance large capital projects in infrastructure development, but the purpose of the ESF had more to do with politics and security than with economics. ESF was provided mainly to countries of geopolitical interest (e.g., Israel, Egypt, Pakistan, the Philippines, Turkey, and Greece).

## The Evolution of United States Foreign Aid Policies

Foreign aid has played a critical role in U.S. foreign policy since World War II. As a percentage of the GNP, U.S. foreign aid has always been small, but in absolute terms the United States has for years been the largest foreign aid donor, with a significant number of countries for which it is the largest foreign aid donor (fig. 3.1, maps 3.1 and 3.2). The number of countries for which the United States is the largest or second-largest donor has declined over time. Several authors have distinguished phases in the evolution of U.S. aid (e.g., Vernon and Sparr 1989; Semmel 1984; Congressional Research Service 1986). During the Mar-

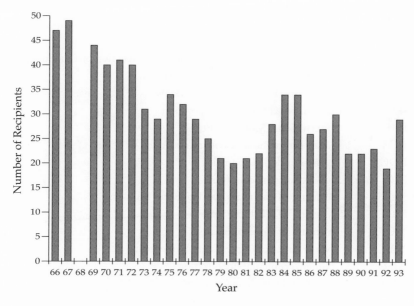

*Fig. 3.1.* The number of countries for which the United States
is the largest foreign aid donor, 1966–93

shall Plan era, grants largely went to European countries to fund purchases of American exports. While the form of aid was predominantly
economic, the purpose was ultimately to shield these countries from the
Communist threat. Strong economies and strong economic ties to the
United States were considered crucial.

In the 1950s and 1960s, the composition of foreign aid changed in
that funding for capital projects increased, as did the formal "tying" of
aid to the purchase of American goods and services (Tarnoff and Nowels
1993, 22), satisfying the interests of American business lobbies. Wars in
Korea and Vietnam, however, were responsible for the infusion of large
amounts of military aid into Southeast Asia.

Two developments arose in the 1970s. The so-called New Directions
legislation placed a new emphasis on development goals to benefit poor
countries, and the Carter Administration added more weight to human
rights considerations. The composition of aid changed to reflect basic
need concerns. This trend implied a move away from capital projects
funding and the "untying" of aid. It also led to increased aid flows to
the poorer countries in Africa. This trend, however, coincided with the

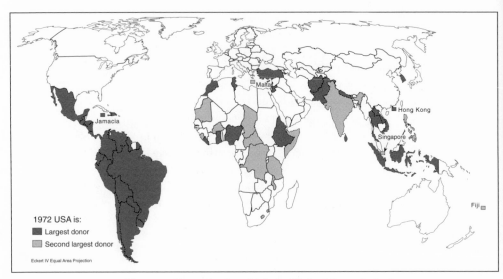

*Map 3.1.* Countries for which the United States is the largest
and second-largest foreign aid donor, 1972

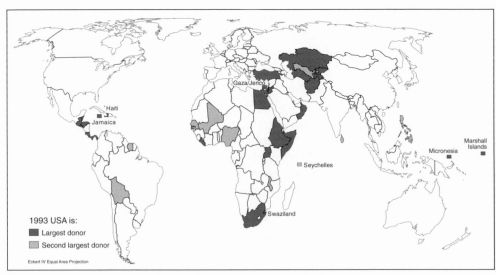

*Map 3.2.* Countries for which the United States is the largest
and second-largest foreign aid donor, 1993

rapidly increasing importance of the Middle East in American geopolitical strategy. Aid to Israel, Egypt, and Jordan increased after the Yom Kippur War in 1973 and after the Camp David Accords in 1978.

A consolidation of the geopolitical orientation of U.S. foreign aid occurred in the 1980s, which was related to the efforts by the Reagan administration to reassert American power vis-à-vis the Soviet Union. Development goals faded into the background, and security aid went increasingly to countries considered vital to American security. In the early 1980s, Central America emerged as a recipient region of vital interest to the United States: most aid went to countries opposed to the leftist regimes in Nicaragua and El Salvador (see, for example, Shultz 1984; Barry and Preusch 1988). The Middle East remained the most important region for U.S. aid; in Asia the Philippines and Pakistan maintained their position as key recipients of U.S. security assistance.

## Domestic Pressures for Change

The U.S. foreign aid budget for 1991 was criticized for "being written in Cold War parlance that was obsolete" (Lowenthal 1991, 7). The reformulation of U.S. foreign aid policy gathered momentum in the 1990s. Outlining the future of U.S. foreign aid, Ronald Roskins, director of USAID, listed six "new" goals: stimulating economic growth, building democracy, promoting well-being, safeguarding the environment, fighting AIDS and drug trafficking, and alleviating the consequences of natural disasters (Roskins 1990, 128). However, USAID could manage foreign assistance only with the cooperation of policymakers in the administration and Congress. USAID did not control half of the funds that it administered, such as the Economic Support Funds (GAO 1993, 7). Since the 1970s, Congress had become increasingly involved in budgetary decision making and earmarked certain amounts for specific countries.

Pressures to change aid practices came from a number of sources. First, business lobbies argued for "aid for trade" to stimulate U.S. exports (Tarnoff and Nowels 1993; Preeg 1993) and contended that the United States benefited less from its aid than other donors. For example, in 1991, 17 percent of all U.S. bilateral aid was tied, compared to the Organization for Economic Cooperation and Development (OECD) donor average of 24 percent. Business lobbies wanted more assistance programs that funded capital projects, fewer cash transfers to alleviate balance of payment problems, more "mixed credits" (official government financing of below-market-rate loans that are blended with commercial and near-commercial funds), and a strengthening of "buy American" provisions that guaranteed procurement of U.S. goods and services.

The second pressure for change emphasized the opportunity, created by the ending of the Cold War, to return to foreign aid programs that aimed at promoting the development of poor countries (see studies by Lowenthal 1991; Zimmerman 1993). Proponents, usually in USAID circles, contended that business goals conflict with development goals, and that aid is a costly form of export promotion that is not very effective. Zimmerman, for example, remarked that "the United States may spend $50 million on a power plant for Egypt and benefit the General Electric constituents of United States senators, but that same money would go much further and have greater impact . . . if it could be spent in ways that empower people" (1993, 193).

Third, there was pressure on the Clinton administration to provide a new definition of U.S. security interests. Now there were fewer compelling reasons to give aid to former Cold War allies such as Turkey, the Philippines, and Pakistan or to support Third World countries formerly threatened by the Soviet Union (e.g., Zaire or Somalia). Nonetheless, aid still needed to be provided to countries threatened by more powerful regional neighbors, as the Gulf War has shown.

## The Clinton Administration's Response
## Prior to the 104th Congress

The response by the Clinton administration to the various pressures for change can be summarized in three points: the passing of legislation in 1992 on foreign aid to the former Communist states, the publication of the so-called *Wharton Report* in 1993, and the proposal of a new foreign assistance act in 1994.

After the Gulf War was over, the transformation of the former Communist block gradually became the center of attention in U.S. foreign policy. In late 1992, Congress passed the Freedom Support Act (FSA) and the Support for East European Democracies Act (SEED), which included legislation on foreign assistance. If the democratic transformations failed, the key argument went, U.S. security interests would once again be threatened.

The *Wharton Report* (1993) recognized that foreign aid policies were torn between conflicting demands and badly needed a new global rationale. It identified new threats to the United States in the form of several global issues, such as environmental degradation, drug trafficking, AIDS, population growth, and migration (see also USAID 1994b). It also proposed that the United States give less military aid and more economic aid (*Wharton Report* 1993, 71).

The most concrete and comprehensive response of the administration was presented in early 1994 with the Peace, Prosperity, and Democracy Act (PPDA) and the budget request for fiscal year 1995. This proposed legislation reflected many of the intentions in the *Wharton Report*, and its central objective was to "streamline legislation governing foreign assistance so that it better conforms to emerging international realities" (USAID 1994a, 1). As such, it repealed the Foreign Assistance Act (FAA) of 1961.

The structure of the PPDA was simpler and more straightforward than the old legislation. All assistance programs were brought under one of six thematic objectives of United States foreign aid (USAID 1994a):

1. promoting sustainable development;
2. promoting democracy;
3. promoting peace;
4. providing humanitarian and crisis assistance;
5. promoting growth through trade and investment; and
6. advancing diplomacy.

The objectives, however, did not all receive equal weight. Development goals and environmental threats were given top priority, and commercial interests were given a relatively low priority in the PPDA; more conventional security interests ranked in the middle.

In the 1995 budget request based on those six thematic objectives, Secretary of State Warren Christopher stated, "I am pleased to present what is truly the first post–Cold War International Affairs budget" (United States Government 1994, 1).

## The Changing Foreign Aid Discourses
### since the 104th Congress

Even though the PPDA seemed to try to appease various constituencies—from trade lobbies to human rights groups to the powerful Israel lobby to environmental groups—it struck a tone that was different from the past. On the surface, it seemed a faithful effort to rethink foreign aid for the post–Cold War, global era. It was also characterized by idealist overtones, especially in terms of new possibilities for international cooperation and a return to true development assistance expressed in terms of the alleged shared interests of all countries in the prosperity of the global village. As such, the PPDA also put a special emphasis on "green aid" and population programs (Nowels 1994).

The passing of the new foreign aid act had been doubtful from the beginning. With the election of a Republican majority in Congress in November 1994, the bill was effectively killed (Nowels 1995). The Republicans came with their own proposals for foreign aid reform, which were in part a by-product of broader plans to balance the federal budget. The new chairman of the Senate Foreign Relations Committee, Jesse Helms, stated, "The foreign aid program has spent an estimated $2 trillion of the American taxpayers' money, much of it going down foreign rat holes, to countries that constantly oppose United States in the United Nations, and many which reject concepts of freedom. We must stop this stupid business of giving away the taxpayers' money willy-nilly" (*Washington Post National Weekly Edition* 1994). He proposed an overall reduction of foreign aid by some 20 percent. Republican plans also emphasized that foreign aid should serve the U.S. national interest, especially in terms of security and commerce.

The Clinton administration no longer had the initiative. There are many signs that in the course of 1995 it started to move back from its earlier ideological position to one based on pragmatism and political viability. If it is true that Clinton in general moved his policy agenda to the right (to accommodate the Republicans and to court the voters with an eye on the presidential elections in 1996), this is particularly true with regard to his foreign aid policy.

Accordingly, the administration started to emphasize real political motives for foreign aid. It moved away from its earlier idealist rhetoric and its previous insistence on global interdependence and shared interests with developing countries around the world. Consequently, it was unavoidable that the earlier enthusiasm for green aid, environmental programs, population programs, and human rights programs dissipated. With the rejection of the PPDA, the budget structure for 1996 returned to its usual shape, except for special lines for aid to transitional countries in East Europe and the former Soviet Union.

## The Geographical Distribution of Aid
## since the End of the Cold War

One of the major issues in the redirection of U.S. aid concerns the balance between economic aid and security aid. Security aid—or, more generally, geopolitically motivated aid—has always formed a large part of U.S. assistance programs. Security aid peaked during the renewed Cold War in the early 1980s and has since declined (fig. 3.2). This decline was especially sharp from 1990 to 1993 and coincided with an increase of economic assistance. The situation stabilized around 1994, and security aid started to pick up again slightly.

Declaratory policies have focused especially on new development goals in U.S. foreign aid policy. As was indicated earlier, the business lobbies do not appear to have been very successful in giving commercial interests a prominent place in the new foreign aid legislation. We have also seen that in this respect the new foreign aid policy is at odds with this administration's overall foreign policy of putting a premium on stimulation of the domestic economy of the United States. For example,

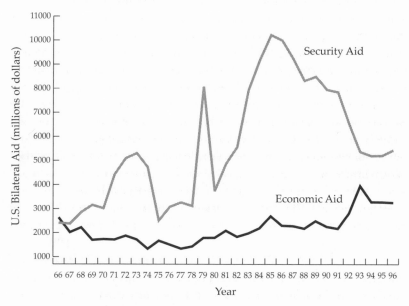

*Fig. 3.2.* Bilateral United States aid to individual countries: economic and security aid in millions, 1966–96

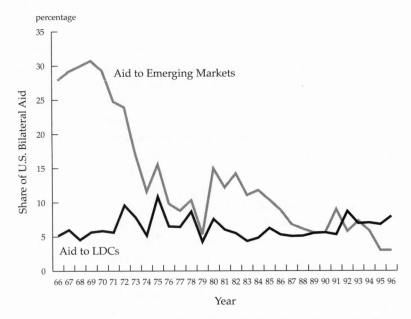

*Fig. 3.3.* Share of United States bilateral aid to "emerging markets"
and to "least developed countries," 1966–96

the Department of Commerce announced in April 1994 its "Big Emerging Markets Strategy" to promote exports to high-growth countries
(*International Economic Insights* 1994, 12), including Argentina, Brazil,
China, Hong Kong, India, Indonesia, South Korea, Mexico, Poland,
South Africa, Taiwan, and Turkey. Figure 3.3 shows the share of all
bilateral U.S. aid sent to emerging markets from 1966 to the present
and compares this with U.S. aid distributed among the least-developed
countries.

Clearly, neither development of the poorest countries nor American
business interests have increased in importance. Aid to least-developed
countries remained stable: between 5 and 10 percent of total aid disbursements. Aid to emerging markets declined in the 1970s and 1980s
and stabilized at a similarly low level (the high levels of aid to emerging
markets in the late 1960s and early 1970s were largely "coincidental"
and are attributed to the geopolitical importance of Southeast Asia at
the time of the Vietnam War). The distinction between economic and
security aid is becoming increasingly problematic with the introduction

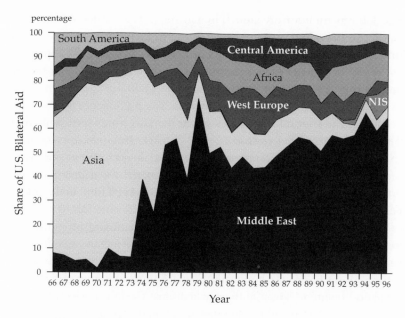

*Fig. 3.4.* Regional shares of United States bilateral aid, 1966–96

of "security threats" like population growth and environmental degradation.

It is difficult to measure the benefits to the donor's domestic economy of commercially motivated aid, and some argue that it is smaller than usually assumed (e.g., Morrissey 1993). Ironically, it is likely that U.S. security aid contributes more to the U.S. domestic economy than almost any form of "economic" aid. For example, in 1993, 90 percent of all military aid was procured in the United States, compared to 62 percent of all economic aid (Tarnoff and Nowels 1993).

The new priorities of foreign aid are reflected in the changing regional distribution of bilateral aid from 1990 to 1996 (fig. 3.4). The Middle East remains by far the largest recipient; the former Soviet Union and East Europe are the fastest growing regions; Africa experiences modest growth; aid to Asia and Central America is decreasing; and aid to South America remains small. This "new" regional distribution is remarkable because it continues the striking "asymmetry" of U.S. geopolitics that was characteristic of the Cold War period, when the United States was more involved in further-away regions on the Eurasian continent than in nearby Latin American regions (Nijman 1993). Oddly, despite the ending of the Cold War and the rapid economic growth of several Latin American countries, Latin America remains an insignificant region in the overall scheme of U.S. foreign aid. Figure 3.4 also underscores the somewhat puzzling retreat from Asia by the United States as a foreign aid power.

One of the major criticisms of U.S. aid was that it was spread too thin to too many countries. In a response, the USAID announced in November 1993 its intent to close missions in twenty-one countries by the end of 1996 (USAID 1994b, 33); these are all recipients of relatively insignificant amounts of aid. These intentions, however, were undercut by the rapid proliferation of new candidates for aid after the demise of communism: between 1985 and 1996, the number of recipients did not decrease but increased substantially, from 99 to more than 130. This expansion is for the most part due to new aid programs in the newly independent states (NIS) of the former Soviet Union and countries in East Europe (although most aid is allocated on a regional basis, virtually all of these countries receive some aid on an individual basis as well).

Besides the increase of aid to the NIS and East Europe, there have been several other important changes in the geographical distribution of United States aid in the past six years (map 3.3). The most significant and consistent decrease of aid on a regional basis occurred in Central America in the wake of returning political stability. The only Latin American countries experiencing an increase are Peru and Bolivia, where aid is aimed primarily at fighting narcotics trade. In Africa, where many countries receive assistance but generally at low levels, there have been many small changes. In most cases, aid shifted from "Cold War orphans" (Richburg 1992) to countries where aid had stronger developmental purposes. South Africa quickly became a large recipient, and almost all of its aid has been labeled "economic." In Asia, the biggest losers are the former Cold War allies Pakistan, the Philippines, and Afghanistan. The only country with an increase in U.S. aid was Cambodia, where assistance programs are aimed at countering drug trafficking. Map 3.4 shows the prevailing purpose, as stated in the budget request for 1996, of aid to all countries receiving $1 million or more and exhibits a clear regional pattern.

Broadly speaking, "development aid" goes to the South—Latin America, Africa, and South Asia—and comprises by far the largest number of recipients. "Security aid" is aimed at a relatively small number of

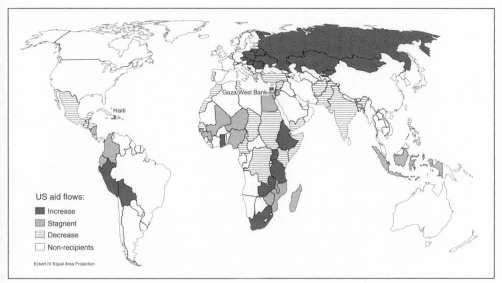

*Map 3.3.* Changes in the geographical distribution
of United States foreign aid, 1989–96

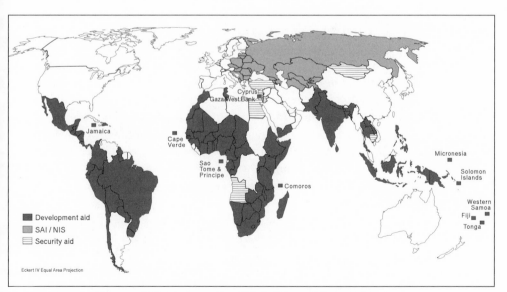

*Map 3.4.* Official categories of United States bilateral aid
by geographical destination, 1996 (budget requests)

countries in the Middle East, but it entails the largest share of all U.S.
bilateral aid. Finally, Special Assistance Initiatives (SAI) for East Europe
and NIS aid to the former Soviet Union are per definition regionally defined. This official categorization begs the question, once again, of
whether the main purpose of SAI/NIS aid programs is economic or
political.

## Conclusions

In the case of the United States, global geopolitical changes coincided with waning domestic support for aid, diverging demands for a
new aid rationale, the need for institutional and legislative renewal, and
an unprecedented budget squeeze. In practice, the effects on foreign assistance programs are not yet fully manifest. Thus far, on the implementation side of foreign aid policy, there is continuity as well as change. It
took several years, since the ending of the Cold War around 1989, for
this change to materialize. The most important changes in the composition and distribution of United States aid can be summarized in four
points. First, overall geopolitically motivated aid has increased at the expense of economic aid. Second, most of this new geopolitical aid goes to
the former communist states that are trying to make the transition to democracy. Third, aid has increased to countries involved in narcotics
trade, such as Peru and Cambodia. Finally, there has been a reduction of
aid to former Cold War allies, such as Zaire, Morocco, Pakistan, Guatemala, and the Philippines.

Foreign aid policy rhetoric moves in cycles. The declaratory policies
of the Clinton administration prior to the 104th Congress articulated
the same general goals and arguments (with the exception of combating
drug trafficking) that were heard in the 1960s and 1970s. Thus, while aid
for the purpose of containment was labeled obsolete, commercial interests and particularly the promotion of (sustainable) development came
to the fore again.

There is a real chance that the cyclical pattern of foreign aid rhetoric
will be broken because the very integrity of foreign aid is now at stake.
Critics of U.S. foreign aid argue that it is something of the past: foreign
aid was useful to the extent that it helped to win the Cold War, but it was
a waste in terms of helping poor countries develop. The latter task, they
say, is better left to the free market and private financial flows.

It seems inevitable that pressures to diminish the U.S. federal budget deficit will take their toll on foreign aid programs: in one proposal for a balanced budget, foreign aid would be reduced by 32 percent by the end of this decade (*New York Times,* Nov. 28, 1994). A shrinking budget implies further regional differentiation and concentration in aid disbursements, the latter especially in the Middle East and the former communist bloc, meaning that true development programs will be hit the hardest by imminent cutbacks.

The present U.S. aid crisis suggests the beginning of the end of foreign aid as we have known it for the past forty-five years: "foreign aid" is increasingly disassociated with "development aid." On the other hand, from a more cynical point of view, one might question whether this is indeed a crisis at all, or if it is business as usual, as it merely ends the worn pretense of U.S. aid for development purposes.

# 4

# Japan
## *A Foreign Aid Superpower*

### Richard Grant

T HE YEAR 1994 marked the fortieth anniversary of the beginning of
the Japanese aid program. Since its modest inception, the Japanese
aid program has developed into the world's largest. In June 1989, Japan
overtook the United States as the largest foreign aid donor in the global
economy—and again from 1991 to the present. In 1993 the Japanese donated $11.47 billion and had far-reaching impacts on the development of
156 recipient countries around the world. Most striking about the evolution of the Japanese aid program is that three decades ago Japan was a
major aid recipient of U.S. and World Bank aid.

Strong government and public support for the continued growth of
Japan's aid program persists. For the future the volume of Japanese aid is
likely to increase: Tokyo has budgeted $70–75 billion for the five-year pe-
riod beginning in fiscal year 1993. According to the annual report of the
Ministry of Foreign Affairs (MOFA), foreign aid will continue to be a
"main pillar" of Tokyo's foreign policy, particularly in addressing post–
Cold War global challenges (MOFA 1991, 73).

The purpose of this chapter is to understand Japan's aid activities
from its origins as a donor in 1954 to the present. The chapter consists of
five sections. In the first I discuss the five stages in the evolution of the
Japanese aid program. I address the domestic policymaking arena for
Tokyo's aid in the second section, and the various geographies of Japan-

ese foreign aid patterns and the quality and emphases of aid in the third. In the fourth section I examine Japan's role in the New World Order. The final section contains a set of conclusions about the possible future directions of the Japanese aid program.

## The Evolution of the Japanese Aid Program

Japan's foreign aid policies have different origins than those of other donors. For instance, Japan was not a direct participant in Marshall aid, from which the system of aid coordination developed; nor does Tokyo have the equivalent of the United Kingdom's Colonial Development and Welfare Acts to justify its overseas aid. Concepts of Christian charity (which underpin at least the unofficial side of Western aid) and the Moslem practice of almsgiving (relevant for most OPEC donors) are "foreign" to Japanese society. There is not an active development lobby; the leading nongovernmental organizations (NGOs) are monitored by governmental institutional organizations (41 percent of their funding derives from government subsidies) (MOFA 1992) or have their roots in Buddhist spiritualism, a connection that emphasizes nationalistic, not international, alms. There is little in Japan to compare with the scale and scope of Western nonprofit charity organizations such as OXFAM or CARE.

Foreign aid is still a very "foreign" concept for most Japanese. For example, Western terms for aid *(enjo)* or development assistance *(kaihatsu enjo)* are hardly ever used. Recently the phrase *keizai kyoryoku* has been used to convey the concept of cooperation with equal but needier foreign partners in development. An emphasis on "self-help" runs through Japan's aid planning and implementation, a focus that derives from Japan's experience of postwar economic development, which depended relatively little on foreign capital. Accordingly, the Japanese program emphasizes loans over grants. Officials believe that this orientation encourages financial discipline and discourages a "welfare" mentality, thereby assisting the recipients' development of independence from foreign aid.

Japan's donor role evolved in five postwar stages. In stage one (1945–53), Japan was a recipient of foreign aid. The Japanese received $5 billion of relief and economic rehabilitation aid from the United States from 1946 to 1951. In addition, Japan received thirty-four loans from the World Bank (valued at $860 million), and these loans were largely used for infrastructural projects, such as bullet train line.

In the second stage (1954–63), war reparations of over $1.2 billion of government funds were transferred to Burma, the Philippines, Indonesia, and Vietnam. In addition, Tokyo loaned about $738 million under the same scheme to the same group of recipients. Japanese business leaders played a key role in negotiating the reparations agreements, ahead of the Ministry of Finance (MOF), establishing an early pattern for Japan's foreign aid.

The policy of trade promotion through tying aid began in 1958, when Japan extended its first yen loan to India. A vehicle for penetrating Asian markets with Japanese plants and material, this extension also stimulated resource flows in both directions. The grant element in Japanese aid was low and tying absolute, but this arrangement was justified because Japan was still recovering economically: in 1958 Japan's per capita income was $280—closer to that of India than to other OECD (Organization for Economic Cooperation and Development) donors. Japan also joined the Colombo Plan in 1954 and participated in technical assistance to South and Southeast Asia. Japan formally joined the Development Assistance Committee (DAC) in 1961 as a founding member.

In the third stage (1964–76), aid expanded significantly. Owing in part to the appreciation of the yen against the dollar, Japanese foreign aid increased tenfold—from $115.8 million in 1964 to $1,149 in 1976. Japanese aid also was diversified and enriched in quality: food aid started in 1968, and general grants were disbursed in 1969. In general, in the 1960s aid complemented Japan's foreign economic strategy and contributed to a "good neighbor" policy.

The fourth period of systematic aid expansion occurred between 1977 and 1988 and was facilitated by the pursuit of several medium-term targets, which doubled the aid budget over a number of years (usually five). The early 1970s also represented a benchmark for Japanese foreign aid and the emergence of assistance beyond Asia. Encouraged by the United States toward more burden sharing and simultaneously responding to changes in the international environment, Japan expanded foreign aid rapidly and initiated programs in Africa, Latin America, and the Middle East. Aware of its vulnerability and threatened resource security, Japan responded to the oil shocks by extending new aid packages to several oil-producing states and even considered extending aid to states bordering natural resource routes (Orr 1990, 55).

Other opportunities to examine Japanese foreign policy goals and to distinguish them from Washington's interests were offered by the "Nixon shock," which entailed Nixon's decision to visit China, with no prior consultation with Tokyo, and the United States' decisions regarding its economy (soybean embargo, flexible exchange rates, etc.), which affected the Japanese economy directly. These U.S. decisions demonstrated that Washington would act in its own interest, potentially endangering Japan's interests.

In response to demands from the United States and other OECD countries, Japan further globalized foreign aid in the 1980s through a series of consecutive five-year plans to double foreign aid budgets. The Japanese also committed to targeting surplus recycling, realizing that if its massive current account surplus ($80 billion in 1987) were simply recycled according to market mechanisms, it would only be attracted to the North. During the 1980s, Japanese aid policy had two broad goals: to share the burden by contributing toward the security of the Western alliance and to support the "comprehensive national security" policy (by maintaining reliable and affordable supplies of raw materials and foodstuffs from foreign suppliers and unimpeded access to foreign markets for Japanese exports and investment).

Japan emerged as the largest aid donor in the world in the fifth stage of expansion (1989 to the present). In 1989, Japan surpassed the United States for the first time to become the top donor in the world. On June 30, 1992, the Japanese announced guidelines and principles for aid giving by introducing a formal Foreign Aid Charter. The four principles set forth in the charter are "(1) pursuing environmental conservation and development simultaneously; (2) avoiding the use of aid for military purposes or for the aggravation of military conflicts; (3) monitoring trends in recipient countries' military expenditures, development and production of weapons of mass destruction, and export and imports of arms; and (4) promoting democratization and introduction of market economies, and attending to the conditions related to basic human rights and freedom" (MOFA 1992, 45). Three of the four guidelines respond to the international community's stipulations that allowed Iraq to become a military power. The charter also reiterates the regional foci of Japanese aid because "historically, geographically, politically and economically, Asia is a close region to Japan" (MOFA 1992, 47). Aid conditionality is a new policy stance for the Japanese.

## The Domestic Policymaking Arena

The Japanese rely on a dispersed administration system for foreign aid. Four government agencies—MOFA, MOF, the Ministry of International Trade and Industry (MITI), and the Economic Planning Agency (EPA)—administrate aid policy, but the EPA is less involved in practice. The group is officially chaired by MOFA. Two separate aid systems operate, depending upon whether loans or grants are extended. In the case of loans, the four main ministries arrive at a common decision for every loan provided. Grants, unlike loans, fall almost exclusively under MOFA's control, with MOF influencing the budgeting stage. MOFA ultimately controls the Japan International Cooperation Agency (JICA), which is responsible for administering grants. A closer examination of the responsibilities of the major divisions in JICA reveals that the relationships among the divisions are more blurred and several ministries are involved in grants. For example, MOF heads the Finance and Planning Division; officials from the Ministry of Agriculture, Forestry and Fisheries typically manage rural development grants; and MITI monitors mining and industrial planning. In practice, the bureaucrats attached to these agencies eventually rotate back to their ministries, to which they retain ultimate loyalty.

Each aid agency has different domestic constituencies. MOFA, the strongest supporter of expanding aid, approaches aid from a diplomatic perspective and favors policies likely to appeal abroad, such as targeting aid to the poorest states and reducing commercially oriented aid. MOFA uses aid as a diplomatic lever as frequently with developed as with developing states. It is adept at applying foreign pressure as leverage to win support for its positions within the domestic decision-making process. By contrast, MITI responds to industrial and trade constituencies for foreign aid and is less receptive to foreign pressure. It ardently opposes reducing the economic orientation of foreign aid and favors targeting aid recipients based on their potential to benefit Japan's trade and industrial interests.

The Japanese Diet plays virtually no role in the process of decision making on aid, in sharp contrast to the United States, where Congress, influenced by large immigrant lobbies, plays a major part in the specifics of foreign aid. In Japan there is nothing like the Foreign Assistance Act in the United States to legitimize aid. The Diet is empowered to pass the annual aid budget, and the legislature only occasionally uses its authority to evaluate aid plans.

MITI's influence no longer predominates as it did in the early stages of Japan's aid, when extensive aid tying and export promotion occurred. MOFA's relative influence in the Japanese bureaucracy has increased in recent years, with the gradual increase of grant aid as a proportion of total bilateral aid, from 38 percent in 1977 to 56.5 percent in 1993 (APIC 1994). Because of the pressure to bring Japan's grant share in line with the OECD average grant of 70 percent in 1990 (OECD[a] 1991, 178), it is likely that the grant share in Japanese aid will increase and empower MOFA even more.

As a result of the compartmentalization of aid, administration policy pronouncements are often vague, leading some in Washington to suspect sleight of hand. The image abroad of a Japanese consensus approach to foreign aid is a myth: the bureaucracies compete vigorously for aid control and influence. No comprehensive reform of the aid apparatus is on the horizon. Only ministry-specific attempts at organizing and streamlining aid activities are being introduced (*Japan Economic Review* 1994, 7).

## Regional Patterns of Japanese Foreign Aid

Over the last thirty years, the Japanese aid program greatly expanded the number of its recipients (156 in 1993) and the volume of its aid contributions over time. The program was very modest in the 1960s; for example, in 1966, Japan was the largest foreign aid donor to only 3 countries (fig. 4.1). By 1972, Japan was the top donor to 3 Asia-Pacific

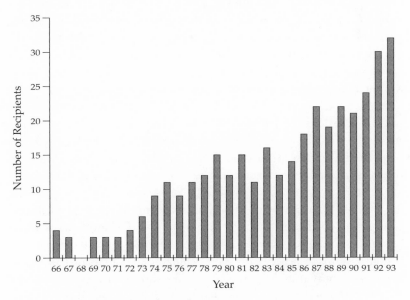

*Fig. 4.1.* The number of countries for which Japan
is the largest foreign aid donor, 1966–93

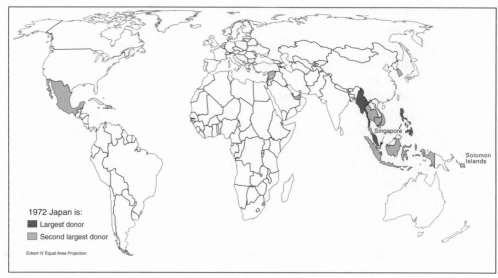

*Map 4.1.* Countries for which Japan is the largest
and second-largest aid donor, 1972

countries and the second most important donor to another 11 recipients.
(See map 4.1 for the geographical distribution of Japanese recipients.)
Japanese aid activity expanded from the mid-1970s onward; in 1974, for
example, the number of countries for which Japan was the top donor
worldwide almost tripled (to 9). Since then, the number of recipients has
grown steadily, expanding significantly in the late 1980s. By 1993, Japan
was the number one donor to 35 countries and the second largest donor
to another 29 recipients.

A large majority of Japanese aid targets are in the Asia–Pacific region
(fig. 4.2). While the geographic emphasis on the region has lessened over
time, from 93.6 percent in 1966 to 66.0 percent in 1993, the volume of
aid has increased to the region. Japan replaced the United States as the
top regional donor after 1986, when Japanese contributions were twice
the level of American. For virtually all recipients of the Asia–Pacific region, Japan was the top donor in 1993 (map 4.2). The intra–Asian distribution has changed dramatically since the 1980s as countries in the
region have made progress in their economic development—there has
been a shift away from South Asia toward Southeastern Asia. The share
shift was largely the result of a sharp rise in aid to China, India, and the

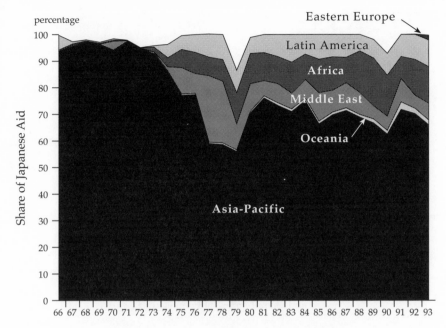

*Fig. 4.2.* Japanese aid to world regions, 1966–93

Philippines (poorer and more populous countries). The content of Japanese aid is also changing. In 1993, Japan terminated grant aid to Thailand, and loans to Malaysia are being shifted to environmental conservation projects.

Aid flows have been returning to the Middle East in the last two years and now are being restored to levels that existed before the Gulf crisis. During the 1970s insecurity over oil supplies made these states major aid recipients; at a peak in 1977, these states accounted for 25 percent of Japanese aid, declining to a low of 4.9 percent in 1992. In the 1980s the major oil producers of the Middle East were no longer large recipients of Japanese aid, partly because they no longer had income levels low enough to qualify. In the 1990s, however, the Middle East is again receiving Japanese attention as an important source of petroleum, an essential commodity for Japanese industries.

Only since 1990 have Eastern European states become Japanese aid recipients. The first loan to Eastern Europe was extended to Poland in 1990 ($21 million to assist economic reforms). Even though the volume

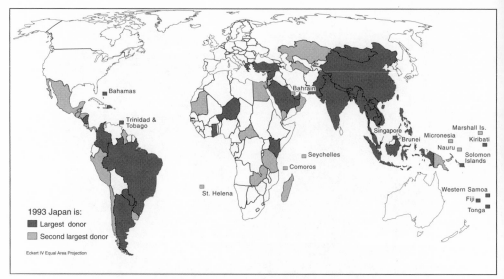

*Map 4.2.* Countries for which Japan is the largest
and second-largest aid donor, 1993

of Eastern European aid is extremely low, at $125.9 million in 1993, it is
growing rapidly (APIC 1994).

Aid is given to most Eastern European states and is typically in the
form of emergency food aid or cultural grants; for example, Hungary received aid for purchasing musical instruments for the state symphony in
1991. Because the Kurile Islands dispute has soured relations with Russia (Pitzl 1995), aid is not given to Russia, especially as only MITI is
in favor of extending aid to Russia (Inoguchi 1993, 147). In 1993 some
of the Commonwealth of Independent States, such as Kazakhstan, Uz-
beckistan, Kyrghyzstan, Tadzhistan, and Turkmenistan, received small
amounts of Japanese aid for the first time.

Africa now ranks as the second-largest regional destination of Japanese aid, whose amounts have risen steadily over time, with the most significant increase over the last decade: Japanese aid to Africa accounted
for 13.5 percent of total Japanese aid in 1992. Although aid to Africa placated some foreign critics of Japanese aid, the Africa program is debated
intensely amongst the bureaucracies. For example, MITI frequently opposes aid to Africa because the majority of funds are grants, which unlike loans are not subject to the deliberation of the four ministries,

meaning that MITI is effectively excluded. MOFA, in contrast, views aid to Africa as a way to debunk the economic critique of the Japanese program.

Although critics argue that Japanese aid especially privileges the Asia-Pacific region, there is no intrinsic reason why a donor should distribute its aid more or less equally among various regions. On the contrary, one could argue that aid can be used more effectively in regions where the donor has close historical, political, and economic relationships and is familiar with local institutions. The norm among DAC donors is to allocate aid to former colonies. Japan is no different in favoring a regional concentration, except none of its major recipients is a former colony.

## The Economic Geography of Japanese Aid

The geography of Japanese aid can be further explored by examining aid giving as it is related to the economic categories of states. Whether Japanese aid is more humanitarian than commercial in nature can be assessed by the volume of aid given to poorer countries compared to aid given to newly industrializing countries (NICs), OPEC members, and strategic countries that provide Japan with exports of valuable raw materials. Aid to the poorest recipients—for instance, the twenty lowest-income countries (LICs) in the world—represents a smaller share of Japanese aid (10.5 percent in 1993) than might be expected. Japanese aid appears to be motivated less by humanitarian considerations than is officially proclaimed (table 4.1). However, Japanese aid allocations to LICs increased in the 1980s from 2.5 percent of total foreign aid in 1966 to 13.9 percent in 1990 relative to the DAC average of 23 percent (OECD[a] 1992, 52), reflecting official policy statements that underscored humanitarian aspects of Japanese assistance. Since the end of the Cold War, the LICs' aid share has declined to 9.0 percent, partly because more and more recipients receive aid each year and aid is allocated for new emergent needs in Eastern Europe and the Commonwealth of Independent States, but mostly to reinstate the very high levels of support to the NICs.

This hands-off approach differs considerably from Japan's involvement in NICs, which is subject to intense public sector review. Tokyo's detached approach toward LICs reflects its uneasiness in cooperating with states that have no long-standing historical or political relationship

*Table 4.1*  The Allocation of Japanese Foreign Aid by Target Group

|            | 1966 | 1970 | 1975 | 1980 | 1985 | 1990 | 1993 |
|------------|------|------|------|------|------|------|------|
| LICs[a]    | 2.5  | 2.9  | 5.9  | 5.6  | 11.3 | 13.9 | 10.50 |
| NICs[b]    | 95.6 | 86.2 | 65.5 | 52.1 | 56.3 | 60.0 | 58.5 |
| OPEC[c]    | —    | 3.0  | 4.3  | 1.8  | .3   | .2   | 1.5  |
| Strategic[d] | 95.5 | 79.8 | 70.2 | 51.0 | 57.1 | 76.1 | 57.4 |

Source: OECD(b) (1966–96).

a. The lowest ranked countries of the world in terms of World Bank's classification of the twenty poorest countries. Countries included are Bangladesh, Burkino Faso, Burundi, Chad, Ethiopia, Laos, Madagascar, Malawi, Mali, Mozambique, Nepal, Niger, Nigeria, Rwanda, Somalia, Tanzania, Togo, Uganda, Zambia, and Zaire.

b. NICs are defined according to the *Economist*'s list of countries with the highest GDP growth rates. NICs include Argentina, Brazil, China, Chile, Czech Republic, Greece, Hong Kong, Hungary, India, Indonesia, Israel, Malaysia, Mexico, the Philippines, Poland, Portugal, Russia, Singapore, South Africa, South Korea, Taiwan, Thailand, Turkey, and Venezuela.

c. OPEC countries include Algeria, Iran, Iraq, Kuwait, Qatar, United Arab Emirates (U.A.E.), Saudi Arabia, Gabon, Libya, Ecuador, and Venezuela.

d. Strategic countries are defined as Japan's top twenty import partners for commodities which it has a comparative disadvantage in producing; for example, food, oil and natural gas, and minerals. Countries include Argentina, Brazil, China, Chile, Indonesia, India, Iran, Korea, Kuwait, Oman, the Philippines, Mexico, Malaysia, Qatar, Saudi Arabia, Singapore, Thailand, U.A.E., Vietnam, and Yemen. These were calculated according to my analysis of Japan's import partners for 1992 using the United Nations *Commodity Trade Statistics* (1993).

 with Japan. Most observers believe that Japan must overcome its seeming indifference toward the LICs to be accepted as a global leader. Recent policy announcements indicate that Tokyo will redressing its aid emphasis in the future. In June 1993, Tokyo announced a "Funds for Development" initiative that provided an additional $70 billion of untied aid for developing countries over the next few years (Ishii 1994, 12), but it is too early for changes to show up in aid data.

Particularly striking is the large share of aid given to NICs, which varied from about 96 percent of bilateral aid flows in 1966 to approximately 60 percent in 1990s. Even at a time when MITI's role in the bureaucracy is diminishing, the share of aid to the NICs continues to expand. A large part of this pattern is explained by the NICs' location in the Asia-Pacific region, the central focus for Japanese aid.

The category of strategic countries is also a very important destination for Japanese aid flows. Countries that provide Japan with valuable exports of raw materials appear to be favored in terms of aid given. This trend seems to be reinforced by a modest but still significant level of aid given to OPEC countries, which are far less a needier group than the LICs. The high levels given to these economic groupings of countries can be attributed to the functioning of Japan's comprehensive security policy in foreign aid policy.

## Aid Project Emphases

Heavy private sector involvement characterizes Japanese aid activities. Private involvement extends to project identification, implementation, and evaluation, not only because of the high proportion of funds spent on large economic infrastructural projects (transport, energy, communications, and river development) but also because of the shortage of aid personnel available to service several aspects of the aid process (1,853 in 1993, fewer than half the comparable United States personnel) (MOFA 1994). The understaffing problem and the economic emphases of aid projects reinforce each other indirectly as capital projects are less labor-intensive than social assistance projects.

Within the economic infrastructure and services category the transportation sector occupies the highest share every year (18.8 percent in 1993); this category includes both land transportation (road and railroad) and marine transportation (port construction and improvement). Emphases of Japanese aid vary across countries, reflecting the request basis of Japanese aid. Japanese officials stress the value of infrastructural investment as a stimulus for sustained economic growth. Following the Foreign Aid Charter, which underscores aid for basic human needs, aid allocations to agriculture and program assistance have been rising. More aid was also directed toward social infrastructure and services in 1993. This increase is again explained by new Japanese emphases on aid for the environment, population, women in development, and AIDS prevention. In many ways, Japan is becoming more typical in its allocations of aid to various project emphases. Overall, Japan behaves more like the World Bank, which contributes 32 percent of its funds to economic infrastructure (Islam 1993, 343).

The environment is a sectoral allocation of Japanese aid that is expanding rapidly. Japanese aid increases to this sector have corresponded to the government's new policy emphasis as specified in the Foreign Aid Charter. For instance, environmental aid accounted for 18 percent of total aid in 1993 and serviced eighteen large environmental projects. This new environmental aid emphasis is a response both to Japan's domestic accomplishments in creating and enacting a whole range of environmental laws and to its abysmal international environmental reputation (Maull 1992), where Japan was been accused of whaling, driftnet fishing, endangered species smuggling, and tropical rainforest destruction.

## Aid Tying

Aid tying can assume various forms, including foreign assistance linked to a specific development project or to the purchase of project-related Japanese services; both forms limit local development options. Another more fungible restriction is partially tied aid, an arrangement that requires the recipient to procure certain commodities in the donor country or specifically designated countries or regions.

In the early years, Tokyo treated foreign aid as part of its postwar strategy toward economic recovery, and all aid was linked to the purchase of Japanese goods and services. Aid tying occurred simultaneously when MITI commanded aid policy. Over the years, Japanese aid has become increasingly less tied, and efforts to delink the commercial aspects of Japanese aid have intensified. Tokyo shifted gradually from tied aid to partially tied aid and then to the present policy of untying 65 percent of foreign aid (in comparison to the DAC average of 42 percent) in 1992.

Despite Japan's maintaining one of the lowest levels of official tying, critics still charge that Japanese aid is informally tied, because the private sector is extensively involved in identifying projects and assisting recipient governments in applying for Japanese foreign aid (Preeg 1993, 99). Furthermore, the exclusive use of Japanese consultants to conduct feasibility studies creates incentives for project designers to specify materials and equipment that can be supplied only by domestic firms. The request basis for the consideration of aid projects, relying on recipients to outline development projects, enables Japanese trading companies to approach developing countries' officials with a potential project. Furthermore, it also is not unusual for a company to lobby its Tokyo contacts for acceptance of the project and to monitor discussion during the approval process (Orr 1990, 60).

In response to informal accusations of tying, Tokyo introduced a policy to untie consultant services in April 1988 (Jepma 1991, 35) with JICA and OECF expanding their activities into project identification. As a result, more foreign suppliers are securing procurement contracts. In

1984, for example, 75 percent of procurement contracts went to Japanese suppliers; only 31 percent went to Japanese firms in 1991 (MOFA 1992), a very small share for the highly competitive Japanese firms. In 1992, the U.S. Department of Commerce established an information and support program to assist domestic suppliers in obtaining Japanese aid contracts (*Business America* 1992). Not surprisingly, MITI and the Japanese business community oppose this policy.

## Japan and the New World Order

Japanese aid agencies have been defining Japan's interests differently since the end of the Cold War. The broad goals have been expanded, and attempts are being made to downplay the self-interest and economic rationale in Japanese aid policies. The previous dual emphasis of the maintenance of international order and the sectarian advantage (as espoused by the "comprehensive national security" policy of the 1980s) led to ambivalence in Tokyo's foreign policy conduct. The goals of Japanese aid are defined today by universal, not national, terms. "The securing of world peace and stability, the furtherance of global economic prosperity, the promoting of universal values such as freedom, human rights, and democracy and the solution of global issues such as environmental problems" (MOFA 1993, 3) are put forward as Japanese objectives.

Fortunately for Japan, the post–Cold War era places a greater emphasis on global and not just Western interdependence and a higher priority on the economic dimension of statecraft. The weighing of priorities toward the economic dimension of power and away from the military suit Japan's foreign policy and enhance its role in global affairs by the extent of its financial and economic resources. Japan is well positioned in the New World Order, in which greater symmetry between global economic and political roles is emerging.

Japanese aid in the 1990s facilitates the U.S.-Japan relationship by responsibility sharing rather than by burden sharing. Responsibility sharing entails a division of labor in global roles in the New World Order: the United States will continue to provide a security umbrella by carrying  the burden of being the world's only military superpower, and Japan will spend huge sums on foreign aid. This arrangement facilitates power sharing and should confer more prestige on Japan as well as provide Tokyo with more leeway in pursuing independent foreign policy actions. For instance, Tokyo was first to resume aid to China after the Tianan-

men Square crackdown, and it broke with U.S. foreign policy again in
1992 by resuming aid to Iran and Vietnam. At the same time, aid facilitates an increasingly important Japanese presence in the Asia–Pacific region. This trend is heightened even more by U.S. aid disengagement
from the region: the gap between Tokyo's involvement and Washington's removal increases over time.

Continuing past policies, the Japanese are emphasizing a pacifist foreign policy. To encourage aid recipients to develop nonmilitarily, the
Japanese judge military expenditures negatively. According to the Foreign Aid Charter, the Japanese monitor "good governance" by paying
particular attention to military trends in developing countries. This policy espousal, which is new, adds a political dimension to an economic instrument and signifies a change from Japan's Cold War practice, when
aid often complemented Washington's efforts to reward strategic allies
and punish Moscow's clients. Thus, the charter is an attempt to address
the North-South problem without the Cold War ideological pejorative.
The criteria for assessing aid recipients do, however, contain ideological
motivations—positive assessments for aid candidacy are awarded to
countries promoting democracy, market reform, and human rights.
Japan appears to be offering its civilian power model (Maull 1991) as a
development prototype for others to emulate.

Despite the rhetoric of paying attention to "good governance," case-
by-case assessments of the application of these principles reveal incon-
sistencies that threaten to erode Tokyo's credibility abroad and respect
for its new diplomatic resolve. Tokyo appears willing to apply its principles only to countries of marginal economic significance, e.g., Malawi,
Kenya, Haiti, and Zaire, or to countries with which it has a political-ter-
ritorial dispute, e.g., Russia; it seems unwilling to exercise the same principles in other cases, such as China, Indonesia, and Thailand, in which
the return on large sums of infrastructural aid investments is at stake.
MOFA's sole support of these principles means continuing compromises
because MITI and MOF are more concerned with the continuation of
market access.

Despite an aid charter that introduces major changes on the declaratory side, little change is evident on the implementation side. In the criteria for assessing recipients, all conditions are to be given equal weight.
Little effort has been made to operationalize the charter, and aid budgets
have not been reorganized accordingly. It is not clear how the major
charter principles will in fact be operationalized. Can any recipient satisfy all the criteria?

## Conclusions

The Japanese have turned increasingly to foreign aid as a source of
world influence and to engage challenges in the New World Order. Foreign aid is an important Japanese policy tool because it serves multiple
purposes. The original bureaucratic organization of the Japanese aid
program indicates the intention of coordinating aid with economic, foreign policy, and other interests. The recent elevation of MOFA's status
within the aid bureaucracy and the related policy pronouncements, i.e.,
the Foreign Aid Charter, indicate that Japanese aid is becoming less
commercial and more multidimensional and complex, serving numerous
political, security, economic, environmental, and global objectives. The
Japanese are attempting to use aid to address the complexities of the
global economy. In this sense, Japanese foreign aid is becoming more like
that of other major donors. However, the Japanese run the risk of following the broad and multipurpose foreign aid programs that emerged
in the United States in the 1960s and 1970s, programs that invited
mounting domestic criticism.

Additional policy emphases are emerging, such as foreign aid for the
environmental sector and most recently "women in development," partly to deflect criticism from Japan's poor international reputation in these
domains but mostly to reflect its new aid philosophy. Japanese aid packages now includes guidelines for reviewing the environmental impacts
of proposed development projects. Furthermore, Japanese aid now aims
to promote forest conservation and afforestation, energy saving, and development of clean energy technology and pollution control. Initially,
these areas will provide the Japanese with opportunities not only in research and development but also in the trading of environment-related
services.

Perhaps the most profound impact of Japanese efforts in foreign aid is
the emergence of Japan's own international development philosophy, favoring a role for government in directing private sector growth versus
what it terms the "excessive free-market reliance" of multilateral institutions. Japan helps promote its development philosophy by making
large financial contributions to multilateral banks. In the 1990s, Japan is
either the most important or the second most important donor to all
multilateral banks, including the European Bank for Reconstruction and
Development (EBRD) (Yasutomo 1993, 326). Efforts to influence development in other important developing countries include the translation
of the official history of Japanese industrial policy into Chinese (*Econo-*

*mist* 1994, 2). Japan is also playing a more significant role in institutions such as the International Monetary Fund and the World Bank. In the World Bank, for instance, Japan's capital share is now second to that of the United States, translating into increased policy influence (Inoguchi 1993, 147). Japan's role in multilateral institutions is being converted from a low-profile policy to a high-profile one in recent years, and World Bank publications reflect that expansion in Japanese policy influence. For example, in 1994 the Japanese paid for a World Bank report on "The East Asian Miracle," which not surprisingly found government intervention to be among the key reasons for development success (*Economist* 1994, 2). Graduates from Japanese aid (e.g., South Korea and Singapore) are starting their own economic aid programs to developing countries based on the Japanese program, thus further confirming the Japanese approach. While Japan's recommendations are received coolly within international fora, their attractiveness to an increasing number of countries seeking to emulate Japan's development experiences is indicative of the weakening of the Western development norm. Furthermore, Japan's many successful development experiences in the Asia-Pacific region are encouraging Japanese officials to continue their high levels of funding for aid programs worldwide.

# 5

# European Foreign Aid
## *South, East, Both, or Neither?*

### Sven Holdar

THE EUROPEAN UNION (EU) and its fifteen member states are the largest source of Western development assistance.* In 1995 the aid programs of the EU-15 accounted for more than half of total Western bilateral aid. The EU-15 dominate aid giving to Africa. Not only the EU member states are large aid donors; the European Commission is also a significant aid donor. The principal influence on EU aid policy has been compromise solutions to satisfy the member states' different regional interests in the Third World. With increasing expansion of the EU over time and with the end of the Cold War, additional regional interests of EU member states have been added to the EU aid agenda. This development has not, however, been part of any concerted strategy. EU aid policy is a mix of national interests, and little coordination exists. In this chapter, I substantiate this characterization of EU aid policies by accounting for the historical development of EU aid policy and relations with the Third World. I give particular focus to why attempts to develop and coordinate EU aid policy have failed. Finally, I comment about the impact of changes in Eastern Europe and the former Soviet Union after 1989.

---

* Belgium, France, Luxembourg, The Netherlands, Germany, Italy, Denmark, United Kingdom, Ireland, Portugal, Spain, Greece, Sweden, Finland, and Austria.

## The Development of European Community Relations
## with the Third World

The European Community's (EC's) involvement in foreign aid was established in the Rome Treaty of 1957, which stated that colonies and former colonies of the EC member states should receive grants from the newly established European Development Fund and become associated with the development of the Community (*EC Courier* 1981, 47). France insisted on this link between Western Europe and its colonies (*Europe-South Dialogue* 1988, 22). Germany and The Netherlands were initially reluctant to agree to this policy of giving certain parts of the Third World privileged status in relations with the EC. The French prevailed, however, and got the other members of the EC to make its interest in maintaining privileged economic ties with its colonies part of EC policy (Muniz 1980, 56; White 1974, 220).

After independence, the French (except for Guinea), Belgian, and Italian former colonies in Africa maintained their economic ties with the EC. These relations were regulated in the Yaoundé treaties (signed in 1965 and renewed in 1969), which started a new, more formal process of relations between the EC-6 and their former colonies. Access to the EC market and European Development Fund (EDF) assistance was formally regulated, and new institutions were created to oversee the implementation of the treaties (*Europe-South Dialogue* 1988, 22).

In the late 1960s pressures grew on the EC to take a more global approach in its aid and trade policies toward the Third World. Organizations like the United Nations Commission for Trade and Development (UNCTAD) and the General Agreement on Tariffs and Trade (GATT), as well as Germany and The Netherlands, pressed for an open policy that would not give special treatment to francophone Africa (Mytelka and Dolan 1980, 255). This pressure resulted in the EC decision in 1971 on a Generalized System of Preferences (GSP) whereby all so-called "Third World countries" would get preferential access for their manufactured exports to the EC (*Europe-South Dialogue* 1988, 22). This decision weakened the French position of favoring only the exports of its former colonies. With the United Kingdom's entry into the EC in 1973, however, France's favoring of exclusionary EC relations with certain parts of the Third World was strengthened. Britain's entry was predicated on its non-Asian Commonwealth members being able to enter into some sort of preferential relationship with the EC similar to what the francophone African states enjoyed through the Yaoundé treaties (My-telka and Dolan 1980, 255). In the negotiations on a new treaty between the EC and the francophone and anglophone former colonies of Africa, the Caribbean, and the Pacific (ACP), France supported the British position. Germany, on the other hand, maintained its position on equal preferential treatment for all Third World countries but eventually retreated and accepted the creation of a special EC-ACP relationship, laid down in the first Lomé Treaty of 1975 (Lomé II was signed in 1979, Lomé III in 1984, and Lomé IV in 1990) (Mytelka and Dolan 1980, 256).

The Lomé treaties gave most ACP exports free access to the EC market. The major exception was agricultural products in areas where ACP exports competed with EC products. Although access was subsequently extended also in this area, tariffs and quotas are still used by the EC to limit some ACP agricultural exports. As in the Yaoundé treaties, economic aid was an important part of the Lomé treaties. Since 1975 the EDF has sent more than 60 percent of its aid to the ACP countries (*EC Courier* 1993, 52). (The five-year commitments of the Lomé treaties are shown in table 5.1.) Money for these programs is based upon fixed contributions by the member states. In the 1960s and early 1970s, France made the largest contribution (Wood 1986, 75). Over time, however, Germany has taken over this role. Of the EDF contributions for Lomé II, Germany provided 28.3 percent, France 25.6 percent, Britain 18 percent, Italy 11.5 percent, The Netherlands 7.4 percent, Belgium 5.9 percent, Denmark 2.5 percent, Ireland 0.6 percent, and Luxembourg 0.2 percent.

The German acceptance of the EC-ACP relationship and France's acceptance of GSP illustrate the compromise on EC Third World policy, which was also demonstrated in the Paris Declaration of October 1972, where the EC heads of state agreed upon a global policy of development cooperation involving all Third World countries as well as a regional African focus in the extension of the Yaoundé treaties into the Lomé treaties (*Europe-South Dialogue* 1988, 76). As part of the former policy, the EC in the 1970s further developed its relationship with the Mediterranean countries as well as with Asia and Latin America.

During the period from 1963 to 1972, the EC had already signed association and preferential trade agreements with big trading partners in the Mediterranean region, such as Greece, Turkey, Spain, Cyprus, and Malta. In late 1972, the EC Commission proposed an extension of new trade and aid agreements to the southern Mediterranean countries. Be-

*Table 5.1*  EU Aid and Loans Provided through the Lomé Conventions
*(millions of ECUs)*

| Category | Lomé I | Lomé II | Lomé III | Lomé IV |
|---|---|---|---|---|
| Total EDF[a] | 2,980 | 4,627 | 7,400 | 10,800 |
| Grants | 2,058 | 2,986 | 4,860 | 7,995 |
| Risk capital EIB[b] | 97 | 284 | 600 | 825 |
| Stabex[c] | 380 | 557 | 925 | 1,500 |
| Sysmin[d] | — | 282 | 415 | 480 |
| Total EIB | 390 | 885 | 1,100 | 1,200 |

Source: *Europe-South Dialogue* 1988; Biståndet och EG 1991.

a. European Development Fund.

b. European Investment Bank.

c. A fund for compensating single-crop exporters for large losses due to fluctuating world market prices. It is primarily a few agricultural exporters in West Africa (Ghana, Sengal, and Côte d'Ivoire) that have benefited from Stabex support.

d. A fund for compensating mineral exporters for large losses due to fluctuating prices on the world market.

tween 1975 and 1977 this resulted in new cooperation agreements with the Maghreb countries (Morocco, Algeria, Tunisia, Libya, and Mauritania) and Mashreq countries (Algeria, Morocco, and Tunisia; Israel, Egypt, Jordan, and Syria) (*Europe-South Dialogue* 1988, 41). Despite these cooperation agreements, however, little aid was extended from the EC. In addition, most support (more than 60 percent of total assistance between 1978 and 1986) was given as soft credits handled by the European Investment Bank (EIB). In the 1980s there were also complaints from developing countries about EC protectionism limiting access to exports, such as textiles and agricultural products (*Europe-South Dialogue* 1988, 43).

As part of the global approach toward the Third World, the EC intensified efforts to cooperate also with countries in Latin America and Asia. New policies were influenced by the addition of new EC members. Britain's membership in 1973, for example, resulted in more EDF aid going to countries in South Asia (India, Pakistan, and Bangladesh), while Spain's and Portugal's membership in 1986 led to pressures on the EC to intensify its economic ties with Latin America and the Mediterranean (Wingborg 1993, 6). Although agreements on economic and cultural cooperation were signed between the EC and the Association of

South East Asian Nations (ASEAN) (1980), China (1985), and the Gulf Cooperation Council (1988), their scope was limited, as was the amount of EC aid (*Europe–South Dialogue* 1988, 80–88).

Although the EC's relations with different parts of the Third World are extensive, they continue to be characterized by ambiguity. The regional ACP approach and the global approach have continued to exist side by side. Even though the economic importance of the ACP countries for Europe has diminished every year, France has continued to defend this special relationship (Mytelka and Dolan 1980). States showing the greatest interest in foreign aid matters, such as Germany, the United Kingdom, The Netherlands, and Denmark (Biståndet och EG 1991, 52), pressed for a more global approach. Recently, it appears that the latter opinion has gained influence. In the 1990s, EU aid to the ACP countries has decreased and the preferential treatment of these countries has increasingly come under discussion because of both the inefficiency of many of these programs and EU member states' growing interest in more economically important regions, such as Eastern Europe, the Mediterranean, and Asia. Still, that this discussion fundamentally would alter the direction of EU aid is not probable. The geography of EU aid is likely to remain scattered, with the EU's own aid being little more than a patchwork of the member states' national interests in the Third World.

## Aid Coordination and the Geography of European Aid

In the late 1960s the concentration of EC aid basically corresponded to that of France (table 5.2). Former French colonies, Zaire (reflecting Belgian interests), and Turkey (largely reflecting German interests) were the largest recipients of EC aid during this period. France's share of the total aid given by the five member states with aid programs amounted to almost 50 percent, putting France in a powerful position to influence the direction of EC aid. Its influence weakened toward the end of the 1960s and in the early 1970s because of two circumstances. First, the United Kingdom became a new member of the EC in 1973 and broadened the EC's connections with Third World countries. Second, a new interest for development issues and the Third World emerged, especially in Northern Europe (e.g., The Netherlands, the Scandinavian countries, and Germany), and resulted in new movements for the expansion of the national aid programs. Aid became a new issue on the political agenda in

*Table 5.2*  The European Aid Donors and Their Major Recipients, 1966–70

| Donor | Total aid[a] | Aid as % of GNP[b] | Main recipients[c] |
|---|---|---|---|
| Belgium | 489 | .46 | Zaire, 62.7; Rwanda, 11.1; Burundi, 9.6; Tunisia, 2.5; India, 2.4; Turkey, 2.2; Indonesia, 1.7; Chile, 1.3; Morocco, 1.3; Pakistan, 1.3 |
| France[d] | 4,350 | .66 | Algeria, 26.1; Senegal, 6.9; Malag, 6.4; C. d'Ivoire, 6.2; Morocco, 5.5; Cameroon, 4.5; Tunisia, 4.4; Niger, 4.0; Indonesia, 3.6; Chad, 3.1 |
| Germany | 2,653 | .32 | India, 13.4; Israel, 10.4; Pakistan, 7.9; Turkey, 5.7; Indonesia, 5.1; Chile, 4.3; Nigeria, 3.1; Morocco, 2.8; Argentina, 2.7; Brazil, 2.3 |
| Italy | 56 | .16 | Indonesia, 21.3; Turkey, 13.4; Tunisia, 12.4; Egypt, 7.8; Somalia, 7.8; Syria, 5.8; Ethiopia, 5.5; India, 5.4; Zambia, 5.4; Morocco, 4.0 |
| Netherlands | 670 | .61 | Indonesia, 35.5; Surinam, 19.5; India, 16.9; Pakistan, 5.5; Nigeria, 3.6; Ghana, 2.2; Turkey, 1.7; Tunisia, 1.7; Uruguay, 1.7; Kenya, 1.5 |
| EEC | 740 | — | Cameroon, 9.6; Malag, 8.9; C. d'Ivoire, 7.8; Turkey, 7.2; Senegal, 7.1; Zaire, 6.0; Mali, 5.4; Chad, 4.5; U. Volta, 4.3; Niger, 4.3 |

Source: OECD(b) (1966–96).

a. Total net in millions US$; includes bilateral and multilateral aid (and contributions to the EEC).

b. The numbers are for 1970.

c. Percentages of the donor's total country-specific bilateral commitments for the years 1966, 1967, 1969, and 1970.

d. Including aid to French overseas territories (e.g., Reunion, Martinique, New Caledonia).

these countries, and consequently their aid programs were expanded and their governments came to take a greater interest in the EC aid program itself.

It was against this background that the EC member states, in the Paris Declaration of 1972, expressed a common interest in further developing the coordination and harmonization of EC and national policies on development cooperation (*Europe-South Dialogue* 1988, 77). The EC Commission was to be given a greater role in these efforts. This was in line with the new EC interest of coordinating the member states' foreign policies with each other. As noted by the EC itself in 1989, however, little came out of this effort (Council of the European Communities 1989). The national aid agencies did not follow any common European foreign aid policy; instead, the EC, in its distribution of aid, incorporated an assemblage of objectives fitting the interests of all member states (*EC Courier* 1993, 52).

*Table 5.3* The European Aid Donors and Their Major Recipients, 1976–80

| Donor | Total aid[a] | Aid as % of GNP[b] | Main recipients[c] |
|---|---|---|---|
| Belgium | 473 | .50 | Zaire, 43.3; Rwanda, 11.0; Burundi, 7.2; Morocco, 4.6; Tunisia, 4.4; Indonesia, 4.0; India, 2.5; C. d'Ivoire, 2.1; Bangladesh, 1.7; Niger, 1.7 |
| France[d] | 14,650 | .64 | Morocco, 9.6; C. d'Ivoire, 6.9; Algeria, 6.8; Senegal, 6.7; Tunisia, 6.6; Cameroon, 5.3; Indonesia, 3.6; Egypt, 3.5; CAR, 3.4; U. Volta, 3.3 |
| Germany | 12,574 | .44 | Turkey, 8.6; Bangladesh, 7.5; India, 7.1; Indonesia, 5.1; Egypt, 4.7; Tanzania, 3.9; Sudan, 3.5; Tunisia, 3.4; Israel, 3.0; Pakistan, 2.9 |
| Italy | 1,755 | .17 | Somalia, 18.9; Pakistan, 13.5; Egypt, 7.4; Ethiopia, 6.8; Indonesia, 6.7; Vietnam, 3.8; Mozambique, 2.9; Morocco, 2.8; Tunisia, 2.8; India, 2.3 |
| Netherlands | 5,743 | 1.03 | India, 13.7; Indonesia, 10.6; Tanzania, 9.0; Bangladesh, 6.6; Surinam, 5.9; Kenya, 4.2; Pakistan, 4.1; Sudan, 3.6; Peru, 2.8; U. Volta, 2.7 |
| EEC | 4,416 | — | Turkey, 7.3; India, 6.7; Senegal, 4.5; Sudan, 3.9; Bangladesh, 3.7; Tanzania, 3.2; Zaire, 3.2; Ethiopia, 3.1; Niger, 2.5; Morocco, 2.4 |
| Denmark | 789 | .74 | Tanzania, 22.8; Bangladesh, 11.1; India, 9.8; Kenya, 8.7; Mozambique, 4.9; Sudan, 4.2; Egypt, 3.8; Malawi, 3.7; Burma, 2.8 |
| Ireland[e] | 90 | .16 | Lesotho, 11.6; Sudan, 3.0; Tanzania, 2.6; Zambia, 2.2; Swaziland, 0.6; Rwanda, .06 |
| UK | 7,361 | .35 | India, 24.0; Bangladesh, 8.4; Kenya, 7.3; Sri Lanka, 6.3; Pakistan, 5.5; Tanzania, 4.6; Zambia, 3.6; Malawi, 2.9; Nepal, 2.2 |

Source: OECD(b) (1966–96).

a. Total net in millions US$; includes bilateral and multilateral aid (and contributions to the EEC).
b. The numbers are for 1980.
c. Percentages of the donor's total country-specific bilateral commitments for 1976–80.
d. Including aid to French overseas territories (e.g., Reunion, Martinique, New Caledonia).
e. For Ireland, percentages of gross disbursements, 1980–81.

The former French colonies in the late 1970s no longer held the dominant position they held in influencing the distribution of EC aid in the late 1960s (compare tables 5.2 and 5.3). Instead, former British colonies in South Asia and Africa (and Turkey) now became more important destinations for EC aid. While France's share of total EC member state aid at this time had decreased to around 30 percent, Britain's, Germany's, Holland's, and Denmark's combined share made up almost 60 percent of the total. Sharing similar views on foreign aid, these four states began to cooperate informally on EC foreign aid policy in the 1970s (Wingborg 1993, 8) but have not been interested in giving the EC Commission more power to administer EC aid and coordination between the EC and member states. Rather, their influence has been restricted to the direction of EC aid and the contents of EDF aid programs (Biståndet och EG 1991, 52–55). Although the 1991 Maastricht agreement on a European Political Union (EPU) asserted that EU aid policy should aim for further coordination among the member states, it is likely that the EU's foreign aid policy (and foreign policy) will continue to be a complement, rather than a substitute, for national foreign aid policies.

What may change is the mix of such interests with the expansion of the EU to include Finland and Sweden. In these countries there are powerful lobbies for aid, and the governments have made efforts to expand their national aid programs. Their aid objectives are similar to those of Denmark and The Netherlands, with a focus on British Africa and South Asia, and with humanitarian objectives playing a large role. It is likely that these Scandinavian countries, as members of the EU, will work with the already existing group for aid cooperation within the EU. It is unlikely, however, that they will work for more coordination under the EU Commission. This would both dilute their high national aid profiles and give more influence to French, Portuguese, and Spanish interests to direct more EU aid to their former colonies in Sub-Saharan Africa, the Maghreb, and Latin America.

The top recipients of EU aid (map 5.1) are Mozambique ($83 million), former Yugoslavia ($72 million), Poland ($49 million), Tanzania ($44 million), and China ($41 million). Aid funding levels indicate a development focus in EU aid, especially aid to Mozambique, Tanzania, and China (in the latter case aid is given for poverty alleviation in contrast to the Japanese focus on infrastructural projects). The EU is also responding to the fall of communism in Eastern Europe and the breakup of the Soviet Union. In particular, Germany and Austria stand out as countries that have most expanded their aid programs (about one-half of Austria's and about one-third of Germany's total aid went to Eastern Europe and the former Soviet Union in 1993). Poland is the number one recipient in the region, but the states of former Yugoslavia are also emphasized in an effort to stabilize the region. Since 1992 these states have also become the largest recipients of assistance from The Netherlands, the United Kingdom, and Sweden. In general, EU donors have retained their traditional regional interests in their distribution of

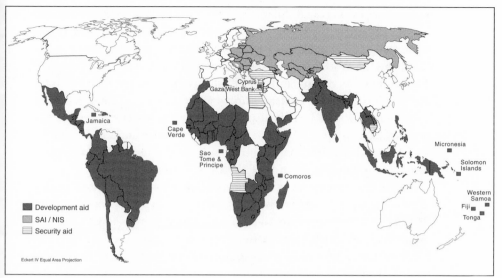

*Map 5.1.* The European aid donors and their major recipients in 1993

aid to the Third World (for example, French, British, and Belgian interests in their former colonies and Danish, Dutch, and German interests in poor countries in Eastern Europe, Southern Africa, and South Asia).

## Go East! The New Direction of European Aid?

At the Group of 7 (G-7) meeting in Paris in July 1989 (attended by Canada, France, Germany, Italy, Japan, the United Kingdom, and the United States), the EC Commission was given the leading role in coordinating Western assistance to the emerging noncommunist regimes in Eastern Europe. This outcome resulted from a compromise between the United States and France, meaning that the American idea for a wide-ranging Western aid program to Poland and Hungary (coordinated by the Europeans) as well as France's proposal for a new European Bank for Reconstruction and Development (EBRD) were accepted as foundations for a new Western policy toward Eastern Europe (Merritt 1991, 21–22). The EU-led assistance program was to take place within the so-called Group of 24 (G-24), which included Canada, the United States, Japan, Australia, New Zealand, Austria, Belgium, Denmark, Finland, France, Germany, Greece, Iceland, Ireland, Italy, Luxembourg, The Netherlands, Norway, Portugal, Spain, Sweden, Switzerland, Turkey, and the United Kingdom; the International Monetary Fund (IMF); the Organization for Economic Cooperation and Development (OECD); the Paris Club; and the World Bank (Biståndet och EG 1991, 19).

In addition to coordinating the Western aid effort, the EC started up new aid programs for Eastern Europe and the Soviet Union. The two main ones are PHARE (Poland and Hungary: Assistance for Restructuring Economies) and TACIS (Technical Assistance for the Commonwealth of Independent States) during 1989 and 1990. PHARE aid today accounts for about two-thirds of the EC's total budget for program aid budget to the former Soviet bloc (in 1992, for example, this total in European Currency Units was ECU 1.5 billion). TACIS accounts for one-third (Ek and Stjernström 1993, 9–19). PHARE and TACIS aid has been evenly divided between the recipient countries, reflecting their population size. Germany has paid most (about 50 percent) of the contributions to these programs (Ek and Stjernström 1993, 60).

France's pet project from 1989, the EBRD, came into operation in 1990. Although it is a non-EC organization, the EC and its member states own the majority of shares in this bank. How much funding the EBRD members should contribute to this bank initially caused some conflict among EC members. France demanded the highest sum, ECU 15 billion, while Britain and The Netherlands argued for only ECU 5 billion. In the end, a compromise was reached: ECU 10 billion. However, like many other East European aid programs, EBRD during its first three years of operation used very little of this capital to fund actual projects in Eastern Europe (Merritt 1991, 240).

While the EC Commission was given a leading role in coordinating aid to Eastern and Central Europe, it was the IMF that in 1990 was given the task of coordinating Western aid to the former Soviet Union. The greater geopolitical significance of the USSR meant that the United States took a more active role with assistance programs for the former Soviet Union than with those for Eastern Europe. Through the IMF, the United States, with the largest voting share, could wield more influence over the direction of Western policy toward the USSR than through the EC Commission. In this way, a geographic division of labor emerged. Over time, the EC and the EC-12 (Belgium, France, Luxembourg, The Netherlands, Germany, Italy, Denmark, United Kingdom, Ireland, Spain, Portugal, and Greece) have taken most of the responsibility for coordinating Western policy toward Eastern and Central Europe, while the United States has taken the leadership role in relation to the former Soviet Union.

In the summer of 1989, both American and European politicians were enthralled by the political changes in Poland and Hungary and competed to propose the largest amounts of aid to this part of the world. However, with the subsequent disintegration of the whole Soviet–East European empire and the Soviet Union itself, and with the deep economic crisis in the Western economies, interest in aiding the former communist enemies faded. Putting taxpayers' money into programs organized by international organizations (EC, EBRD, IMF) and protected from public control and aiding countries with very diffuse future economic and political prospects did not entice European, U.S., and Japanese politicians (Merritt 1991, 43). A proposal for a single general aid fund for Eastern Europe (with special powers, and to which all G-24 would contribute) was rejected by the G-24 countries in 1990 (Merritt 1991, 239). Ideas in the EC Commission for a new Marshall Plan for Eastern Europe and the Soviet Union never came to fruition (Merritt 1991, 236). In addition, the amounts of aid contributed by the Western donors to the G-24 program (except for Germany) were small. Because most of the funds actually sent were in the form of loan deferrals and export credits, the EC Commission criticized the United States and Japan for flagging in their contribution of funds to the G-24 program and the EC member states for lacking the will to cooperate within the G-24 framework (Merritt 1991, 251).

Of the aid contributed within the framework of the G-24 program, Germany's has been the biggest share. It is especially in regard to the former USSR that German aid has dominated (over 70 percent of the total in 1991 and 1992). These high figures are to a large extent due to Germany's payments for the withdrawal of former Soviet troops from the former German Democratic Republic and their reintegration into Russian society. In both European and Western aid contexts, it is Germany that has argued for the highest contributions of aid to the reconstruction of the East (Holdar 1993a, 180). Overall, however, Germany has received little support for this stand from the other European and Western governments.

Although map 5.1 may give the impression that the West has spent large amounts on aid to Eastern Europe and the former USSR and that the EU has been leading in this effort, its numbers do not tell the whole truth. First, if we examine the trends over a three-year period, it is only

Germany and Austria that consistently contributed large amounts of aid to this part of the world; in 1991 and 1992, for example, Germany's and Austria's Eastern and Central Europe (ECE) and former Soviet Union (FSU) aid disbursements made up more than 0.15 percent of their GNPs, while the OECD average was 0.04 percent (Development and Co-operation 1994, 133). Compared to Western net assistance to the Third World, which in 1990, 1991, and 1992 on average made up 0.33 percent of the OECD member states' total GNP, the amounts of aid disbursed to the East were small (Development and Co-operation 1994, 160). Second, of the aid that was initially promised to the East only limited amounts have actually been paid out. A recent example is Western aid to Russia: of a total of $28 billion committed in 1993 only $5 billion had been paid out by the end of the year (Sachs and Wyplosz 1994). Third, a significant part of what Western politicians have termed "aid" to Eastern Europe and the former USSR has consisted of export credits, food aid, and loan deferrals—instruments used to satisfy Western companies, farmers, and banks rather than the citizens of Eastern Europe. In the East European policy of Western and EU member states, such "aid" as this instead of monetary assistance to create a foundation for economic and political stability in the former Soviet bloc reflects the primacy of short-term national interests over long-term Western interests. No coherent Western or European strategy has yet been developed to deal with the problems of Eastern Europe and the former USSR (see Kramer 1993).

In terms of EU and member states' internal policies, the disintegration of the Soviet bloc can be said to have created a new sphere of interest for Germany. In addition to French interests in its former colonies; British interests in the Commonwealth; Spanish and Portuguese interests in Latin America; and French, Italian, and Spanish interests in the Mediterranean region, German interests in Eastern Europe have now been added to the agenda of EU external relations. As former president of the EU Commission, Jacques Delors, has noted, an important reason for adding Eastern Europe to the EU agenda is to keep Germany firmly inside the Community; i.e., balancing interests inside the EU is an important motivation for EU East European policy (Merritt 1991, 39).

As before, the resulting EU policy has not been a policy transcending the member states' national aid policies. Instead, the EU has failed in terms of both aid and trade. Aid has been limited and mostly tied. The member states have not been willing to give up authority to general funds administered at the EU level. Trade concessions have been made (especially to Poland, Hungary, and the Czech Republic, which have signed association agreements with the EU), but these have been limited and have largely excluded important areas such as agricultural products (Merritt 1991, 40–43). Although the United States has given the EU a leading role in Eastern Europe, and Germany has contributed the lion's share of Western assistance to this region, the EU lacks a sense of direction as well as the instruments to deal with developments in Eastern Europe. This is demonstrated by the failure of EU mediation efforts in the former Yugoslavia (despite the large commitments of economic aid and of peacekeeping units of the EU member states) and by (1) the failure to create a comprehensive program for assistance to Eastern Europe, (2) the small amounts of aid actually given, and (3) the slowness of giving East European countries trade access to the EU market.

## Conclusions

The historical development of EC aid programs and the geography of EC member states' aid show that the EU lacks a consistent strategy to guide its and the EU-15's relations with aid-recipient countries. The EU still acts primarily as a customs union in its relations with Third World countries (trade and aid issues are closely linked), and it is a mix of the national interests of member states that guides the distribution of EU aid, a mix related to changes in the relative power of member states within the Community. In the 1950s and 1960s, French colonial interests dominated the distribution of EC aid. Since the early 1970s these interests have had to retreat in face of a coalition of Northern European countries (Denmark, The Netherlands, Germany, and Britain) that favored a more global approach and directed more of EC aid to former British colonies in Africa and South Asia.

The changes in Eastern Europe and the Soviet Union have not led to any major redirection of EU aid. It is principally Germany that has pushed for (and sent most) aid to Eastern Europe and the former Soviet Union. However, together with the EU Commission, which coordinates the Western aid effort to Eastern and Central Europe, Germany has been unsuccessful in getting the other European and Western donors to start any major financial programs for assisting these postcommunist societies.

The principal changes in EU aid policy for the future are not likely to be influenced by the Maastricht agreement, which calls for a European

Political Union with common foreign and security policies, including foreign aid. The foreign policy interests of the most influential members of the EU (France, Britain, and Germany) are simply too different to be fused into any common European external policy. Rather, the major influence on EU aid policy, as before, will be the addition of new members. Two developments are important in this regard. First is the reunification of Germany (incorporating the GDR into Germany and the EU). With the consolidation of economic development in the former GDR and with the end of the economic crisis in Germany, it is likely that Germany will take a more active role in influencing other EU member states to send more assistance to Eastern Europe and the former Soviet Union. Demands for more aid to Eastern Europe are also likely to be strengthened with Austria's new membership of the EU. Second, the addition of  Finland and Sweden will strengthen the already dominant Northern European aid lobby in the EU, which is likely to increase attention to a global approach toward the Third World and to weaken the idea of preferential treatment of former European colonies in Sub-Saharan Africa, the Caribbean, and the Pacific as laid down in the Lomé conventions.

# Part Three

*Regional Experiences*

# 6

# Foreign Aid to the Middle East
## *Change or Continuity?*

### Alasdair Drysdale

T HE "NEW WORLD ORDER" in the Middle East was ushered in by
two momentous events—not one, as elsewhere—for in many re-
spects the Gulf crisis unleashed by Iraq's invasion of Kuwait in 1990
eclipsed the collapse of the Soviet Union in its regional impact
(Freedman 1993; Keddie 1992). An Arab writer aptly termed these parallel upheavals "Sovietquake" and "Arabquake," and since the beginning
of the decade their ramifications have almost completely dominated
Arab political discourse.

During the Cold War the United States and the Soviet Union contested the Middle East more closely than most other geopolitical regions
because of its strategic location at the junction of three continents,
where major sea lanes are forced to converge through a series of narrow
straits and waterways. In addition, the presence of some two-thirds of
the world's proven petroleum reserves ensured that the Western industrial countries were vigilant about maintaining access to the region's resources. Conveniently, internecine ideological conflicts and unresolved
territorial disputes provided the superpowers with numerous opportunities to involve themselves deeply in the affairs of the region and wage a
surrogate war for influence through their clients. For these reasons,
Middle Eastern states were among the major recipients of military and
economic assistance from the superpowers and their respective allies

during the Cold War. Several countries became adept at charging strategic rent and extracting generous amounts of aid from their patrons, occasionally playing the United States and the Soviet Union against one
another to achieve maximum leverage.

The Middle East has been unique within the "Third World" in being
both a major beneficiary of external assistance and a key source of economic support for countries within the region. Although almost all in-
terregional aid goes from one Arab country to another, functionally it
can legitimately be considered "foreign" aid. Moreover, through such
agencies as the Islamic Development Bank, the OPEC Fund for
International Development, the Saudi Fund for Development, and the
Kuwait Fund for Arab Economic Development, the richest Middle
Eastern states have loaned large amounts of money outside the region,
particularly to other Muslim countries (Wilson 1989). The Middle East
simultaneously has some of the world's most generous aid donors and
some of its largest recipients.

In this chapter I examine foreign aid to and within the Middle East in
the context of the "new world order" and the global and regional events
that precipitated it. I show that with the obvious exception of the suspension of aid from Russia and Eastern Europe, which primarily
affected Syria and Yemen, the end of the Cold War has had little or no
effect on external assistance patterns. The United States remains the
overwhelming donor of importance to the region, especially to Israel
and Egypt, and I examine its relationships in detail. The Gulf crisis also
had a substantial impact on the flow of aid and especially inter-Arab aid.
In the short term, it resulted in a sudden and large infusion of outside
assistance and prompted a redistribution of inter-Arab aid in favor of
those countries that opposed Iraq's invasion of Kuwait. Eventually, however, the immense cost of the war, the diversion of the region's wealth
into a massive new arms race, and lingering bitterness among Middle
Eastern regimes combined to force a serious reassessment of intrare-
gional aid.

## Aid Distribution Patterns: An Overview

In dollar terms, Egypt has consistently been the largest recipient of
combined multilateral and bilateral official development assistance
(ODA), with Israel a close second (table 6.1). Typically, these two countries have received over half of all ODA in the region (and a much larger

*Table 6.1* Official Development Assistance Receipts
to Middle East Recipients, 1993

|  | Contribution per capita ($) | Fraction of GNP (%) |
|---|---|---|
| Egypt | 40.8 | 5.9 |
| Yemen | 23.4 |  |
| Morocco | 29 | 2.8 |
| Jordan | 59.7 | 4.4 |
| Tunisia | 28.9 | 1.7 |
| Algeria | 13.4 | 0.7 |
| Turkey | 7.7 | 0.3 |
| Iran | 2.2 | 0.2 |
| Syria | 29.8 |  |
| Oman | 8.8 | 0.1 |
| Saudi Arabia | 2 |  |
| Israel | 242.5 | 1.8 |

*Source:* World Bank 1995, 198–99.

proportion of military assistance, a separate aid category). Israel far out-ranks all other countries in the Middle East—in fact, virtually all other countries in the world—in per capita ODA receipts: in 1993 these to-taled $242, compared with $60 in Jordan and $41 in Egypt. However, aid accounted for a far greater share of Egyptian and Jordanian GNP (see table 6.1). The Gulf war had a huge impact on ODA receipts, which for the region as a whole more than doubled between 1989 and 1990 and peaked at $12.2 billion in 1991.

Although Kuwait was the first Arab country to initiate an organized foreign aid program, establishing the Kuwait Fund for Arab Economic Development in 1961, it was not until the explosion of oil prices in 1973 that inter-Arab aid became a significant source of income within the re-gion. The Arab states earned approximately $1 trillion from oil exports in the ten years after 1973, and some of this was recycled within the re-gion in the form of aid. Since 1973 members of the Organization of Arab Petroleum Exporting Countries (OAPEC) have typically given a far larger share of their GNP in ODA each year than the Organization for Economic Cooperation and Development (OECD) countries. Kuwait, during the second half of the 1970s, distributed between 8 per-cent and 15 percent of its GNP in foreign aid, perhaps the highest pro-portion for any country at any time. Between 1973 and 1989, Saudi

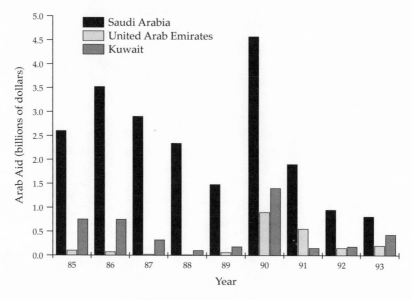

*Fig. 6.1.* Arab aid, 1985–93

Arabia, the world's fourth-largest aid donor, gave grants and concessionary loans to developing countries amounting to $59.4 billion, equivalent to an average of 5.5 percent of its GNP (*Middle East and North Africa* 1994, 762). In 1990 it gave 3.4 percent of its GNP, or $4.5 billion, more than the United Kingdom and the great majority of OECD members (fig. 6.1). However, Arab aid plunged after the Gulf war. Saudi Arabian assistance, for example, fell to $811 million in 1993 (only 0.70 percent of its GNP). Nevertheless, even in 1993 that far exceeded the share of OECD states, which collectively gave 0.30 percent of their GNPs as ODA, or that of the United States, which gave only 0.15 percent. In 1990, OAPEC members distributed $6.3 billion in ODA, comparable to Germany, and more than any single OECD country with the exception of the United States, Japan, or France.

## United States Aid to the Middle East

The most striking feature of U.S. aid to the Middle East—or more accurately, perhaps, the entire American foreign aid program—is the degree to which it is dominated by just two countries: Israel and Egypt.

Between 1979 and 1995, they received some $75 billion in U.S. aid, a level of bilateral assistance that is without parallel. Equally striking is the imperviousness of this aid to change in spite of the end of the Cold War and the much-altered circumstances in the region following the Gulf war. Even in the current budget-cutting climate of American politics, Israel and Egypt received $5.1 billion of U.S. aid in 1995. In the 1996 budget the House of Representatives slashed almost $3 billion from the roughly $15 billion President Clinton requested for foreign aid but maintained the allocation for Israel and Egypt at previous levels. In other words, the Israeli and Egyptian shares of all U.S. aid are climbing and together will reach 43 percent in 1996 (Doherty 1995, 1760). At least in the case of Israel, aid is completely divorced from real need: with a per capita GNP in 1993 of $13,760—comparable to Spain—Israel will receive at least five times more U.S. aid than all of Sub-Saharan Africa and roughly one-quarter of all U.S. aid. Annual per capita U.S. aid to Israel is roughly $600, compared with a little over $1 to Sub-Saharan Africa.

Other Middle Eastern countries receive comparatively small amounts of U.S. aid. For example, in 1996 the Clinton administration requested an appropriation of approximately $2.25 billion in economic assistance for the Middle East. Of this, 89 percent was for Israel and Egypt. The remaining 11 percent was divided among Turkey ($105 million), Jordan ($15 million), Yemen ($9.4 million), the West Bank and Gaza Strip ($76 million), and Morocco ($27.8 million). Because its aid is so highly concentrated geographically, the United States is a major donor in a limited number of countries and a minor one in many more. In the case of Egypt, the United States provided approximately 30 percent of the total $2.4 billion in economic assistance pledged in 1994, the largest portion. Its share of military aid was considerably higher. By contrast, in 1994 it accounted for only 13 percent of Jordan's economic aid, 5 percent of Morocco's, 5 percent of Lebanon's, and 2 percent of Yemen's. Of the $2.4 billion pledged to the Palestine Authority in the West Bank and Gaza Strip between 1994 and 1998, the United States accounted for $500 million.

Since the mid-1970s the U.S. program to Israel has flourished, steadily growing in complexity and size. Gradually the aid package has assumed the form of an entitlement and spilled horizontally outside the confines of the foreign aid budget, making it increasingly hard to calculate its total magnitude. When off-budget assistance is figured in, total annual U.S. aid to Israel may be closer to $4.2 billion a year than the gen-

erally accepted figure of $3 billion (Wenger 1990, 12). Many of the extras
can be traced to forty-three pieces of special legislation enacted over the
years to benefit Israel (Neff 1990, 18). During the mid-1980s the U.S.
Congress converted all aid to Israel from loans to grants. Aid to Israel
also lacks many of the strings normally attached to U.S. foreign aid. For
example, economic aid is not designated for special projects, so there is
no United States Agency for International Development (USAID) office
in Israel. Essentially, Israel can use economic aid as it deems fit and
therefore does not have to meet rigorous accounting requirements.
Equally unusual is that Israel alone is allowed to use a portion of its military aid to purchase locally made equipment. Historically, the United
States has required recipients of foreign military sales (FMS) funds to
spend them on U.S.-made products, thus directly benefiting American
corporations and workers (Rabie 1988). Besides the regular aid package,
Congress has occasionally approved supplemental assistance. For example, following the Gulf war it allocated an additional $650 million, osten-
sibly to offset reconstruction costs after Iraqi missile attacks. The Bush
administration also approved a five-year $10 billion loan guarantee for
housing Russian immigrants. In 1993 the U.S. Congress authorized the
Pentagon to "drawdown" $700 million in military equipment from
Europe, as the Cold War came to a close, and transfer it to Israel. In
1996, Israel is scheduled to receive $1.8 billion in FMS assistance and
$1.2 billion in economic support funds (ESF)—a total of $3 billion.
Furthermore, this assistance is "considered politically untouchable by
Congress" (*New York Times*, Mar. 26, 1995, E3).

The end of the Cold War and collapse of communism diminished
Israel's global strategic importance. The Gulf war undermined its asser-
tion that it was a strategic asset to the United States within the Middle
East and would be available to assist it in any local crisis. Arguably, the
Gulf crisis demonstrated that Israel was a strategic liability: the United
States beseeched it not to retaliate against Iraqi missile attacks for fear
that Israel's retaliation would force the Arab members to abandon a
coalition led by the United States. In effect, at a time of extreme crisis
Israel's military might could not be used in the Middle East in association with the United States without harming the latter's regional interests. The end of the Cold War essentially eliminated the military threat
to Israel from its main foes, and since Iraq's defeat in the Gulf war,
Israel's military superiority has been unchallenged. Despite this recon-
figuration of the political and strategic environment, both regionally and

globally, there are no indications that the U.S.-Israel aid relationship will be reassessed.

Between 1974 and 1995, Egypt received approximately $20 billion in economic assistance from the United States and some $21 billion in military aid. In 1995, it obtained $2.1 billion, of which $1.3 billion was in FMS and $815 million in ESF assistance. This was more than the rest of Asia and Middle East combined, excluding Israel, and more than double all of Africa. The United States is by far Egypt's largest aid donor and has helped to create a situation in which Egypt is "indisputably hooked on external finances" (Weinbaum 1986, 121).

Between the mid-1950s and the early 1970s, Egypt obtained most of its economic and military assistance from the USSR, but President Sadat reestablished relations with the United States following the 1973 Arab-Israeli war and sought American help in negotiating disengagement agreements with Israel during 1974 and 1975. To encourage this realignment, the United States allocated increasing amounts of aid. In 1977, Sadat traveled to Israel to address the Israeli parliament, signaling a new seriousness in Egypt's search for peace. Two years later, Egypt and Israel signed a peace treaty, which provided for a phased Israeli withdrawal from the Sinai peninsula in return for full diplomatic relations. Egypt was immediately ostracized by the rest of the Arab world, and aid from the Arab oil-producing countries was suspended. The United States made up the difference to reward Sadat and bolster his domestic position.

As in the case of Israel, the end of the Cold War has had no impact on the U.S.-Egypt aid relationship, in part because Egypt has presented itself effectively as a reliable ally in a turbulent region, most especially during the Gulf crisis. Recently Egypt has positioned itself as a bulwark against Islamist movements and lined up against neighboring Libya and Sudan, two of the regimes the United States is most concerned about in the region.

The impact of U.S. aid has been controversial (Sullivan 1990). Whereas American aid to Israel comes with few strings attached, aid to Egypt is encumbered in numerous ways and only a small amount is in direct cash transfers (Weinbaum 1986, 125). At the very least, American aid has fostered a dependent relationship, although since the mid-1980s all transfers have been in grant form. Egypt has clearly lost some autonomy because the United States has, with the International Monetary Fund (IMF) and the World Bank, strongly encouraged free market reforms and economic liberalization. Because of its size and influence, Egyptian critics sometimes describe the local USAID bureaucracy as a "shadow cabinet." In 1990 and 1991, after years of resistance, Egypt finally started to implement key recommendations in the areas of pricing and subsidies, the exchange rate system, interest rates, and the money supply (Lofgren 1993, 411).

American aid has also been an instrument for economic penetration: since the mid-1970s, when Egypt began its policy of economic liberalization, many U.S. companies have moved into Egypt. In the words of Robert Pelletreau, Assistant Secretary for Near Eastern Affairs in the State Department, "US assistance has . . . developed Egypt as a major market for US products, especially agricultural goods" (1995, 434). American aid is tied to the purchase of American goods and services and thus benefits U.S. corporations just as much as, if not more than, Egypt (Zimmerman 1993, 93). In 1994 "more than 85 percent of the $815 million congressional earmark [for economic assistance] was spent in the US for goods and services" (Pelletreau 1995, 434).

American and other international aid has been a crutch of sorts for the Egyptian regime. Despite elements of dependence, however, the relationship is not completely asymmetrical. With Washington committed to delivering $2 billion of aid each year as long as Egypt stays at peace with Israel and continues to serve U.S. strategic interests in the region, American leverage over Egyptian internal and external policies is limited. Egypt grasps that, because U.S. aid is politically motivated, Washington is unlikely to withhold it. Egypt, like Israel, has successfully made the transition to the "new world order" with its aid relationship with the United States intact.

## Inter-Arab Aid

Patterns of inter-Arab aid must be seen in the context of the "Arab Cold War" (Kerr 1971, 26). Since the 1950s the Arab world has been internally divided along numerous shifting axes. The most serious and persistent division pitted radical Arab nationalist regimes aligned with the Eastern bloc against conservative monarchical regimes tied to the West. Generally speaking, the former espoused pan-Arabism and sought to overthrow the royal families, who they believed stood in the way of Arab unity and the liberation of Palestine. This intense struggle created severe turbulence in the region, especially from the mid-1950s until the early 1970s. To some extent, the Arab Cold War also pitted haves against have-nots, because many of the more radical regimes lacked oil (Iraq and Libya were exceptions) whereas the monarchical regimes often had huge reserves. Iraq's invasion of Kuwait in 1990 was, in some senses, a continuation of this confrontation, bringing to a head unresolved conflicts over the social and geographical distribution of wealth. As one Arab writer put it in the aftermath of the Gulf war, "How was it that the 15 million Gulf Arabs had foreign investments and financial reserves of around $600 billion, while the other 185 million Arabs had foreign debts of some $200 billion?" (Khouri 1991, 6).

When large-scale inter-Arab aid began flowing in the 1970s, it was a way in which the conservative states could exercise some political leverage within the region and enhance their prospects of survival by co-opting their foes into dependent relationships. Wealth gave them the power of *al-manh* (providing) and *al-man'* (withholding), which could be used to influence the behavior of regimes that looked to them for financial assistance. In a sense, they were paying protection money, buying off and pacifying adversaries like Egypt and Syria, which as "frontline" states in the Arab confrontation with Israel needed huge amounts of cash to pay for their arms purchases and disguise their severe economic problems. Their largesse to the countries that bore the main military burden protected the oil-producing states to some degree from the criticism that they were doing nothing in the conflict with Israel. Thus between 1973 and 1979, Egypt received an estimated $13 billion in assistance from Saudi Arabia, Kuwait, the United Arab Emirates, and Qatar.

As oil prices softened in the 1980s, Arab oil revenues plunged from $178 billion in 1980 to only $41 billion in 1986 (Sadowski 1992, 4). Consequently, Arab support declined sharply during the decade: between 1980 and 1989, Saudi Arabian aid fell from $5.6 billion to $1.4 billion and Kuwaiti assistance from $1.1 billion to $169 million. The United Arab Emirates, which distributed $1.1 billion in aid in 1980, gave only $2 million in 1989. At the same time, the Arabian peninsula countries turned their attention from the conflict with Israel to the Iraq-Iran war. Alarmed by the prospect of an Iranian victory, the rich Arab oil-producing states began financing Iraq's war effort—in effect, supporting another oil-producing state. According to one estimate, Saudi Arabia may have spent as much as $23 billion supporting Iraq between 1980 and 1988 (*Middle East Review* 1993/94, 2). Kuwait, to its lasting regret, also generously helped to pay for Iraq's voracious appetite for arms. The concurrent war in Afghanistan between the Soviet Union and largely Islamist rebels placed further demands on the Arabian peninsula's financial resources. Consequently, much aid was diverted from former Arab beneficiaries. Perhaps the biggest loser was Syria, which had in any case angered its benefactors by supporting non-Arab Iran during the Iran-Iraq war and by mistreating the Palestinians in Lebanon's civil war. Despite earlier pledges, Syria received only $500 million in Arab aid annually between 1986 and 1988, and by the late 1980s, just as the Eastern bloc was collapsing, this source of funding suddenly ended.

Iraq's invasion of Kuwait in 1990 sharply exposed Arab divisions as states and regional actors chose, or were compelled to choose, sides in the conflict. In the short run, the poorer Arab states that supported the Allied war effort to expel Iraq from Kuwait were richly rewarded. Syria, at the moment of its greatest isolation, seized the opportunity to maneuver its way back to center stage by providing vital Arab nationalist cover to the U.S.-led coalition. In return, Saudi Arabia and the other Gulf states delivered more than $2 billion in aid, and the Europeans and Japanese pledged an additional $700 million in credits (Drysdale 1993). Egypt did even better: Saudi Arabia immediately awarded it $1.5 billion in loans and grants and, with Kuwait, forgave $6.6 billion of its debts (Sadowski 1991, 5). Contributions from Western and Arab governments in the Gulf war doubled Egypt's foreign exchange reserves (Lofgren 1993, 411). Another beneficiary was Turkey, which was compensated for the economic dislocations associated with enforcing UN sanctions on Iraq. In 1991, Saudi Arabia gave it $1 billion worth of free petroleum to supplement $1.6 billion in cash it had already received.

The long-term consequences of the war on patterns of inter-Arab aid have been less favorable even to those countries that supported the allied coalition. The war made it plain that resentment among the Arab have-nots against the haves had played a key role in the crisis and, at least initially, convinced many both inside and outside the region that, unless Arab oil wealth was more equitably distributed, the economic chasm between Arab states would persist as a source of regional conflict. If anything, however, the Gulf crisis has further diminished the enthusiasm of the Arab Gulf states for pan-Arabism and encouraged them to be more open in placing their own state interests first. The Gulf crisis perhaps irrevocably changed the Arab political discourse, resolving the long-standing tension between the imperatives of the territorial state and those of the Arab nation in favor of the former (Karawan 1994, 439). Consequently, the sense of moral obligation among the rich states to help their poorer neighbors has been undermined. Resentment lingers against some of the poor states, which despite years of financial aid turned on them quickly in their crisis. Even if their governments pledged support, their populations often sympathized with Saddam Husayn. To some Arabs, the lesson of the Gulf war was that the rich had not shared enough of their wealth with the poor. But those with the money learned an altogether different lesson: that they had to look out for themselves.

Following the war an energetic new arms race was unleashed in the Gulf region, depleting even further the financial resources of the principal Arab aid donors. Strictly speaking, there were several parallel, overlapping arms races. Thus, Saudi Arabia feared not only Iraq, which at the time of the Gulf war had the fourth-largest army in the world and even after its defeat deployed 50 percent more battle tanks than Britain, but also Iran and Israel. These developments fueled an enormous appetite for arms in the 1990s, with the result that Saudi Arabia "has become the principal, and insatiable, recipient of those arms sales which, in the 'new world order' . . . western governments expressed pious intentions about cutting to a minimum" (*Middle East Review* 1993/94, 2). Between 1990 and 1994, Saudi Arabia placed orders for $30 billion of arms with U.S. corporations. The kingdom's military buildup also envisioned tripling the size of the armed forces to 200,000. Kuwait, in its 1991–92 budget, increased defense spending sixfold, to 43 percent of the total. In the remaining Gulf Cooperation Council (GCC) states, the response was essentially the same. Iran, meanwhile, began its own military buildup in response to this activity. Between 1991 and mid-1993, total arms orders from the Middle East—primarily the GCC states—exceeded $50 billion, with U.S. orders accounting for well over half of the total. These expenditures, combined with residual war costs, left the Gulf states with little spare cash to distribute as aid. Between 1990 and 1993, Saudi Arabian aid fell from $4.5 billion to $811 million.

## Conclusions

The end of the Cold War barely disrupted external aid patterns to the Middle East, primarily affecting the Soviet Union's small number of clients. Despite fears within the region, western aid was not, in any significant way, diverted away from the Middle East to assist the former Soviet bloc's transition to capitalism and democracy. In particular, U.S.

aid disbursements today closely resemble those at the height of the Cold War: Israel and Egypt continue to secure a large proportion of American assistance to the Middle East. The U.S.-Israeli and, to a lesser extent, U.S.-Egyptian aid relationships are so well entrenched that it is difficult to imagine any fundamental change in their magnitude. Even in the current frugal climate in Washington, aid to Israel and Egypt (so long as the region remains at peace) seems to be immune to budget cuts. If anything, U.S. assistance to the region is likely to increase in the future as Israel and its neighbors make peace.

Predicting future inter-Arab aid patterns is far more problematical because historically these have fluctuated sharply in accordance with ever-shifting calculations about whether the interests of a particular donor state would best be served by providing or withholding aid. However, in the aftermath of the Gulf war, all of the traditional donors have much less to give. Indeed, one analyst has argued that "cash will never again be the great instrument of control and appeasement" (*Middle East Review* 1993/94, 3). However, prudence (and history) dictate a far less emphatic conclusion. As long as the Middle East is divided between haves and have-nots, pressures to share Arab wealth will be formidable.

# 7

# Foreign Aid to Africa
## *The Rise and Fall of*
## *Structural Development Aid*

### Ton Dietz and John Houtkamp

IN 1990, Africa received \$26 billion of official development assistance (ODA) from all sources combined. More than 44 percent of all world aid went to Africa during that year. During the early 1980s aid to Africa was around \$11 billion annually, and it received about 32 percent of all world aid flows (OECD[a] 1987, 1993). Development aid has become a structural phenomenon in most African countries. Various indicators can be used to show the relative importance of aid to Africa. Excluding South Africa (and Libya), each African received an average amount of foreign aid of \$45 in 1990, or 13 percent of the average per capita income, approximately \$350. In comparison with South Asia—on average even poorer than Africa—the difference is striking: an average South Asian received \$5 of aid money on average, and aid was less than 2 percent of the GNI in 1990 (World Bank 1992).

For the African politico-bureaucratic elite, aid has become so important that the government machinery revolves around shots of aid money. The new enslavement results in heavy problems if aid suddenly stops, as some "communist widows" experienced during the implosion of the Soviet empire and some other countries experienced when resistance to "structural adjustment recipes" of the World Bank and the International Monetary Fund (IMF) or to "democratization" resulted in postponed aid.

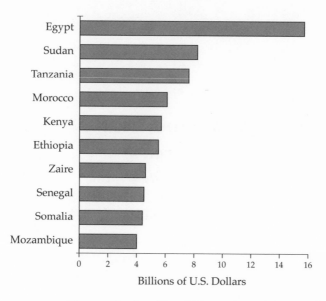

*Fig. 7.1.* Foreign aid to Africa: major recipients, 1980–89

Within Africa there are major differences in aid receipts and in "addiction." During the 1980s the ten countries given the most aid received 56 percent of $115 billion ODA to Africa during the decade (fig. 7.1). In 1990 the most aid went to Egypt ($5.4 billion), followed by Kenya and Tanzania (both $1.2 billion), Morocco ($1.1 billion), and Ethiopia and Mozambique (both $1.0 billion) (OECD[a] 1993). In terms of aid dollars per capita, Gabon, Botswana, Egypt, and Mauritania led the list: all received more than $100 per capita. Aid as a percentage of GNP was very high in Mozambique (66 percent), Tanzania (48 percent), and Somalia (45 percent). At the other end of the spectrum, the oil giant Nigeria stands out: with only $250 million of aid in 1990, $2 per capita, and less than 1 percent of GNP, aid is negligible there, at least for the time being (World Bank 1992: 240–41, 256–57).

## Aid Patterns: Recent Changes

It was not the fall of the Berlin Wall in 1989 or the implosion of the Soviet empire in 1990 that caused a "post–Cold War" rearrangement of aid patterns. "Moscow's retreat from Africa," as Light (1992) called it, probably started around 1984 and gave room for much aid expansion by the Western powers from that time onward (partly catalyzed by a response to calamities such as the 1984 drought in the Horn of Africa). If we compare the volumes of aid to individual countries in 1989 with those in 1983, we see that Western aid to Algeria increased by 160 percent, aid to Ethiopia and Mali more than doubled, and aid to Mozambique, Guinea, Benin, and Uganda more than tripled (total aid to Africa during this period increased by 170 percent). However, extreme increases were not restricted to the so-called Cold War enemies of the West: aid to Nigeria, Ghana, Malawi, and Cameroon more than tripled between 1983 and 1989. And not all Western enemies experienced dramatic increases in aid volumes: aid to Sudan and the People's Republic of Congo even diminished (for Angola the situation was unclear).

What happened after the final collapse of the Eastern bloc? If we compare the aid situation of 1991 with that of 1989, total aid to Africa had increased with 145 percent. Only one of the former friends of the East bloc, however, increased its aid receipts above average: Algeria. Most dramatic increases had to do with the Gulf crisis and not with the final demise of Soviet power, although of course the Gulf war as such could only be possible as a result of it. Aid to Egypt more than tripled in these two years (mainly from the United States, the Arab donor countries, and Japan), and it was already very high. Aid to Morocco, another Western ally in the anti-Iraq front, more than doubled, mainly a result of increases in Arab and French aid volumes. But Zambia also showed a remarkable increase in its aid volume during this period, to which most donors contributed. On the other hand, a large number of African countries experienced a decline in aid volumes between 1989 and 1991: Somalia, Kenya, Botswana, Lesotho, Central African Republic, Zaire, Nigeria, Senegal, and Mauritania.

In 1992 and 1993 the impact of the Kuwait crisis on aid disbursements petered out: aid to Egypt decreased from $5.0 billion to $2.3 billion and aid to Morocco from $1.2 billion to $0.8 billion. Most other African countries (22 out of the 37 for which the World Development report gives figures) experienced a slight increase in aid volumes in 1992, followed by aid decreases for a majority of African countries (25 out of 37) in 1993, which is the year all major Organization for Economic Cooperation and Development (OECD) donor countries, with the exception of Japan, started to diminish their total aid volumes (World Bank 1995, 196–99). If we compare the aid disbursement figures, however, the total level of aid (in current dollar terms) in 1993 was still higher than it was in 1989 for 24 out of 37 African countries and approximately 40 percent higher for Africa as a whole. Four countries even experienced more than a doubling of aid levels between these two years (Sierra Leone, Zambia, Algeria, and Namibia) and another six countries had an increase beyond 50 percent (Ivory Coast, Burkina Faso, Zimbabwe, Rwanda, Morocco, and Egypt). Among the former communist allies, only Algeria experienced a more than average increase of Western aid levels. Support for the Algerian government's fight against radical Islamism was a more important reason for this increase than the post–Cold War realignment.

No overall picture can be given yet for the period after 1993. From data published since 1993 in the *Africa Research Bulletin (ARB)*, one recent change becomes evident: the increase of aid to South Africa after the dissolution of apartheid. Japan has clearly taken the lead. In 1994, Japan signed an agreement for $1.3 billion to assist the new South Africa, making it the largest single donor to South Africa; this was also Japan's largest single aid agreement with an African country. A minor but interesting new development is the increased aid to Africa from other Asian  countries: South Korea, Taiwan, India, Indonesia, and Turkey had all become donors to African countries by 1993. There are also indications that Israel is regaining the donor position it had before being ousted almost everywhere in 1973; Israel's involvement in Eritrea is especially worth mentioning. Another interesting recent phenomenon is that South Africa, besides becoming a major receiver of aid, has started to give development aid, e.g., to Mozambique, Zimbabwe, and Angola. To Gabon it made a most symbolic donation: electoral equipment for the presidential elections of December 1993. There is evidence that Western development aid to African countries is partly used now to purchase South African goods and services, which furthermore indirectly supports the rapid expansion of South African private sector activities throughout Africa. Such development aid has included the deployment of private armies to clean up the mess of civil wars in countries like Angola and now even in Sierra Leone. Aid from African countries to other African countries is not confined to South Africa. The Rwanda crisis of 1994 elicited emergency aid from many corners of the world, including countries like Tunisia and Gabon.

In African government circles there is a general fear that the disappearance of the Cold War will result in lower donor attention for Africa, a relocation of aid flows from Africa to Eastern Europe, and an internal refocusing of attention toward South Africa. The 1993 decision by the U.S. government to cut back aid to Africa was seen as the first evidence of a developing trend. In addition, World Bank loan commitments to Africa went down in 1992 and 1993. The *Africa Research Bulletin* wrote, "The Cold War's demise . . . has proved a setback for black Africa. Superpower rivalry once gave crucial purchase to poor lands with prized real estate for military bases, or a grip on maritime 'choke points', or large reserves of strategic minerals. . . . Africa's leverage has markedly weakened" (*ARB* June 31, 1994). Another possibility, posed by Nigerian political scientist Claude Ake, is that "the post–Cold War period may well sharpen rivalries among capitalist powers liberated from their siege mentality." The journal *West Africa* added that "the present flux may be a 1990-style scramble for influence in Africa. . . . the very economic weakening which Sub-Saharan Africa has been demonstrating makes it in fact more vulnerable to predators" (1993, 2229). If they are right, bilateral aid can be expected to play a key role. Some see France's recent policy as a clear sign of its mission to become the preeminent power in post–Cold War Africa; the opening of offices of the French Development Bank Group in Ghana and South Africa, France's involvement in the Rwanda crisis, and the French president being the first world leader to visit postapartheid South Africa are given as examples. On the other hand, France's pressure for the devaluation of the franc CFA (Communauté Financière Africaine), in existence since 1948 with a fixed parity of 50:1 to the French franc, was seen by many as the beginning of a new era of French involvement in its former colonies, or even as betrayal of its African domain.

## Current Trends in Nongovernmental Aid to Africa

Nongovernmental flows of aid to (and within) Africa started well before independence; in fact, such aid dates back to the activities of Catholic and Protestant missions, Islamic brotherhoods, and charity organizations. During the 1980s, however, the flow of NGO aid has risen quickly, partly because government and multilateral donor agencies started to increase their funding to northern—and especially European—NGOs (e.g., OXFAM [UK], NOVIB [The Netherlands], Misereor [Germany]) and through them to a multitude of nongovernmental development organizations in Africa, with varying degrees of NGO independence from the governments in receiving countries. Riddell (1992,

66) suggested that total "voluntary" contributions from the North to Africa were in the range of 15 percent of net foreign aid in the late 1980s—close to $3 billion a year. On the basis of an OXFAM report, the *Africa Research Bulletin* even estimated that NGOs invested $6.4 billion in Africa in 1989: "more than the World Bank's net transfers to the region and more than six times the figure for direct foreign investment" (*ARB* Aug. 30, 1993).

From the donor's perspective, two examples illustrate the trend. From Germany, the average disbursements by private voluntary agencies grew from $78 million in 1970 (11 percent of all German aid) to an annual average of $387 million between 1980 and 1984 (10 percent) and $577 million (13 percent) between 1985 and 1988 (Schultz 1991, 52); however, it is unclear how much aid was directed to Africa. Part of the politically sensitive aid (e.g., to Namibia and to South Africa) was channeled this way, and "there is a fairly wide-ranging consensus among most aid specialists in West Germany that NGOs play a very useful role in extending aid beyond the scope of official assistance and that they are particularly well suited to implement a basic needs-oriented development strategy. . . . Some further increase of government support for NGO aid activities therefore has general political backing and is likely to continue in the future" (Schultz 1991, 61).

In The Netherlands, the absolute and relative levels of aid via NGOs increased: from Dfl 29 million (or 3.7 percent of total Dutch development aid) in 1970 to Dfl 331 million (6 percent) in 1990, of which 32 percent went to Africa. Moreover, commitments were formulated to increase the relative importance of Dutch NGO aid to African NGOs for the 1990s (Stuurgroep 1991, 13).

With more emphasis on structural adjustment with a human face, multilateral donors started to channel money to and through NGOs. An early and notable example is the World Bank's huge social fund ($750 million for a six-year period) to be used by Egyptian NGOs after 1986. Increasingly, NGOs are being used to speed up the decentralization and privatization of government services—for example, in the sphere of health care, as in Kenya, and in transport infrastructure, as in Mali. There is increasing complexity in NGOs—international and local, non-state and pseudostate, intermediary and grassroots—and a tendency for NGOs to take over development tasks that state institutions, now withdrawing, are no longer willing or able to perform.

Attention to the relative importance and impact of NGO activities in

Africa is increasing because of an unfolding debate about state-civil relations. The most important recent example is the collection of studies
by Wellard and Copestake (1993). In our opinion, much more work is
needed.

## Aid and Africa's International Economic Position
### *Private Capital Flows*

Until this point, we have restricted our analysis to what is called "net
official development assistance," or "ODA net," that is, grants and loans
below certain ceilings of interest rates, grace periods, and amortization
periods. There are also other official flows (closer to market rates and
practices), and there are private flows, such as direct investments, portfolio investments, and export credits at market rates. For Africa as a
whole, foreign aid dominates the picture (Riddell 1992, 60). Our discussion here focuses on 1990.

Non-ODA ("other") official flows were dominated by multilateral
donors in 1990, while Italy and Germany were important net providers
of this source of capital as well. The U.S. net contribution was negative,
largely because of a big difference of almost $2 billion between gross and
net receipts of "other official flows" from the United States by Egypt.

The picture for private flows (consisting of private investments, portfolio investments, and bank credits) was extremely negative for Africa in
1990. Almost all private sources were, on balance, withdrawing from
Africa, either disinvesting or receiving far more credit repayments than
providing new credits at market rates. French private sources were leading the outflow of capital, with $1.1 billion out of $2.0 billion for the European Community (EC) as a whole. But private sources from the
United States also added to the trend: −$0.3 billion. Private outflow, al-
most as high as non-ODA inflow, was 10 percent of the value of total
foreign aid inflow in 1990. The situation with private flows continued to
deteriorate during the 1980s: from an annual positive (though decreasing) inflow of $6.2 billion (1982), $4.3 billion (1983), $1.5 billion (1984),
$1.1 billion (1985), and $0.8 billion (1986) to a negative inflow of −$1.4
billion (1987), −$1.6 billion (1988), −$2.5 billion (1990), and −$1.7 million
(1991). Although 1989 showed a positive figure of $2.1 billion, 1989–91
total private flows to Africa were −$3.4 billion. Within Africa the figures
for private flows show an extreme variation as well: for the 1989–91 period there were very negative flows for Nigeria (−$2.4 billion), Egypt

(–$2.0 billion), Ivory Coast (–$1.5 billion), Tunisia (–$0.6 billion), and Congo (–$0.3 billion). On the other hand, considerable positive flows were reported for Kenya ($1.0 billion), Liberia ($0.9 billion), and Algeria ($0.9 billion).

The overall negative picture of private capital flows is dramatically illustrated by the behavior of wealthy Africans themselves. If it is true that "the stock of African savings deposited outside the continent exceeds the continent's entire annual output" (*ARB* Oct. 9, 1994), more than $400 billion generated in Africa supports development elsewhere, a sum equivalent to almost twenty years of the current level of foreign development assistance.

Finally, in a comparison of the figures about capital flows with another important source of funds, the workers' remittances, World Bank figures suggest a massive stream toward Africa of more than $6 billion in 1990, equivalent to a quarter of all foreign aid (and this estimate is based only on officially measured remittances). Although Africa as a whole received large amounts of foreign aid, the bulk of it went to only a few countries: Egypt ($3.7 billion), Morocco ($2.0 billion), and Tunisia ($0.6 billion).

## Capital Flows and Debts

Official development assistance to Africa has always contained a rather large grant element, and foreign aid has been relatively important as an element of all capital flows. In the course of time, however, Africa built up a considerable debt. In 1970 the total long-term debt to foreign public and private creditors combined was only $9.3 billion. By 1990 it had increased to $233 billion: of this, private nonguaranteed credit was only 4 percent; all other debts are either public or publicly guaranteed. If we include IMF credit and short-term debt, the total debt comes to $269 billion, equivalent to $441 per capita and comparable to a full year's GNP for Africa as a whole and almost three times the value of African exports of goods and services. In relative terms, the accumulated debt of Africa is more problematic than that of Latin America or South Asia. Though huge, Latin America's accumulated debt was equivalent to only 42 percent of GNP and South Asia's to 31 percent (World Bank 1992).

Within Africa, six countries are responsible for 60 percent of all accumulated foreign debts to Development Assistance Committee (DAC) countries and multilateral institutions in 1990: Egypt ($40 billion), Nigeria ($36 billion), Algeria ($27 billion), Morocco ($24 billion), Ivory

Coast ($18 billion), and Sudan ($15 billion). Debts almost three times the current annual level of total exports are already an almost impossible burden; for some countries the situation is far worse. Sudan's and Mozambique's debts are more than fifteen times the current annual level of total exports, Tanzanian and Ugandan debts more than ten times.

In 1970 the total debt service (amortization and payment of interest) resulted in a return flow of $966 million or 40 percent of the net foreign aid inflow ($270 million interest payments). In 1990 total debt service had reached a level of $22.2 billion, which is almost 90 percent of the level of net foreign aid disbursements. It is 23 percent of the exports of all goods and services and 8 percent of total African GNP. The return flow of interest payments alone amounted to $8.1 billion in 1990 (World Bank 1992, 258–61). The huge interest burden, coupled with ailing economies, has resulted in large interest arrears, which reached $14 billion in 1992, three times that of 1987, despite debt write-offs and reschedulings. Some donors started to pay African countries' debt arrears to other donors, as in the case of France's payment of Congo's arrears to the World Bank or the combined move of Belgium, The Netherlands, the United States, Canada, Norway, and Switzerland to settle Rwanda's debt to the World Bank and thereby enable the new RPF government to open new credit lines.

## Aid and Trade Patterns

Does the geography of aid resemble the geography of trade during the 1980s? Unfortunately, the figures for exports and imports for many African countries, as presented by the United Nations' International Trade Statistics, do not go much beyond the early 1980s and their reliability is questionable. Using incomplete data for the most important northern countries, however, can give us some insights. Before looking at those data, it is important to realize that for almost all northern countries, Africa's importance as a trade partner dwindled during the 1980s despite increasing aid. It is clear from statistics that Africa's position in the world market has deteriorated dramatically during the 1980s. All northern purchasing countries show a more marginal position for Africa's exports. With the exception of Belgium and Portugal, the same is true for Africa as a buyer of northern goods and services.

In the years after World War II, the pattern of trade bilateralism between a European mother country and its African colonies more or less collapsed. This first happened in the 1950s with the relationship between Great Britain and its overseas territories. By 1982, in only three of eleven cases studied was Great Britain the most important import partner, the United Kingdom accounting for 13 percent of all imports of its former colonies. Britain was the most important buyer in four cases, buying 17 percent of all exports of its former colonies. For the few countries where Britain still dominated aid flows (mainly Malawi and Uganda), there is some evidence that the United Kingdom also remained the most important trade partner. For those countries with trade statistics available for 1988 or 1989, it is clear that almost everywhere Britain's position further deteriorated to a level of 12 percent of imports and 14 percent of exports. The British position was taken over by the United States (by far the most important buyer of Nigerian produce), Japan (important in Southern Africa), and other European countries, especially Germany.

As with aid, the French position remained considerably stronger. In 1982, France was the most important provider of goods and services in fifteen of seventeen former colonies. In 1988, it still dominated in all ten countries for which trade statistics are available, though at an average level of 27 percent of all imports, lower than the 34 percent of 1982.  With a few exceptions, in the French case the geography of aid closely resembles the geography of trade (exceptions are Morocco, which exhibited trade dominance without aid dominance, and Algeria, which exhibited aid dominance only).

There is not much scope for trade improvements in the near future. In general, African export products do not have strong bargaining power on the world market, and the deterioration of relative prices may be expected to continue. The only continent expected not to gain from the General Agreement on Tariffs and Trade (GATT) agreement of late 1993 was Africa. The dwindling position of Africa as a trade partner in global import and export networks has not been counterbalanced by a growing intra-African trade network. In a meeting between the Organization of African Unity, the Economic Commission for Africa, and the African Development Bank in late 1992, there was dissatisfaction with the "abysmally low share of intra-African trade which accounts for less than 5% of total [African] trade" (*ARB* Jan. 30, 1993).

## Aid to Africa and Economic Development

Economic self-interest of donor countries is an important incentive for the global aid industry. Partly through the tying of aid, goods and services are procured in donor countries to a considerable degree. Even in a relatively liberal country like The Netherlands, close to 70 percent of all aid money is in fact spent on goods and services procured in The Netherlands (Jepma 1991, 71). However (on paper, at least), development aid is directed not primarily at the further development of northern economies but at the development of continents like Africa. One would expect there to be some correlation between the level of aid and the level of economic growth (and other development indicators). If we look at the African experience in the 1980s, the evidence shows a real drama. Despite relatively high levels of aid per capita ($229 per capita between 1980 and 1989), the development performance has been traumatic. If we compare per capita GNP in current U.S. dollar values, the situation in 1990 was worse than in 1980 in many African countries. But even this would give too rosy a picture: if we use the German mark instead of the U.S. dollar value, only fifteen of thirty-eight African countries would have a current per capita GNP value in 1990 higher than in 1980.

There has been much debate about the impact of international financial institutions' structural adjustment programs (SAPs) in African countries, which started during the 1980s. These programs were meant to counter the downward trend. According to a World Bank report published in 1989, "the evidence points to better overall economic performance in countries that pursue strong reform programs than those that do not" (World Bank 1989, iii). Looking at the countries with such structural adjustment loans (SALs) for the period until mid-1987, however, Malek (1991, 4–6) concluded that "the rates of return on World Bank program aid have been rather disappointing and most other economic indicators do not register significant improvement in the SAL group." If we add our own data for the last years of the decade to Malek's data, a comparison between GNP per capita for 1990 and that for 1980 shows a combination of extremely bad performance for the countries that Malek defined as "strong SAL countries" (Nigeria and Tanzania), very poor performance (Ivory Coast, Madagascar, Kenya, and Malawi), poor performance (Ghana, Niger, Togo, Zaire, and Burundi), meager performance (Congo, Mauritania, and Central African Republic), and only in two cases a performance that could be regarded as "promising" (Senegal and Guinea). If we compare the trend in SAL countries with that in non-SAL countries (again following Malek's definition), there are both relatively good performers during the 1980s (Cameroon, Chad, Rwanda,

Burkina Faso, and especially Botswana) and extremely poor performers (Mozambique).

Maybe there needs to be more time before the final verdicts are given on structural adjustments, but the evidence so far is not at all convincing that SAPs alleviate development problems. The *Africa Research Bulletin* (July 30, 1993) was not very positive: "Ghana is perhaps the only African country to have accepted the spirit as well as the letter of the World Bank's list of market reforms over the past decade. But after 10 years of structural adjustment the country has yet to receive the promised rewards." And, having reviewed an analysis about Africa in the *UK Financial Times*, the *Bulletin* wrote, "Its focus on the impact of the structural adjustment programs, 10 years after inception, leaves a mark of pessimism about both the effectiveness of these measures and the ideological reasons for their prescriptions," and "Twelve years after the adoption of SAPs on the continent and more than $170 billion in net development assistance, the Sub-Saharan economy is shown to be still falling" (*ARB* Aug. 30, 1993). The World Bank's own project activities in Africa also came under attack. Summarizing an article written in the UK-based *Guardian* on the occasion of the fiftieth anniversary of the World Bank, the *Africa Research Bulletin* wrote, "Across Africa, projects funded by the bank have become synonymous with financial mismanagement, environmental degradation, the displacement of vulnerable populations and corruption," and "In myriad cases, bank projects, supposedly targeted on the poorest of Africa's poor, not only increased inequality and hunger, but exacerbated ethnic conflicts." A bleak sign of Africa's deteriorating position is that almost 50 percent of global food aid allocations went to Sub-Saharan Africa in 1993–94, against less than 10 percent in 1970–75. The *Africa Research Bulletin* continued, "It is a region that cannot afford the cost of commercial food imports at a time when global surpluses earmarked for food aid are also diminishing" (*ARB* Aug. 7, 1994). The African crisis has not yet come to an end, and by the end of the 1990s, Africa will be even more dependent upon aid than it was at the start of the 1980s. We agree with Riddell's conclusion (1992, 77) that more and more of the poorer economies will not only be aid-dependent but also become aid-driven.

With human rights, democracy, good governance, environmental sustainability, and more northern niceties as added requirements for continued aid, one can see the contours of neocolonialism in the early part of the twenty-first century. Some political leaders have tried to resist this; Kenya's President Moi is a good example. During the difficulties he had between 1990 and 1992 with the IMF, the World Bank, and some bilateral donors, which resulted in donors using the withholding of aid as a political weapon and the Kenyan economy coming to a grinding halt, he "urged donor countries and agencies to help developing countries when they are still on their feet economically, instead of waiting to assist them when they are devastated." The Kenyan press became demanding as well: "Kenya needs this money and needs it quickly. There is an emotional aspect to the business of aid which cannot be ignored, a perception that the colonialists are trying to rule Africa again from afar" (*ARB* Jan. 30, 1993). The same concern was voiced by the democratically elected parliament of Benin, resisting conditions the government had negotiated with aid donors and writing a letter to the IMF asking it to "avoid giving the impression that Benin is under foreign control" (*ARB* Aug. 7, 1994).

## Aid and the Development of a Rent Mentality

Aid has become so important in Africa that it doubtless has a profound impact on the style of government. In the virtual absence of private capital stock and of an indigenous private capital tradition, governments in independent Africa have long seen themselves as the engines of growth, the design and implementation machinery for development. To finance development, foreign aid funds were increasingly received, and many governments became more dependent on aid funds than on internal savings in various forms of taxes to finance development investments. In more recent years, ever more governments have been forced to ask for donor assistance to finance salaries of civil servants—or, in some cases, salary arrears, such as in the Central African Republic in early 1993 (*ARB* Jan. 30, 1993) or in Mali in 1994 (*ARB* Mar. 31, 1994)—as well as maintenance costs of existing "development facilities," "reconstruction costs of facilities damaged or neglected during civil wars," emergency operations, costs of elections, demobilization and social reintegration of refugees, and even costs like the printing of currency notes, as in Sierra Leone in 1992 (*ARB* Feb. 3, 1993). The basis for government legitimacy and maneuverability became the donor community instead of the national parliament, despite donors' efforts for increased democracy and accountability. Ferguson's analysis of aid as an "anti-politics machine" in Lesotho—as a source of depoliticization and increased bureaucratic power of a state in which "expatriate" and "local" elements mingle—might be true for a major part of Africa nowadays (Ferguson 1990).

Government elites (politicians and bureaucrats, including the military) are no longer primarily dependent for their future funds on the success of their investment strategies or on collecting taxes from the private sector. They became dependent on "the image of acceptability" for donor agencies. Donor funds increasingly failed to work as sources of productive or facilitative capital and increasingly became a "rent fund," in which image became the source of rent capital. For African governments in this position, image and reality could be completely different things, and often government bureaucrats became very much divorced from the socioeconomic reality. A large part of the African population opted out of contacts with government, and chose a strategy to avoid formal spheres by investing in deepening informal networks.

If we compare tax revenue with development aid for those countries where figures are available for the year 1990 (World Bank 1992; OECD[a] 1993), we can see the extent of aid dependency. For Uganda, Malawi, Mali, Central African Republic, and Mauritania, aid is more important than taxes for government funds, and for some other countries—Zaire, Sierra Leone, Kenya, Ghana, Guinea, Lesotho, and even Egypt—aid is almost as high as taxes.

If African government elites become so entrenched in donor dependency to finance their official expenses, to support their individual forms of "primitive accumulation" and their "economies of affection" (another useful concept introduced by Hyden), and to "buy their internal political survival," one can expect the rent mentality to become a predatory force, killing long-term dedication to real economic growth. One danger is that "democratization" as a new pillar of the image to uphold may only result in decentralizing the rent mentality (often along ethnic or clan lines). With increased donor pressure for accountability, monitoring and evaluation, and cost sharing, the rent-dependent elites will professionalize their "image defense," often with expatriate support. And if the pressure becomes too much, elites might decide to go on the rampage and resort to the deep end of a predatory rent mentality: warlordism. What started as aid to structural development then degrades to complete destruction and "take what you can." The examples of Mozambique and Angola, Sierra Leone and Liberia, Sudan and Somalia, Rwanda and Burundi become too numerous to neglect as exceptions. Development aid degrades to emergency aid, under external military protection.

# 8

# Foreign Aid to Central America
## *Is the Era of Aid Over?*

### William M. LeoGrande

T HE UNITED STATES foreign assistance program in Latin America
was a child of the Cold War. Born when Washington's rivalry with
Moscow began to manifest itself in the Western Hemisphere, it flourished during decades of superpower competition and waned dramatically after the Soviet Union disappeared.

Having resisted Latin American requests for aid during the 1950s,
Washington lavished resources on the region after the Cuban revolution,
which seemed a portent of communist gains elsewhere. Beginning with
the Alliance for Progress and continuing through the late 1980s, U.S. aid
programs served to bolster friendly regimes, both economically and mil-
itarily, and to provide Washington with political leverage over them.
Sometimes that leverage was used to push recipient governments to the
right, or even to destabilize them; at other times, it was used to foster human rights and social reform.

## Central America in the 1980s

During the last decade of the Cold War, Washington's attention focused on Central America, which was torn by internal wars in
Nicaragua, El Salvador, and Guatemala. Over $5 billion in economic and
military aid was pumped into the region between 1981 and 1988 by the

Reagan administration, whose aim was to secure victory for anticommunist forces regionwide. The recipients of Washington's largesse were happy to get it, strings and all. They had little alternative, because few received any significant assistance from outside the Western Hemisphere.

The government of El Salvador needed help to close a significant fiscal gap created by the expansion of the military budget during the civil war. Part of that cost was defrayed by U.S. military aid and part by budgetary support from Economic Support Fund (ESF) assistance. Economic aid was also critical to keeping the economy afloat despite falling gross domestic product (GDP) due to war damage.

The government of Guatemala faced similar problems, albeit of a much smaller magnitude. It, too, had difficulty financing its counterinsurgency program, in part because traditionally low tax rates limited government resources. During the early 1980s Guatemala's abysmal human rights record made it an international pariah, and it received very little bilateral assistance from any source. An economic crisis at mid-decade, characterized by slow growth and heavy debt, led Guatemalan elites to support the creation of an electoral democracy in the hope that this would open the coffers of the United States and Western Europe for bilateral assistance.

In Nicaragua the Sandinista government also faced an economic crisis because of the Contra war and the government's ongoing political conflict with the private sector. Washington's efforts at economic denial effectively blocked most multilateral aid to Nicaragua after 1981. Instead, the Sandinistas sought bilateral assistance from Western Europe and the Soviet bloc. The Soviets were generous with military assistance but unwilling to provide economic aid commensurate with what the Nicaraguan economy needed to maintain critical imports. Aid from Europe declined as donors became impatient with Nicaragua's authoritarian politics. The result was economic collapse.

For Costa Rica the early 1980s were a time of economic readjustment brought on by debt. The central fear of the Costa Rican political elite was that cuts in government spending would require dismantling the nation's social welfare system. Thus the country would lose the programs that had given it some immunity to the political instability so prevalent elsewhere in the region. For Costa Rica foreign aid was a means of cushioning the adjustment process and preserving the heart of the social democratic contract.

In Honduras motives were less lofty. The Honduran government, especially the armed forces, sought increased aid from the United States as compensation for its cooperation with U.S. regional policy. Large amounts of the resulting flow of resources disappeared in graft.

As Central America's armed conflicts subsided in the 1990s, the region's need for outside aid shifted from financing hostilities to financing peace. For El Salvador and Nicaragua in particular, the process of demobilizing combatants and reintegrating them into productive economic activity was costly. External assistance played an important role in supervising demobilization, distributing land to former combatants, and financing local development projects in formerly strife-torn areas.

Throughout the 1980s and early 1990s, U.S. economic aid (i.e., all nonmilitary programs) constituted the largest block of assistance received by the Central Americans, often amounting to half of total annual aid flows. For countries other than Nicaragua, multilateral sources were the next most significant. Bilateral donors, especially in Europe, were generally reluctant to devote significant resources to a region torn by so many armed conflicts. A single year's worth of U.S. economic aid to El Salvador in the mid-1980s amounted to more than the country received from all other bilateral donors during the entire decade. Only in Costa Rica and Nicaragua did non-U.S. bilateral aid rival the level of multilateral aid—in Costa Rica because European donors sought to bolster a stable democratic polity, in Nicaragua because multilateral aid was so low. As the region's wars subsided in the early 1990s, however, non-U.S. bilateral aid increased significantly, from both Europe and Japan.

Japan had virtually no presence as a donor in Central America during the 1980s, providing no more than a few million dollars annually to any one country. Only when peace was restored did Japan begin to provide any significant assistance, and even then the amounts rarely exceeded $50 million annually to any one country—less than what was provided by the European Economic Community or the United States.

## After the Cold War

The end of the Cold War abruptly changed the calculus of U.S. interests in Central America. Without the Soviet menace, Washington faced no plausible national security threat in the region. Moreover, the end of the Cold War coincided with successful diplomatic efforts to resolve the wars in Nicaragua and El Salvador. In Nicaragua the Marxist Sandinista government agreed to hold a free, internationally monitored election in

1990, which was won by a coalition of opposition parties, thus bringing the Contra war to a conclusion. In El Salvador the guerrillas reached an accord with the government in 1992 that ended their two-decade rebellion. Thereafter, Washington's interest in the region diminished rapidly.

These events translated into a radically reduced foreign aid budget for Latin America. "Trade not aid" was the Clinton administration's slogan, and scarce foreign aid dollars flowed away from Central America toward Eastern Europe and the former Soviet states. For fiscal year 1996, the administration requested just $167 million in economic assistance for all of Central America—down 71 percent from Clinton's first budget request in 1993, and down 86 percent from the peak level of U.S. aid, $1.2 billion in 1985. Moreover, it was certain that the Republican majority in Congress would cut Clinton's aid request even further (effectively a 25 to 30 percent cut for programs other than Egypt and Israel, which remained sacrosanct) (Lippman 1995).

Costa Rica "graduated" from United States Agency for International Development (USAID) programs and was thus slated for no economic assistance at all in fiscal year 1986 other than $1.6 million for the Peace Corps program. Nicaragua and El Salvador, only recently free of bloody civil conflicts, suffered dramatic declines in aid despite the danger that economic difficulties could undermine their fragile democratic systems. Nicaragua, which received almost $300 million in 1990 after the Sandinistas lost election, was slated for just $39 million in Clinton's budget for fiscal year 1996. El Salvador, which received almost $500 million annually in the late 1980s and $230 million as recently as 1993, was slated for just $43 million in economic aid in 1996 (USAID 1996, 26). The sharp drop in aid prompted the Salvadoran president Alfredo Cristiani to upbraid Washington publicly. "We are critical of the fact that the United States is more worried about Europe than about what happens in its own yard," he complained. "In the democratic processes that are beginning [in Central America], if economic results are not palpable and positive for people, the disillusionment can be dangerous" (Farah 1994).

USAID's program for Latin America during the Clinton administration emphasized "sustainable development," which meant open markets, broadly shared development to lift the standard of living of the poor, democracy, and environmental protection (USAID 1996). Military and ESF assistance virtually disappeared, especially from the Central American program. None of the countries in the region was slated for any ESF in 1996 or for any military assistance other than a few hundred thousand dollars in military training funds—a total of just $1.5 million regionwide (USAID 1996, 26).

## Aid as Leverage

The first Latin American crisis testing Clinton's prodemocracy policy came in May 1993, when Guatemala's elected president Jorge Serrano attempted to assume dictatorial powers with the support of the armed forces. Washington's response was swift and decisive. The administration suspended aid and warned that unless democracy was restored Guatemalan exporters would lose preferential access to U.S. markets. That threat produced an unlikely alliance of conservative businessmen and the progressive popular movement that demanded Serrano's resignation. Faced with growing popular unrest, the military changed sides, Serrano departed, and the Guatemalan Congress selected the human rights ombudsman Ramiro de Leon Carpio as president. This move was an unusually effective use of aid and trade as an instrument of coercive diplomacy.

Unfortunately, even de Leon Carpio proved unable to bring the Guatemalan armed forces under control. The human rights situation got no better, and the Guatemalan government continued to refuse to conduct serious investigations into several prominent cases, including the 1990 murder of the U.S. citizen Michael DeVine and the disappearance of the guerrilla leader Efrain Bamaca, captured in 1992. The DeVine case had led the Bush administration to cut $3.3 million in military aid to Guatemala in 1990 (although the overt assistance was immediately replaced with covert military assistance channeled through the CIA) (Weiner 1995). The Bamaca case was brought to public attention by his wife, Jennifer Harbury, a Harvard-educated lawyer who camped out in front of the presidential palace in Guatemala City and began a hunger strike, demanding to know her husband's fate (DePalma 1994). In March 1995 the Clinton administration cut off the last overt military assistance flowing to Guatemala—$200,000 in IMET funds—on human rights grounds (Greenhouse 1995).

### *Reinforcing Democracy in El Salvador*

In January 1992 negotiations between the Salvadoran government and the Frente Farabundo Martí para la Liberacíon Nacional (FMLN) finally brought the war to an end. A critical factor in convincing the Salvadoran military to accept the peace accord was the 1990 decision by the U.S. Congress to cut military aid by 50 percent. With the war stalemated and U.S. aid diminishing, the armed forces had little alternative but to accept a negotiated solution.

When Bill Clinton came to office in January 1993, the Salvadoran peace accord that ended the war was still in danger. The guerrillas had agreed to lay down their arms in exchange for significant reforms in the armed forces, particularly the removal of officers responsible for human rights abuses. An investigatory group set up under terms of the accord, the Ad Hoc Commission, identified over one hundred officers for removal. But in January, President Alfredo Cristiani, under pressure from the army, announced that he would retain fifteen of the most senior officers named, including Defense Minister Emilio Ponce. On March 12, the Clinton administration announced it was freezing the disbursement of $11 million in military aid until the Salvadoran government complied fully with the recommendations of the Ad Hoc Commission. The pressure was effective. Fearing that the obstinacy of the fifteen officers named was endangering the interests of the armed forces as an institution, junior officers added their voices to those demanding that the fifteen depart. In March, Ponce tendered his resignation, and President Cristiani announced that all fifteen would leave their posts on June 30.

As the Salvadoran election campaign moved into high gear in the last few months of 1993, death squads launched a campaign of assassination against former FMLN leaders running for office. At the same time, the government seemed to be intentionally stalling the registration of new voters to disenfranchise communities likely to support the left. The FMLN warned that if such obstruction continued, it would boycott the March 1994 election.

In October 1993 the Clinton administration followed the recommendation of the House Appropriations Subcommittee on Foreign Operations and froze the disbursement of $70 million in economic aid because of the slow pace of the electoral registration process. Once again, brandishing the stick brought results. The Salvadoran government accelerated voter registration and eventually managed to enroll more than half of the estimated 750,000 unregistered voters. In March 1994 the Salvadorans held their first election in which parties from the entire political spectrum were free to participate. Despite some instances of local fraud, all sides accepted the result, which was a victory for the incumbent conservative ARENA party.

For El Salvador the most important source of hard currency was neither trade nor aid, but remittances—dollars sent home by Salvadorans in the United States. During the 1980s a million or more Salvadorans fled to the United States to escape the war. By 1994 they were sending home almost $1 billion a year—more than the earnings from coffee, El Salvador's main export, and nearly as much as all its export earnings combined (Wilkinson 1994).

In 1990, Congress had granted Salvadoran refugees "temporary protected status" because of the ongoing war. President Bush renewed the special status in 1992 and 1993, and President Clinton renewed it in 1994. By 1995, however, the war had ended, and reasonably fair elections had been held. Moreover, in November 1994, California voters approved Proposition 187, an anti-immigration measure that exemplified a growing national hostility to Washington's immigration policy. In January 1995 the Clinton administration announced that the Salvadorans' protected status would not be renewed, though deportations would be delayed for at least nine months. Most analysts concluded that few refugees would ever actually be deported, but the mere possibility of it produced vigorous protests from the Salvadoran government.

The prospect of significant deportations was a graver threat to El Salvador's postwar reconstruction than the decline in U.S. bilateral assistance. "Many families who receive remittances reside . . . in the principal ex-conflict zones where the greatest civil war fighting took place," the U.S. ambassador Alan Flanigan warned. "These are among the poorest areas in El Salvador. The effect of significantly reduced remittances would be economically disastrous for these areas. In fact, it would probably lead to increased illegal immigration to the United States" (Wilkinson 1994).

## Nicaragua's Ongoing Turmoil

In Nicaragua national reconciliation was much harder to achieve than in El Salvador. Shortly after Violeta Chamorro defeated the Sandinista Daniel Ortega in the 1990 elections, her United Nicaraguan Opposition (UNO) coalition fractured over her policy of conciliation toward the Sandinistas—particularly her decision to retain Ortega's brother Humberto as minister of defense. By 1992, Chamorro and her loyal supporters had joined in coalition with the defeated Sandinistas against right-wing elements in the UNO.

Ecstatic at the electoral defeat of the Sandinistas in 1990, the Bush

administration was bitterly disappointed at the continuing influence of
the Sandinista party in Chamorro's government. In 1992, at the instiga-
tion of Senator Jesse Helms (R-N.C.), Bush held up disbursement of
$104 million in economic aid to pressure Chamorro to reduce Sandinista
influence in the military and police, investigate several politically sensi-
tive killings, and compensate U.S. citizens for property expropriated after the 1979 revolution. Half the aid was released in December 1992
after Chamorro fired the Sandinista chief of police.

In April 1993, President Clinton released the other $52 million in sus-
pended aid as part of a new policy of disengaging the United States from
Nicaragua's partisan squabbles. Both sides had been looking to Washington for support. Alfredo Cesar, leader of the anti-Chamorro faction in
UNO, traveled regularly to Washington to consult with Senator Helms
and lobby against aid for Nicaragua. His brother-in-law Antonio Lacayo,
Chamorro's principal adviser, also trekked north to lobby—or as he him-
self put it, "to panhandle"—for aid (Marquis 1993a). The Clinton administration tried to end this unhealthy dynamic by declaring its support
for Chamorro as the elected president of Nicaragua while at the same
time declaring neutrality on Nicaragua's myriad policy battles.

But disengagement was not so easy. In May a large secret arms cache
owned by Salvadoran guerrillas exploded accidentally in Managua. In-
vestigators concluded that it had been built in 1990 or 1991, after
Chamorro became president, thus raising the issue of how subordinate
to civilian authority the Sandinista army really was. In Washington, Jesse
Helms exploited congressional anger over the arms cache to win approval for a proposal freezing all aid to Nicaragua unless President Clinton certified that its army was not engaged in international terrorism.

Responding to this congressional initiative, the Clinton administration froze economic aid in July 1993 and demanded significant changes
from the Chamorro government as the price of resuming assistance—
specifically, a deadline for the removal of Humberto Ortega as minister
of defense, a full investigation of the killing of a sixteen-year-old boy by
Ortega's bodyguards, and progress on the compensation issue. "The basic theme was: How could we ever go back to the Hill for aid to
Nicaragua?" an administration official explained. "We have nothing positive to report" (Marquis 1993b). Clinton's policy had slipped back into
the same track as Bush's.

In December, after a summit meeting with the Central American
presidents, Clinton released $40 million in aid to Nicaragua on the

grounds that Chamorro has made substantial progress on the issues of concern to Washington. Regular aid was resumed in 1994 when Chamorro not only announced that Humberto Ortega would be replaced in 1995 but also sent to the National Assembly a new military code that strengthened civilian control over the armed forces. Ortega retired on schedule, but Senator Helms continued to press for a cut-off of aid to Nicaragua because Chamorro's government had not yet settled the property claims of U.S. citizens (Rohter 1995).

During the 1980s, Washington spent some $2 billion in economic and military aid to purchase the cooperation of the Honduran armed forces in the wars in neighboring Nicaragua and El Salvador. When those wars ended, so too did Washington's interest in Honduras. Military assistance, which reached a peak of $81 million in 1986, fell to just $2 million in 1994. Beginning with the Bush administration, U.S. officials set about trying to reverse the effects of previous policy by reducing the political influence of the Honduran armed forces. "What we're doing now is damage control," said one U.S. official, reflecting on the legacy of the 1980s (Wilkinson 1993).

## The Future of Foreign Aid in Central America

The Summit of the Americas in December 1994 set a broad agenda for inter-American relations into the next century and underscored the diminishing role of U.S. aid programs. On the economic front, free trade was the centerpiece. The participants agreed to work toward concluding negotiations for a hemispheric free trade zone by 2005 (Brooke 1994). Summit documents called upon the participants to create favorable investment climates to attract capital, both foreign and domestic, to serve as the engine of growth. Some mention was made of the importance of international financial institutions for helping to restructure debt and finance infrastructural development, but bilateral assistance programs were nowhere to be found.

Washington's bilateral aid program in Latin America began when the United States became concerned about the growth of Soviet influence in the region. Economic assistance was conceived as a means of bolstering the legitimacy and economic performance of friendly regimes to undercut the appeal of Marxism. Military assistance was used to build internal security forces to suppress domestic leftist movements. The end of the Cold War has left the U.S. aid program in Latin America without a clear raison d'être and without a strong domestic political constituency to defend it in an era of budgetary cuts.

As U.S. bilateral aid declines, the size of European and Japanese programs will soon rival Washington's. But despite the United States' historical sensitivity to European encroachments in Latin America, Washington evinces no particular concern about this development. Because the United States hopes to build a trading bloc in the Western Hemisphere to rival the European Union, free trade agreements and increased direct foreign investment have become the preferred policy instruments.

# 9

# Foreign Aid to Eastern Europe
## *Assistance to Transitions*

### Wieslaw Michalak

F EW REGIONS have been affected more by the "new world order" than Eastern Europe and the former Soviet republics. Indeed, the end of the Cold War and the dawn of the "new world order" were possible because of the collapse of the socialist experiment in this part of the world. The artificial bipolarity of East-West relations has been removed and replaced by a multitude of conflicting aspirations, interests, and policies. Initially, the West responded to the events in the other Europe with enthusiasm, proclaiming the ultimate victory not only in the ideological quest for a better society but also in the race for world hegemony (Dahrendorf 1990; Fukuyama 1992; Szacki 1994). However, the early euphoria was quickly replaced by a much more cautious and sober reexamination of policies once the monumental magnitude of the economic collapse of the East was fully realized (Schöpflin 1993). No blueprints were available because such a massive transition from a totalitarian to a democratic society had never been attempted before. The forty years of social and economic experimentation in Eastern Europe and over seventy years of communism in the Soviet Union left the economies and societies of the region in ruins.

During the course of the 1990s, it became clear that the countries in the region were faced with three principal problems. First, the costs of reforms, liberalization, and stabilization were far greater than expected.

The Gulf crisis and the collapse of the CMEA (Council for Mutual Economic Assistance) deepened the economic crisis. Moreover, the sheer scale of Eastern European expectations for Western economic aid exceeded anything Western politicians and societies were prepared to commit. Second, none of the multilateral institutions had either the resources or the infrastructure to service the massive capital needs of the region. Third, because of great uncertainties about the transition, compounded by a lack of experience and expertise about the region, flows of private capital were reduced to almost nothing. Many Western investors have a far better knowledge and experience of Southeast Asia or Southern Africa than Eastern Europe. One of the unwelcome and controversial consequences of the collapse of the East was the volume and scale of aid needed to sustain the process of democratization, market reforms, and peace in Europe (Balcerowicz 1994).

From the start, the leaders of the transforming states placed their high hopes of sustained reform in speedy and generous assistance from donors such as Western Europe, the United States, and Japan. Later, almost the same degree of significance was attached to the largest donors by the successor states of the former Soviet Union. The high hopes of these countries quickly evaporated when it became apparent that a coherent, long-term Western strategy was lacking and both the European Union (EU) and the United States were reluctant to get seriously involved in the process of transition. The unqualified enthusiasm of Eastern Europeans toward the West was gradually replaced by a feeling of disappointment and even bitterness.

In this chapter I examine Western aid to Eastern Europe and the former Soviet Union in the context of the "new world order." The West responded to the "velvet revolution" in the East with a multitude of bilateral initiatives and multilateral financial transfers. I discuss the magnitude and significance of these initiatives and the consequences of Western foreign aid.

## Western Aid for the "East"

During the July 1989 Paris summit of the Group of 7 (G-7), the European Commission accepted the request to coordinate aid for the East. Later, in her annual speech in Guildhall, Margaret Thatcher enthusiastically supported new prospective cooperation between the European Union (EU) and Eastern Europe (Van Ham 1993, 126). The most tangible result of this new European policy was a proposal for association agreements for the reforming countries with the EU along the lines of agreements with Turkey. Moreover, Eastern Europe would receive economic and financial aid, a number of significant trade concessions, and increased market access to the EU. After the initial timid changes in Poland and Hungary, political events in Eastern Europe quickly overtook these early initiatives, and once the 1989 reforms seemed irreversible, calls for a more active Western approach gained force. The strategies devised by various Western governments focused almost exclusively on assisting Eastern Europe in the transition toward market economies. The main instruments of this assistance were transfer of capital for macroeconomic stabilization, technology, know-how, and improved market access of Eastern exports to the West. The latter was encouraged by International Monetary Fund (IMF) short-term financing, World Bank structural adjustment loans, and the systemic transformation facility mechanism (IMF 1994b). The coordination of other transfers was left mainly to multilateral lending organizations. It was hoped that a quick and substantial injection of capital would stabilize Eastern economies to the point where it became profitable for private investors to take over the function of supplying capital for the systemic transformation. The objective of technical assistance was to provide the initial critical mass of capital and institutions capable of absorbing financial aid and to attract substantial foreign investment (UNECE 1995). In short, the aim of Western donors was to provide the initial impetus for the economic transformation. Once the right economic framework was in place, it would be a task of private investors to provide the bulk of capital.

Most recipients in Eastern Europe saw objectives of the foreign aid differently. To start with, in their opinion the West underestimated the depth and nature of the crisis in the East. The various stabilization funds, although helpful, would not be able to cope with all the requirements of the systemic transformation and dramatic social changes caused by them. A genuine conversion to a market economy would demand not only freeing prices and removing trade restrictions but also mass privatization, construction of the entire financial structure, and, perhaps most important, creation of the foundations of civil society. Moreover, there was a severe shortage of domestic capital in Eastern Europe. The widely publicized "capital overhang" of the late 1980s did not materialize. Western economists were wrong; none of the countries in the region had sufficient savings to privatize, let alone restructure and modernize the industrial base and infrastructure, no matter how radical their plans might be (Sarcinelli 1992). Eastern Europe would need much more significant, long-term financial help. In short, a new Marshall Plan for Eastern Europe was needed.

The United Nations Economic Commission for Europe (UNECE) was one of the strongest advocates of such a plan. UNECE argued that only carefully prepared and detailed long-term financial plan could make a significant impact on the economies in transition (UNECE 1993). Many Eastern governments also insisted that Western assistance would be most effective if a program of reforms was drawn together with the recipient countries. The overall effort should be coordinated and monitored by an international institution such as the EU, which through a network of donors, recipients, and consultants would help to clarify the specific requests, monitor disbursements, and provide a forum for new ideas and exchange of experiences. In short, East European reformers envisaged a much greater role for the West whereby the donors would inject the initial financial boost but also serve as partners and coordinators of the entire transformation process (Ners 1992, 48–49). The parallel to the Marshall Plan was not merely a rhetorical figure of political language. It expressed a genuine belief that the West (and Western Europe in particular) had not only a self-evident interest in the success of the transformation but also a moral obligation in helping its Eastern cousins. These sentiments were voiced particularly strongly by some high-profile Eastern European politicians, such as Lech Walesa, Vaclav Havel, Boris Yeltsin, and Arpad Goncz (see, for example, Walesa 1991; Havel 1994).

In response to these proposals, during the G-7 Western Economic Summit in Paris, the European Commission was given a mandate to coordinate aid for Poland and Hungary on behalf of all the countries of the Organization for Economic Cooperation and Development (OECD) (Pelkmans and Murphy 1991). Following a meeting, the commission established Poland and Hungary: Assistance for Reconstructing Economies (PHARE) and later Technical Assistance for the Commonwealth of Independent States (TACIS) (Treverton 1992). Since then, a multitude of aid programs has emerged, administered by multilateral institutions created specifically for that task, such as the European Bank for Reconstruction and Development (EBRD), or already existing organizations, such as the European Investment Bank (EIB), the IMF, as well as the International Bank for Reconstruction and Development (IBRD), commonly known as the World Bank, and its agencies, particularly the International Development Association (IDA) and the International Finance Corporation (IFC). In addition, a large number of bilateral programs and initiatives from the EU members, the Group of 24 (G-24), were introduced.

## Distribution of Aid

Right from the start it became clear that despite the official rhetoric insisting on using the collective label of "East Europe," this vast geographical area could not be treated as a single unit. The "Socialist bloc" ceased to exist, for all practical purposes, and Western assistance had to acknowledge this new diversity. On the basis of similarities of approach toward reforms and the state of the economy and polity in each country, at least six distinct areas have emerged:

1. The Visegrad Four (Czech Republic, Hungary, Poland, and Slovakia), the most enthusiastic supporters of democratic transition and market economies (over time, increasingly so, with the exception of Slovakia);

2. The Balkans (former Yugoslavia, Bulgaria, Albania, and Romania), characterized by a slower pace of transition and intensified ethnic conflicts;

3. The Baltic states (Estonia, Latvia, and Lithuania), determined to achieve total and unconditional independence from Russia and some sort of Western security guarantees;

4. The western former Soviet republics, including Ukraine and Belarus, too big and important to Russia to hope for an analogous independence any time soon;

5. Russia itself; and

6. The rest of the former Soviet empire in the south and Asia.

Most bilateral and multilateral institutions appear to use this classification, although it was never discussed or agreed upon formally. The needs of each of these regions were assessed according to different criteria and priorities. Officially, Western assistance to the East was guided by the "Triple R Agenda" of reform, reintegration, and regional security (Laux 1991, 12). The final goal of this agenda would be to construct a new post–Cold War order in Europe wherein the political and security interests of all major participants are guaranteed (Meyer 1992).

The sheer number of aid initiatives makes analyzing them difficult. It is virtually impossible to obtain a clear-cut and comprehensive statistical picture of these efforts since 1989. The figures frequently quoted by the media and politicians are usually intentions of foreign aid, not the actual disbursements. This is an important point because of a wide gap between the reality and what passes as the amount of aid in Western media. Moreover, because the existing sources usually refer to a cumulative total of aid since 1989, any comparisons are impossible. There is also a larger issue: methodological discrepancies between various donors about what actually constitutes aid. Very often, concessionary short-term loans are reported together with bilateral and multilateral commitments of other credits at commercial rates. Polish, Russian, or Bulgarian debt relief is sometimes reported as aid, sometimes not. These differences in reporting techniques often reflect ideological and policy variations between donors and recipients. There is also a degree of competition between donors for high-profile projects that can be reported in their annual reports as successes (UNECE 1994). Similarly, the wide publicity given in the West to many bilateral programs of aid seems to be tailored for domestic political consumption. EBRD, the World Bank, and IMF have very similar objectives in Eastern Europe. Consequently, some commentators have questioned the necessity of creating EBRD in the first place. Even though OECD has been designated as the center for collecting and processing aid data, UNECE, the European Commission, and individual governments maintain their own databases, adding to the confusion. Unfortunately, the result in some cases is that "the information provided by the donors is neither complete, timely nor, in some cases, arranged in accordance with standard definition of assistance" (UNECE 1993, 18).

According to data on Western commitments of international aid from both bilateral and multilateral sources, the total amount intended for Eastern Europe between 1989 and the end of 1994 was just over $206 billion (table 9.1). The larger component of this total is multilateral aid, $115 billion; bilateral institutions committed a total of $90 billion. In terms of geographical distribution, the largest share of aid was committed to the former Soviet Union (it was not possible to desegregate these data further). The rest of the East received pledges of aid amounting to 39.8 percent of the total. However, most of this, 28.5 percent, was destined for the Visegrad Four; 9.9 percent was for the Balkans, and 1.4 percent for the Baltic states.

By far the largest donor and creditor to the region was Germany,

Table 9.1 Commitments of Aid to Eastern Europe
and the Former Soviet Union until the End of 1994

|  | Multilateral (US$million) | Bilateral (US$million) | Total (US$million) | Per capita (US$) | Fraction (%) |
|---|---|---|---|---|---|
| Czech Republic | 3,105 | 4,631 | 7,736 | 751 | 3.7 |
| Hungary | 6,924 | 7,244 | 14,168 | 1,375 | 6.9 |
| Poland | 10,912 | 22,330 | 33,242 | 866 | 16.1 |
| Slovakia | 1,473 | 2,191 | 3,664 | 691 | 1.8 |
| Albania | 707 | 923 | 1,630 | 479 | 0.8 |
| Bulgaria | 2,766 | 1,397 | 4,163 | 490 | 2.0 |
| Macedonia | 283 | 137 | 420 | 191 | 0.2 |
| Romania | 4,609 | 3,559 | 8,168 | 360 | 4.0 |
| Slovenia | 450 | 359 | 809 | 405 | 0.4 |
| Yugoslavia | 2,756 | 2,407 | 5,163 | n/a | 2.5 |
| Estonia | 448 | 283 | 731 | 538 | 0.3 |
| Latvia | 550 | 416 | 966 | 372 | 0.5 |
| Lithuania | 749 | 520 | 1,269 | 334 | 0.6 |
| Total Eastern Europe | 35,732 | 46,397 | 82,129 | 709 | 39.8 |
| Former Soviet Union | 78,600 | 37,600 | 116,200 | 780 | 56.3 |
| Not specified | 1,326 | 6,807 | 8,133 | — | 3.9 |
| Total | 115,658 | 90,804 | 779 | 100.0 | |

Source: European Commission 1995; UNECE 1995.

which pledged over $81 billion in aid. Of this total, almost $68 billion
was designated for the former Soviet Union (excluding the Baltic states).
This total included, among other things, emergency assistance, grants,
credits, and financing for dismantling some nuclear weapons in Russia,
Ukraine, Belarus, and Kazakhstan as well as for constructing new housing for the Russian armies leaving the former German Democratic Republic (GDR) territory. Germany was also the primary donor of aid to
Belarus, Bosnia-Herzegovina, Croatia, Czech Republic, Hungary, Macedonia, Moldova, Romania, Slovakia, Slovenia, and Ukraine. The United
States was the second-largest donor, committed to some $19 billion, and
the primary donor of aid to Armenia, Latvia, Poland, Tajikistan, and
Yugoslavia. Other donors who committed relatively large amounts were
France, Japan, and Austria. Italy pledged some $7 billion and ranked as
the primary donor to Albania. France was the second-largest donor to

Romania and third-largest to the Czech Republic and Poland. Sweden
was the largest donor to Estonia and Lithuania, and second-largest to
Latvia. Turkey was the largest donor to several southern former Soviet
republics—Azerbaijan, Uzbekistan, Turkmenistan, and Kyrghyzstan.

These amounts, although impressive, can be compared to the flows of
financial aid within Germany since 1989. The net government transfers
from Western to Eastern parts amounted to about $108 billion in 1995
alone and totaled some $554 billion or $32,588 per capita since the collapse of the Berlin Wall (IMF 1995). Moreover, these figures do not include any of the private capital and loans. Because Treuhandanstalt was,
at least theoretically, a private holding company, direct subsidies to most
East German industries were not included as official aid. The unification
costs have forced the federal government in Germany to raise taxes and
run up a budget deficit equal to some 6 percent of the gross domestic
product (GDP) only four years after the fall of the Berlin Wall. By comparison, the finance needed to transform the economies of the East to a
level comparable with that of even the poorest members of the EU, let
alone Germany, is significantly greater. It is worth noting here that of
the $206 billion cumulative aid committed to Eastern Europe, about two-
thirds was accounted for by debt restructuring and other forms of "special financing" designed to service interest on debt accumulated by the
East mostly during the 1970s and 1980s. In other words, about two-
thirds of the total amount of aid committed to Eastern Europe was used
to repay Western creditors and never reached the East.

Comprehensive and current data on the actual disbursement of aid
are not available. The best approximation provides a database maintained by the Organization for Economic Cooperation and Development
(OECDa 1994). According to data on disbursement of official multilateral and bilateral aid by recipients for 1991 and 1992 (table 9.2), only $12
billion of the pledged aid actually made it to Eastern Europe (this, however, does not include private and certain bilateral programs). The major
recipients in 1991 were Poland, which received 43.1 percent of the total;
Hungary, 11.6 percent; and Russia, 9.7 percent. In terms of regional distribution, 78.8 percent of aid in 1991 was disbursed to the Visegrad
Four, the Balkans, and Baltic Republics, and 21.2 percent to the rest of
the former Soviet Union. The share destined for the latter increased to
45.3 percent in 1992. The largest single recipient, however, remained
Poland at 29.9 percent, followed by Russia, 29.4 percent, and Ukraine,
8.5 percent.

*Table 9.2* Major Recipients of Official Aid Disbursements between 1991 and 1992

| | 1991 | | 1992 | | 1991 and 1992 Total | |
|---|---|---|---|---|---|---|
| | Amount (\$million) | Fraction of Total (%) | Amount (\$million) | Fraction of Total (%) | Amount (\$million) | Fraction of Total (%) |
| Former Soviet Union | 1,233.6 | 21.2 | 2,990.0 | 45.3 | 4,223.6 | 34.0 |
| Armenia | 2.7 | 0.04 | 27.3 | 0.4 | 30.0 | 0.2 |
| Azerbaijan | 0.3 | 0.04 | 27.3 | 0.4 | 30.0 | 0.2 |
| Belarus | 187.0 | 3.2 | 273.2 | 4.1 | 460.2 | 3.7 |
| Georgia | 0.3 | 0.01 | 24.3 | 0.4 | 24.6 | 0.2 |
| Kazakhstan | 111.5 | 1.8 | 11.6 | 0.2 | 123.1 | 1.0 |
| Kyrghyzstan | — | — | 23.5 | 0.3 | 23.5 | 0.2 |
| Moldova | — | — | 9.7 | 0.1 | 9.7 | 0.1 |
| Russia | 563.5 | 9.7 | 1,942.1 | 29.4 | 2,505.6 | 20.2 |
| Tajikistan | — | — | 11.7 | 0.3 | 11.7 | 0.1 |
| Turkmenistan | — | — | 8.6 | 0.1 | 8.6 | 0.1 |
| Ukraine | 368.3 | 6.3 | 559.4 | 8.5 | 927.7 | 7.5 |
| Uzbekistan | — | — | 61.7 | 0.9 | 61.7 | 0.5 |
| East Europe | 4,583.6 | 78.8 | 3,617.4 | 54.7 | 8,201.0 | 66.0 |
| Albania | 329.6 | 5.7 | 377.5 | 5.7 | 707.1 | 5.7 |
| Bulgaria | 312.2 | 5.4 | 147.6 | 2.2 | 459.8 | 3.7 |
| Czech & Slovak Republics | 410.3 | 7.0 | 234.8 | 3.5 | 645.1 | 5.2 |
| Estonia | 15.4 | 0.3 | 120.1 | 1.8 | 135.5 | 1.1 |
| Hungary | 676.4 | 11.6 | 212.9 | 3.2 | 889.3 | 7.1 |
| Latvia | 3.4 | 0.05 | 83.5 | 1.3 | 86.9 | 0.7 |
| Lithuania | 4.0 | 0.1 | 99.5 | 1.5 | 103.5 | 0.8 |
| Poland | 2,505.5 | 43.1 | 1,976.7 | 29.9 | 4,482.2 | 36.1 |
| Romania | 326.8 | 5.6 | 364.8 | 5.5 | 691.6 | 5.6 |
| Total | 5,816.9 | 100.0 | 6,607.4 | 100.0 | 12,424.3 | 100.0 |

Source: OECD(b) (1986–96).

It is reasonably clear from these data that the countries that introduced the most radical reforms received the largest proportion of aid. Almost half of the entire amount of aid disbursed between 1991 and 1992, 48.4 percent, went to the Visegrad group. The Balkans received a smaller proportion, amounting to 15.1 percent. Russia's share, increasing in aggregate terms, amounted to 20.2 percent. Former western Soviet republics, including Ukraine and Belarus, received a combined share of 11.2 percent, and Baltic states received 2.6 percent. The smallest share, totaling 2.5 percent, was allocated to the former southern Soviet

republics. The increasingly uneven distribution of aid throughout Eastern Europe tends to be a self-perpetuating process because countries
that had the most success in satisfying the conditions of multilateral
donors, the IMF in particular, also had the most success in attracting
private capital. Both the Czech Republic and Hungary not only received
the largest shares of direct foreign investment but also were the only
countries in the region able to access Western capital on the financial
markets (UNECE 1993). By contrast, non-Russian republics of the former Soviet Union had considerable problems in obtaining aid.

The discrepancy between the finances committed and disbursed is
not merely of accounting significance. The lack of capital is arguably the
single most detrimental factor complicating the transformation process
in many Eastern European countries (EBRD 1992). Moreover, the large
discrepancy between what is claimed to have been donated and what is
announced as received can lead to a deterioration in a country's relations
with other creditors, further reducing the flow of capital.


## Aid Assessment

Western aid has been criticized by nearly all governments in Eastern
Europe. Of course, there is no agreement between these countries about
the effects of various programs. Countries such as the Czech Republic
and Hungary avoid any open confrontations, fearing reduction in their
credit rating and restricted access to Western financial markets. For the
same reason, both countries did not request a reduction of their foreign
debt. Instead, they attempted to fulfill their financial obligations at any
cost. Perhaps the most severe critics of the foreign aid programs are former Soviet republics and Russia in particular (Chowaniec and Harbinson 1994, 142).

The most frequent complaints focus on the delays in meeting pledges
of aid, conditions attached to most pledges, complexity and costs of administering aid, and lack of coordination between various programs and
recipients. For example, it was alleged that a disproportionate share of
aid is destined for consulting and administration fees (Ners 1992, 10;
*The Economist* 1993; UNECE 1994, 247). Both salaries and service fees
are several times higher in the West than in the East. Nevertheless, most
aid programs employ almost exclusively Westerners and only in very few
instances local experts. Consequently, even language skills are very limited among these Western "experts." There is a certain irony that only a

very tiny proportion of people administering, monitoring, and planning aid to countries that want to distance themselves from Russia actually speak any other East European language than Russian. This situation has created a certain degree of ambiguity in some of the relations with non-Russian recipients.

Perhaps the best-publicized case associated with mismanagement of aid to Eastern Europe is the EBRD, which until 1993 actually spent more money on its headquarters and salaries in London than on aid to Eastern Europe, the reason that it was created in the first place (Weber 1994). At the EBRD's first annual meeting in Budapest in April 1992, East European politicians sharply criticized the bank for failing to meet the region's financial needs. In the words of the *Financial Times*, "the EBRD has not yet provided that it is anything more than an expensive political gesture" (*Financial Times* 1992, 12). The EBRD's management crisis has focused attention on the fundamental contradictions in the bank's operations despite the best efforts of Western governments to present its former boss, Jacques Attali, as the sole cause of all its problems. The bank was established to provide additional resources to Eastern Europe. But like any other commercial institution, it also had to meet standards of extreme prudence in its investment policies; one of the reasons that it has been criticized for its cumbersome administrative procedures. For example, the bank used to be barred from making investments that would share more than 40 percent of government-owned enterprises, which, until recently, meant the vast majority of enterprises in Eastern Europe. The EBRD lends under fully commercial terms, as a result charging higher rates of interest than the EIB. Even some Western politicians openly declared impatience with some of the more drastic cases. The General Secretary of the Council of Europe, Catherine Lalumiere, for example, called for a reexamination of the way in which Western aid is given to Eastern Europe. She asserted that almost all of the $42 billion donated to OECD by its members had gone "to businessmen and financiers with private consultants as mediators" (RFE/RL 1993b).

Perhaps the most controversial aspect of Western aid is its conditionality. Already in August 1989 when the EU created PHARE, aid to the East was made conditional on progress toward economic and political reforms. Eligibility criteria have changed from case to case; however, they have all stressed a clear commitment toward the creation of a market economy, a multiparty democracy, free elections, human rights, and the state of law. In addition to the conditions routinely attached by the

EU to foreign aid (EU is the coordinator of G-24 aid), there were a number of detailed targets specified by the IMF and the World Bank. Of course, countries like the Visegrad Four already committed to a program of radical reforms could satisfy such conditions much more easily than the rest. However, an additional complication was the short-term nature of most conditions compared to the long-term needs of the transition to a market economy. Moreover, very few of these conditions have taken into account the vast societal costs of radical economic restructuring. In particular, Russia and Ukraine criticized the IMF for failing to grasp the specific local conditions under which transformation was taking place in these countries (IMF 1994a).

Especially controversial has been the role of aid in the pace and timing of market liberalization, the sequencing of reforms, and privatization. Whereas Poland and Hungary embarked on an almost unconditional conversion to democracy and a market economy, the former Soviet Union and Russia in particular restricted themselves to a more limited and gradual program. Some Russian politicians have even voiced their readiness to suffer continuing economic austerity rather than to subjugate themselves to the indignity of foreign aid and economic assistance. Although there is no doubt that such rhetoric is intended largely for the domestic political arena, there is a certain degree of support for such views. Over time, more extreme political parties emerged in the reestablished Duma as one of the consequences of this hesitant and ineffective political and economic program of reforms. It has never been quite accepted by Russian politicians that Western economic assistance would not come free (Van Brabant 1992).

Western conditions for aid have been based upon the assumption that economic reform could be successfully pursued only within a democratic environment, and democracy could succeed only in a capitalist system of free enterprise. Because this view is not universally shared, it has reinvigorated some traditional anti-Western sentiments in Russia. For example, in August 1993, Victor Chernomyrdin, then the Russian prime minister, argued that "[his government] has no intention of going with an outstretched hand to ask for any kind of help. Russia wants equal cooperation on the world market in every direction, including the sale of arms. But those who run the world market are not one bit interested in seeing the country make progress. They want Russia finally to fall apart" (RFE/RL 1993a). Consequently, Western politicians (in particular, ones from the United States) put increased pressure on lending and aid institutions to ease their conditions for approving credit to Russia. Both the IMF and the World Bank have been singled out for strong criticism. Nevertheless, both organizations warned that despite official rhetoric of Russian authorities the pace of reforms has been extremely gradual (IMF 1994a). Accordingly, to qualify for greater Western aid, Russian authorities should speed up the pace of the reform. In particular, hard budget constraints on state enterprises are needed to control budget deficits and inflation. Otherwise, as a leading Russian reformer, Grigorii Yavlinsky, stressed, Western aid will be useless unless it is linked to the creation of a completely new economic infrastructure (RFE/RL 1993c).

## Implications of Aid for the "New World Order"

It is extremely difficult, and perhaps premature, to speculate about the future of the transition and place of Eastern Europe in the "new world order." The countries of the region continue to make limited progress toward market economies and democratic political systems. Foreign aid, however, appears to play a relatively minor role in this process. Economic performance has improved significantly in Poland since 1992, and the growth has spread to virtually all countries of Central and Eastern Europe in 1994 and 1995 (UNECE 1995). In 1994 and 1995 the GDP continued to fall only in Macedonia and Yugoslavia. According to forecasts, for the late 1990s, the average growth rate for the region should reach around 4 percent. Unfortunately, with the exception of Turkmenistan, the entire geographical space of the former Soviet Union experienced significant decline for the fifth year in a row. The strategy of Western aid institutions has worked only to a very limited extent. Even though the rate of decline is slowing down, it is expected that the Russian economy will decline by approximately 4.5 percent. Thus far, only the Czech Republic and Hungary were able to break from the circle of aid dependence and borrow private capital directly from Western financial markets.

Regional disbursements of official aid were highly concentrated in the Visegrad Four and Russia. The data suggest that there is a large gap between the assessed capital requirements of Eastern Europe and the multilateral resources allocated so far. Because of data limitations, it is nearly impossible to assess the impact of this aid on the transition process. If the comments of the recipients are taken at the face value, however, Western aid has not been particularly successful. Even though in 1993 most Eastern European countries received a net transfer of capital from abroad, its contribution to investment appears to be relatively small. Most aid has been consumed by debt rescheduling and repayments, trade guarantees and credits, and administrative costs of distributing aid. The position of Russia is especially peculiar because recently there was a massive net outflow of capital from this country (UNECE 1995). This capital flight is a consequence of the lack of confidence in the Russian reforms and industry by the Russians themselves.

None of this bodes well for the "new world order." In the eyes of East European recipients, the major difficulty with foreign aid is not simply that it is not large enough but, more important, that what is available is not used particularly well. Unfortunately, it is not at all clear that any amount of foreign aid can accomplish all the things that are expected of it (Grieve 1993; Klaus 1994). After all, despite a massive infusion of capital, Eastern Germany was for a long time one of the most economically depressed areas of the former East European bloc (UNECE 1993). Even though there are signs of revival, the rest of Eastern Europe has no hope of receiving anything like comparable amounts of aid, which amount to no less than 40 percent of the GNP of the eastern part of Germany. It is very likely that criticism of the West in this respect is merely a substitute for decisive and radical market reforms. If, however, Western donors use aid simply as an extension of their foreign policies, then aid to Eastern Europe failed to fulfill these objectives. In 1997 there are clear signs that Eastern Europe is developing very unevenly. That in itself, of course, does not represent anything new; after all, it was one of the most economically polarized parts of Europe well before the communist takeover (Wandycz 1992). However, it is the increasing gap between Russia, non-Russian former Soviet republics, and the rest of Eastern Europe that will provide a challenge to the "new world order." Simply put, there is an implicit assumption in most Western analyses that the more democratic (however the term is defined) Russia will become, the more restrained and peaceful her actions will be. Indeed, the logic of foreign aid to Russia seems to rely heavily on this relationship (Kissinger 1994). Unfortunately, this is not necessarily so. A less autocratic and more democratic Russia will not necessarily be more restrained. There is ample historical evidence that economic pluralism can coexist with autocratic forms of government and military expansionism (Gellner 1994, 26). In any case, there are increasing signs that popular support for a full-fledged democracy is weakening. Even democratically elected Russian politicians increasingly stress the national interests of Russia in Europe, Asia, and beyond. Although this is an oversimplification, it is a reason the rest of Eastern Europe attempts to distance itself from Russia—thus the race for EU membership between the Visegrad Four, competition for Western aid, investment, and trade, NATO membership, and so on (Kennedy and Webb 1990; Langguth 1992). Logically, these developments should culminate at some point in some kind of confrontation between Russia, attempting to regain its control of Eastern Europe, and Eastern Europe, trying to hide behind Western guarantees of security, political institutions, and economic integration (Crouch and Marquand 1992; Ash 1993).

The West is attempting to help as much as it can economically. To its own electorates it justifies aid by allocating it to those countries that show the most promise, i.e., the Visegrad Four. At the same time, too much focus on this region will inevitably cause a clash of the Visegrad Four with Russia and large non-Russian republics, which compete for the same aid and control over the same geographical area. Consequently, the hesitant appearance of Western aid may be explained in a significant part by this uneasy balance between the needs of Eastern Europe and geopolitical realities there. If these assumptions are correct, the future of Eastern Europe looks reasonably clear. The Visegrad Four and possibly parts of the Balkans, such as Bulgaria or Slovenia, will be gradually and quietly absorbed within the Western, or to put it more bluntly, German orbit (Pradetto 1992). This process will be gradual for two reasons: first, because Russian fears of isolation will be observed very closely in Germany (Ash 1993), and, second, because the Baltic and non-Russian former republics aspire to membership in the EU (Brzezinski 1994). It is unlikely in any foreseeable future that the EU will risk alienating Russia further by formally embracing these states. A more likely scenario is a quasi-formal integration within the Scandinavian economic area. Russia itself, although seriously weakened by the prolonged crisis, will attempt to regain its lost influence at least within the former Soviet geographical space. For various reasons, mostly beyond the scope of this essay, the West will not be able or willing to challenge openly these aspirations (Kissinger 1994; Ash 1993; Mesarovic 1994). However, the ambiguous position of Russia caught between its superpower past and its only slightly bruised will to project its power outside its borders may, in effect, recreate the old confrontation lines in Europe. This hypothetical scenario does not necessarily imply a return to another Cold War. Nevertheless, it is very likely that in spite of Western aid some form of confrontation between Russia and other parts of Europe will develop sooner or later.

## Conclusions

After the initial euphoria over the end of the Cold War had died down, it became disturbingly clear that the Eastern European transformation was going to be extremely costly (Pomian 1994; GAO 1995a, 1995b). According to the United Nations, the needs of the recipient countries in Eastern Europe and the former Soviet Union are likely to be substantially larger than initially estimated and well beyond the realistic amount of available international funds. For example, it is planned by Germany and the EU that over an adjustment period of twenty years, the eastern part of Germany will reach a level of per capita income close to that of the western part. Countries of Eastern Europe and the former Soviet Union, according to a similar scenario, might attempt to reach income levels comparable to those of Greece, Portugal, and Spain by 2010. Based on estimates of the current labor productivity and various assumptions about the nature of production in these countries, the annual net capital inflows needed would be $80 billion for Eastern Germany, $100 billion for Eastern Europe, and $160 billion for the former Soviet Union (UNCTAD 1992). With the sole exception of eastern Germany, these volumes of financial transfer are, of course, totally unrealistic, and they clearly illustrate the ambiguity of Western aid and its political objectives in the post–Cold War Europe.

The EU's aid efforts for Eastern Europe were slow to start because there was neither a team of specialists who even spoke the relevant languages nor an infrastructure in place to deal with the ever-increasing pace of events (Nello 1991; Schröder 1991). When rhetoric had to be followed by sustained action, a number of traditional problems arose that have been difficult for the EU and the United States to resolve. First, it became clear that not all donors have been willing to provide sufficient information concerning their bilateral aid programs. Second, there has been an increasingly acute problem of coordination among numerous agencies, governments, and institutions. Third, the quality of Western aid has varied dramatically. And fourth, Western aid has concentrated on Russia, whereas the non-Russian former Soviet republics and parts of the Balkans have long been almost excluded from any substantial aid.

Despite many protestations to the contrary, there is no doubt that foreign aid to Eastern Europe has been an instrument of foreign policy of various Western creditors rather than an extension of economic policy informed by a genuine understanding of Eastern European regions. This conclusion explains the regional bias of Western aid toward Russia, which traditionally ranks far higher than any other Eastern European country on the list of American or Western European political priorities. Despite many concessions and extended aid programs, many East European reformers have been disappointed by Western aid and assistance. Both Poland and Hungary aired their discontent over the Europe Agreements with the EU that would not liberate trade in textiles, agricultural products, steel, and coal—that is, nearly all economic sectors where Eastern European goods remain competitive. This criticism points to the reality that the EU's protectionism has not reversed under the influence of the changes in the East (Mastropasqua and Rolli 1994).

The goal of speedy reintegration of Eastern Europe into the world economy calls for a much more balanced distribution of aid between Russia, non-Russian states (in particular Ukraine), and Eastern Europe. Such a "new world order" would be the best assurance that Russia would abandon its efforts to recreate the Soviet empire and, once again, turn Eastern European states into subordinate satellites and threaten the West. In this scenario, Western aid should be used to facilitate the establishment of democratic systems of government throughout the region and the creation of civil societies and market-based economies. In this context, Western aid to the East in the "new world order" is a matter of self-interest based upon a wider definition of security rather than just upon a humanitarian generosity.

## 10

# Foreign Aid to the Asia–Pacific Rim
## *Asian Variations*

### Leo van Grunsven and August van Westen

O VER THE PAST DECADE, a steady stream of publications has dealt with the rise of the Asian-Pacific Rim to the position of the most prominent growth region in the world economy. Indeed, it has become a cliché to describe the region as the economic powerhouse in the twenty-first century. An equally steady stream of publications has highlighted the role of private capital flows, particularly foreign direct investment (FDI), as well as international trade in the growth processes in the region, which gained momentum in the 1960s. Many interpret prevailing analyses of the "economic miracle" in the region as a vindication of the "trade not aid" doctrine. International trade opportunities, particularly preferential access to Western markets afforded to the Asian newly industrializing economies (NIEs) by the United States and European countries during the Cold War, have played a significant role in the rise of these economies and, more recently, in the economies of the members of the Association of South East Asian Nations (ASEAN).

It is also acknowledged that the Asian NIEs (particularly Taiwan and South Korea) could not have achieved "economic take-off" so rapidly without the rather massive foreign aid afforded to them by the United States in the early Cold War period. For instance, Kuo stated that U.S. aid to Taiwan between 1951 and 1965 amounted to about $100 million annually, which comprised 30 percent of domestic investment each year

and constituted the main financial source of domestic investment before
1961. About two-thirds of U.S. aid investment went to the public sector,
a large share of which was used for an expansion of infrastructure, including electricity, transportation, and communications. The remainder
went to the private sector (i.e., manufacturing industry) and the private-
public mixed sector. Thus, the contribution of U.S. aid to manufacturing industries was through the construction of infrastructure as well as
through direct aid. Although U.S. aid was a key factor in the tremendous
achievements of Taiwan, success was as much a function of the efficient
utilization of this financial source as of the volume of funds granted by
the United States (Kuo 1994).

From the Taiwanese and South Korean experiences, as well as from
the role of aid from the former Soviet Union in Indochina (which started after the first Indochinese War), one important conclusion can be de-
rived. Although its contribution to economic growth and development
has varied with the efficiency of its allocation, in terms of volume of financial flows foreign aid has played a significant role in the Southeast
and East Asian region during the Cold War period.

In this chapter we consider recent aid disbursement in the Southeast
and East Asian region from a recipient perspective. The first section presents an overview of recent trends in official development assistance
(ODA) disbursements to the region. Although the donor perspective is
largely omitted from this chapter, the analysis in the first section also includes trends in the donor composition of ODA disbursements to specific countries. Next, the discussion shifts to the significance of aid in the
development process. Subsequently, we discuss a number of issues surrounding foreign aid from the recipient perspective. While the focus of
our discussion is on Southeast and East Asia (defined here as the
ASEAN countries, which include Vietnam, Myanmar, Laos, Cambodia,
China, the Republic of Korea, Taiwan, and Hong Kong), for comparative purposes we also refer to South Asia (India, Pakistan, and Bangladesh) in the next section.

## Trends in ODA Disbursement

As is the case for other least-developed countries (LDCs), "foreign
aid" to the Southeast and East Asian region has been and is provided by
an array of development assistance agencies. Most countries have a
number of large and small bilateral donors as well as large and small

multilateral suppliers (e.g., the World Bank, the Asian Development Bank, and the UN system). In addition, nongovernment organizations (NGOs) from donor countries further crowd the development scene. These suppliers have employed various forms of aid and financial disbursement arrangements, reflecting the range of objectives behind the provision of foreign aid. In the recipient countries, not only government departments and agencies but also local NGOs and private community organizations have been at the receiving end of aid. Indeed, as McCawley noted, there are many players in the "assistance industry" in Asia (McCawley 1993, 8). For this reason, it is a daunting task to assemble a comprehensive and accurate quantitative picture of total aid disbursement to the region.

In the analysis here, we have chosen to focus on net ODA flows from members of the Development Assistance Committee of the Organization for Economic Cooperation and Development (OECD). These flows are well documented, in terms of magnitude by source and destination, by the OECD. In addition, they capture a sufficiently large part of total official flows—from both bilateral and multilateral sources—for the purpose of economic development and welfare (our chief interest here) to discern the main trends in such disbursements. ODA receipts by the Southeast Asian countries, in nominal terms at least, increased significantly after the mid-1980s. Receipts by the East Asian countries show a similar trend. Each year since 1986, ODA receipts by the Southeast and East Asian countries combined surpassed those received by South Asia. In the early 1990s, Southeast Asia surpassed South Asia in the amount of ODA received. The share of Southeast and East Asia in total ODA disbursements to the LDCs stood at roughly 10 percent in the mid-1980s and climbed to some 15 percent in 1993.

Such regional or subregional aggregates obviously mask substantial differences between countries (see fig. 10.1 and maps 10.1 and 10.2). The following observations should be made. First, it is not surprising that the position of the newly industrializing countries (NICs), formerly recipients of substantial volumes of foreign aid, has been reduced to an insignificant level in the 1980s and 1990s, although not in all cases on a per capita basis. Transfers have been rather erratic, and some of these countries show negative transfers in some years. Their relatively insignificant position can also be deduced from table 10.1, which shows the share of individual countries or groups of countries in Southeast and East Asia in total ODA receipts over the period 1987–93.

Second, the increase in the volume of ODA disbursements to East

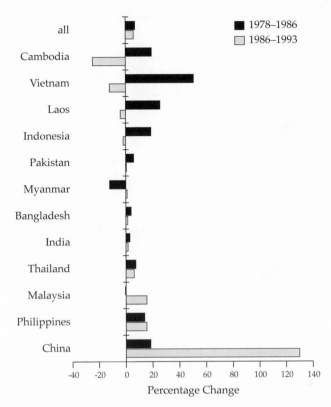

*Fig. 10.1.* Percentage change of net ODA receipts
to the Asia-Pacific region, 1978–93

Asia has been almost fully absorbed by China. China's ODA receipts
have grown tremendously throughout the 1980s and early 1990s. In
terms of volume, it became the largest ODA recipient in Southeast and
East Asia in the mid-1980s and has maintained this position since, absorbing roughly one-third of total ODA disbursements to the region in
the period 1987–93 (table 10.1). In 1992, China also surpassed India.

Third, in Southeast Asia, patterns and trends at the national level are
quite differential. These are best discussed by considering first the
ASEAN countries and next Myanmar together with the countries in Indochina. Among the former, Indonesia clearly remains the leader in
ODA receipts in terms of volume. After 1986 its receipts have increased
significantly. ODA disbursements to Thailand have grown as well,
though not significantly. In absolute terms, it is the third largest recipi-

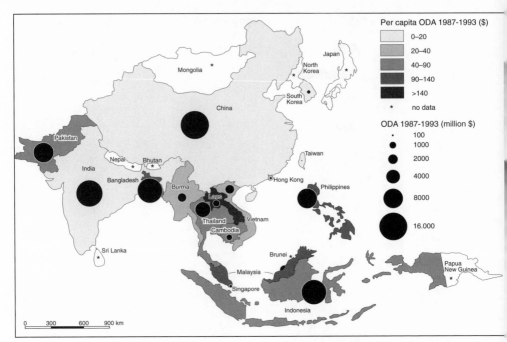

*Map 10.1.* ODA receipts of individual countries in Southeast, East, and South Asia from all sources, 1978–86, aggregate volume and per capita

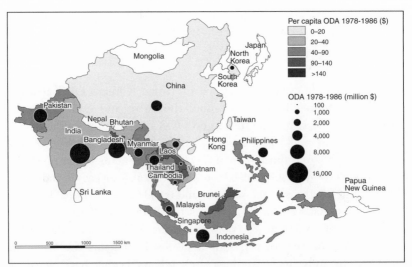

*Map 10.2.* ODA receipts of individual countries in Southeast, East, and South Asia from all sources, 1987–93, aggregate volume and per capita

Table 10.1 Share of Individual Asian Countries in ODA Disbursements, 1987–93 (%)

| | 1987 | 1988 | 1989 | 1990 | 1991 | 1992 | 1993 | 1987–93 |
|---|---|---|---|---|---|---|---|---|
| Indonesia | 25.20 | 27.74 | 28.79 | 24.53 | 28.01 | 23.51 | 24.08 | 25.77 |
| Malaysia | 7.35 | 1.76 | 2.19 | 6.68 | 4.33 | 2.34 | 1.19 | 3.47 |
| Thailand | 10.19 | 9.57 | 11.57 | 11.46 | 10.78 | 8.71 | 7.29 | 9.79 |
| Philippines | 15.59 | 14.52 | 13.22 | 18.16 | 15.74 | 19.27 | 17.72 | 16.59 |
| Vietnam | 2.25 | 2.51 | 2.02 | 2.71 | 3.57 | 6.51 | 3.07 | 3.43 |
| Myanmar | 7.44 | 7.66 | 2.88 | 2.43 | 2.68 | 1.29 | 1.21 | 3.25 |
| Laos | 1.18 | 1.31 | 2.18 | 2.16 | 2.14 | 1.85 | 2.46 | 1.95 |
| Cambodia | 0.29 | 0.31 | 0.47 | 0.59 | 1.36 | 2.32 | 3.77 | 1.49 |
| China | 29.58 | 33.81 | 33.71 | 29.54 | 29.87 | 34.32 | 38.90 | 33.18 |
| NICs | 0.92 | 0.80 | 2.96 | 1.75 | 1.53 | −0.11 | 0.31 | 1.08 |
| Total | 100.00 | 100.00 | 100.00 | 100.00 | 100.00 | 100.00 | 100.00 | 100.00 |

Source: OECD(b) (1966–96).

ent; however, in per capita terms, it has received a larger amount than Indonesia. Particularly striking is the surge of ODA disbursements to the
Philippines from 1985 on, which is also reflected in significant gains in
per capita terms. Over the period 1987–93, the Philippines absorbed
about 17 percent of ODA flows to the Southeast and East Asian region
and a quarter of the flows to Southeast Asia.

Quite in contrast to the Philippines is the trend shown by Malaysia.
Though in aggregate absolute volume nowhere near the level of its fellow ASEAN countries (Singapore excepted), it did receive a substantial
amount of ODA during the 1980s in per capita terms. Currently, because of its strong economic performance (to which ODA contributed)
aid donors are reclassifying it as a post-aid recipient.

Fourth, a clear distinction between the countries in Indochina (the
battleground between the superpowers during the Cold War) and Myanmar immediately emerges from even a cursory glance at the figures. Although remaining the poorest countries in the region (and perhaps
because of it), they are probably the most interesting and illustrative cases about the economic and political behavior of Western donor and recipient countries in the region in the post–Cold War era. Myanmar
stands out in the drama that has been unfolding since the end of the
1980s. Although it was a recipient of significant amounts of ODA in the
1970s and 1980s, disbursements to it were suddenly cut by more than
half in 1989 and since then have kept declining to a quarter of the level
received annually during the second half of the 1980s. Per capita receipts

have declined accordingly. Already for more than three decades, Myanmar has been ruled by an authoritarian military regime. Since 1988 the regime has held control over the country through the State Law and Order Restoration Council (SLORC), which took power after harshly suppressing massive pro-democracy demonstrations. The international community has responded to the 1988 suppression, to the events in the aftermath of the elections, and to the SLORC's behavior since by initially slashing aid disbursements and subsequently declaring Myanmar a pariah among the recipient community. Thus, the potential positive impact of the SLORC's abandonment of the Burmese experiment with autarkic socialism in 1988, opened up the economy to permit private sector expansion and attract investment, was effectively nullified.

In contrast, other countries in Indochina (Vietnam, Laos, and Cambodia) have made great strides toward development in recent years and have received a positive response, as is evident from substantial increases of ODA disbursed to Laos from 1989, and to Vietnam and Cambodia from 1992 on. In the course of the 1980s, the authorities in Laos had already started to steer the economy away from the Soviet model, when its failure—and, with it, the failure of Soviet aid to contribute to the economic development of the country—became apparent. For the implementation of economic reforms, Laos successfully turned to the International Monetary Fund (IMF). The reliance on this source, as well as other Western sources of aid, became even stronger after Soviet aid came to a halt. The path of economic reform that has been sustained since the end of the 1980s has provided the necessary justification and legitimization for substantial increases of ODA disbursements from Western donors.

In 1986 wide-reaching domestic reforms *(doi moi)* were introduced, with the aim of moving the country away from a command economy and closer to the world's free market economies. The economic reform process was strengthened in 1989, and further actions in the early 1990s underscored the conversion to a free market. The U.S. economic embargo was relaxed in 1992, followed in 1993 by the withdrawal of the automatic veto over infrastructure loans provided by international financial institutions to Vietnam. These two events enabled the international institutions to commence action (Brown 1993), as well as other countries (notably Japan) to terminate their policy of refusing to grant ODA. All these factors together resulted in substantial increases of ODA disbursement in 1992 and 1993 and the expectation of further sizable increases thereafter.

The 1970s and 1980s were a period of national devastation for Cambodia. During the 1980s the Vietnam-installed People's Republic of Kampuchea (PRK) depended on an unknown amount of economic aid from the Soviet Union and Eastern Europe for areas under PRK control to maintain a modicum of economic sustenance. The political conditions and Vietnam's role permitted only some humanitarian aid from the UN and private groups. Efforts to negotiate a comprehensive settlement in Cambodia eventually resulted in the Paris Agreements in 1991; national elections came two years later. In September 1993 a new constitution was promulgated and a coalition government formed (Brown 1993). As Cambodia remains a desperately poor country, its economic recovery and reconstruction depends on substantial amounts of ODA from both multilateral and bilateral sources. As part of the 1991 agreements, in 1992 the International Conference on the Reconstruction of Cambodia (ICORC) was formed to coordinate bilateral and international agency economic assistance programs. In June 1992 in Tokyo, $880 million was pledged by international donors. ICORC, comprising thirty-one donor countries and eleven international agencies, met again in September 1993 and pledged $119 million in new aid with an additional $135 million to be committed in 1994 (Brown 1993). Thus, the international community made a firm commitment to assist in Cambodia's reconstruction effort.

## ODA and Economic Development

In general, the volume of ODA appears modest when compared with the magnitude of gross domestic investment (GDI) in Asian countries. The relative weight of ODA is especially limited in the fastest-growing economies of Southeast Asia (such as Malaysia and Thailand), where aid amounts to less than 2 percent of investment activity. Much the same applies to the giant nations of China and India, at 1.7 percent and 4.5 percent on average (1991–93); a consequence of ODA flows tending to favor small nations. Rather more substantial, however, is the role of ODA in the poorer nations of South Asia and Indochina, and also in the Philippines. Generally, aid amounts to rather less than 20 percent of gross investment in the region, but with some exceptions. In Bangladesh the volume of ODA tends to equal roughly half the value of gross investment per year; in Laos, foreign aid actually often exceeds the flow of combined domestic and foreign investment. In both cases, the importance of ODA is probably more likely to reflect the lack of other inward financial flows and domestic savings (related to the overall economic conditions) than the proof of an extraordinary aid effort.

Although this pattern has been fairly consistent over recent years, it is also apparent that the role of ODA in investment activity tends to gradually decrease. Most clearly, this is the case in Malaysia and Thailand, where the size of the aid flows dropped from 4 to 5 percent of GDI by 1987 to around 1 percent in 1993. A decrease is also apparent in Indonesia as well as in the very different contexts of Pakistan and Bangladesh. While the declining role of foreign aid in Southeast Asia can be attributed to both a drop in ODA and a surge in entrepreneurial activity, this is not the case in Bangladesh and Pakistan, where it is likely that diminishing donor activity is solely responsible.

But the significance of foreign assistance to the development process should be looked at in qualitative terms as well as quantitative ones. The efficiency of its use or allocation also has to be considered. For the qualitative aspect, it is useful to consider first the purpose for which individual Asian countries revert to development assistance funding. Perhaps not surprisingly, this defies easy generalization. Over time, country-specific divisions of labor have emerged between national agencies and donors, reflecting specific local conditions. On the whole, though, infrastructure investment tends to rank as the major destination for foreign aid disbursements. This trend is strongest in Thailand and India, where more than half of annual foreign aid tends to be spent on infrastructure. Major targets of this infrastructure investment include energy supply and transportation networks, followed by water supply (for consumption), sanitation, and telecommunications. In India and Pakistan, for instance, foreign assistance is of special importance for the energy industry; in China, for the transportation system. The share of infrastructure in ODA receipts tends to be a little less in the more advanced countries. Where economic performance has made remarkable progress, as in South Korea, Taiwan, Singapore, and Hong Kong, the modest flows of ODA still made available are more often used for social development purposes (health, education, and housing in particular).

In the poor countries of South Asia, economic sector investment generally constitutes the second most important use of foreign aid. In Bangladesh and China investment in the economic sectors actually exceeds infrastructure development as the first target of foreign development funding. In most South Asian countries, top priority in allocations is assigned to the development of agriculture: irrigation works, crop improvement, fertilizers, pesticides, extension services, etc. In China the economic sector targeted varies from year to year but is often composed of extractive industries and manufacturing.

Donor countries, through their ODA disbursements, may have considerable influence on the recipient country's economic policies. As is illustrated by the post-1993 ODA commitments of donors to Vietnam (Curry 1994), multilateral and bilateral donors have become progressively more willing to provide additional support to the Indochinese countries. This, however, is subject to the condition that the economic reform process be continued—i.e., the transition from a centrally planned to a market economy. Although the state has remained the major agent in their economies, both Vietnam and Laos have put in efforts to meet this conditionality (Cambodia's situation is different). Their willingness stems from an awareness of the necessity of reform as well as a need to create an environment conducive to obtaining resources from external sources via official development assistance.

The new economic environment has created substantial opportunities for private entrepreneurship and opened Indochina to a host of foreign influences. In the eyes of the governments, the perils of economic development are becoming as evident as its benefits. One issue is the growth of "guerrilla capitalism" in the economy, focused mainly on short-term economic gain; another is the cultural impact of foreign contacts; a third one is the increase of inequality. As Brown noted about Vietnam, entrepreneurship and making money have replaced "liberation" and "unification" as society's goals. For its part, the Vietnamese government is leery of the deleterious effect of Western culture. Vietnamese youth are all too eager to swill Coca-Cola, dance to Western rock, and covet blue jeans as a mark of cultural sophistication. Underemployment and the increasing gap between rich and poor as Vietnam becomes more prosperous are also problems, particularly in the South. These and other symptoms of the erosion of traditional values are troubling to many Vietnamese both within and without the government (Brown 1993). The inequality issues confronting the governments also include the increasing rift between the urban and rural areas in overall level of development. In the rural areas, poverty is still much more widespread and more acute than in the urban areas. Yet even within farming communities, inequalities have been growing. However, the conditionalities attached to ODA, the disbursement modalities, and the purposes for which aid is provided all put severe constraints on Vietnam as to the directions it may take and, hence, its options to minimize what it perceives as adverse effects of reform and the speed at which it proceeds.

It is clear that Western donors have succeeded in directing the economic policies in Vietnam and Laos (Arndt 1992), thus achieving an economic and strategic goal that has long eluded them. However, the overriding concern with economic reform has meant little attention being devoted to the capacity to handle the ODA inflow and issues of administrative coordination. In such a context the issue of the efficient use of ODA, impinging on the absorption capacity, readily comes to the fore. Thus, in the Indochinese countries "underperformance" of ODA in economic terms is not an unrealistic proposition.

An important point to note here is that the issues of absorption capacity and efficiency are not unique to countries like Vietnam and Laos. They also apply to some of the ASEAN countries. The Philippines stands out as the one market economy that has experienced a significant expansion of ODA inflows during the last decade. Aid has increased not only because of the country's relatively poor economic performance in a region where high growth figures have become common but also because of its political transformation since a combination of a popular uprising and a coup by the more liberally inclined segment of the traditional elite managed to sweep away the Latin American–style dictatorship of the Jurassic Marcos family. Since February 1986 the Philippines have served as the beacon of Western-style democracy in Southeast Asia, an example badly in need of more economic progress to convince other Asians—or even its own population.

Without compromising the idea that foreign aid may contribute to economic development, there is evidence that the nature, strategy, and implementation of official development assistance has not been without unintended consequences. In many instances ODA has led to the aggravation of the foreign debt problem; the concentration of benefits in the hands of the business sector, the upper middle class, and the donor countries; the further deprivation and marginalization of the poor and the powerless; and the exacerbation of land and income disparities (Tadem 1990). For sure, the agenda of aid donors has been shaped by a multitude of considerations other than substantial improvement of the livelihood of the majority of the people in the aid-receiving countries.

## Foreign Aid and Political Change: The Recipient Perspective

The agendas of donors have entered the arena of economic and political power structures, the political system, and government-society relationships. In aid-receiving developing countries, the new agenda of donors has resulted in a weaker tolerance for "bad" governance and authoritarian political regimes that show little respect for those basic human rights that formerly Western societies generally accepted or courted.

In the Southeast and East Asian regions, Western-style political structures are still the exception rather than the rule. Therefore, it is not surprising that political liberalization, democratization, and the granting of individual freedoms now rank high on the publicly voiced agendas of Western donors with respect to the countries in these regions. Underlying is the newly professed belief that these are in fact preconditions not only for genuine development to take place but also for the Southeast and East Asian regions to claim an equal standing in the international discourse on global affairs. It also reflects an optimism "that democratic political evolution in the region can be encouraged and supported, provided they are appropriately designed and there is sufficient political commitment to sustain them" (Koppel 1993, 31).

However, at this point the governing elites in the region perceive this Western donor agenda as highly inappropriate and a source of controversy and confrontation. Perspectives of recipients on political liberalization and human rights in the context of economic development (economic reform, political power, and governance) are basically incongruent with the views expressed by Western countries. A status quo in the structures or system of governance, political power, and government-society relationships is still considered as essential for continuing rapid economic progress. Thus, in the Indochinese countries (i.e., Vietnam and Laos), the conditionality of economic reform may well be preliminary to another type of return, namely political. Obviously, linking economic and political reform does not go down well with the—still communist—regimes. Although they are willing to conduct economic reform, their primary emphasis is on maintaining "social and political stability," which requires keeping a grip on political power (Brown 1993, 16). The brutality of the Tiananmen Square incident in 1989 provides a vivid illustration of the determination of the Chinese authorities to maintain the status quo. In the Southeast Asian countries, sentiments are similar and backed by a more or less substantial show of force. To them, the Philippines provide proof that democratization does not necessarily lead to development.

The question then is to what extent Western donor agendas in this area have any real prospect of being accomplished. There are many influences here. One is the extent to which the position of the recipient is changing in the relationship with its donors. This relates to the extent to which there is still a strong need for foreign aid. Economic achievement impacts national self-confidence, which is reflected in the attitudes and particularly the assertiveness toward donors.

The case of the ASEAN countries is perhaps the easiest to draw conclusions about. Here the position of the recipients remains basically one of noncompliance with the wishes of the Western aid donors. Their attitude toward Western donors increasingly emphasizes the strengthening of their own position and the consequent weakening of the Western donors' position, at least in this area. A clear expression of this attitude is the articulation—more loudly and openly—of the legitimacy of indigenous norms and the rejection of external imposed norms (Koppel 1993) in regard to domestic political arrangements. Governments claim legitimacy of the existing political and social structures on the basis of historical and cultural specificities, which lead to a distinctive set of Asian values (emphasizing, for example, collectivism rather than individualism), as well as on the basis of economic growth and elements of good governance that otherwise would be difficult to establish or maintain (e.g., the leveling between ethnic or social groups and the "one nation" concept). In addition, governments also mention the necessity of keeping at bay domestic forces that could undermine not only national but also regional stability and security (e.g., the growing constituency for Islamic fundamentalism). They want this claim to be heard and its legitimacy to be taken seriously outside the region, all the more so because they do not consider that existing political and social structures deviate in a fundamental way from a universal democratic norm. Rather, in the view of the political elites, they should be regarded as local determinations of what the norm means (Koppel 1993), reflecting Asian specificities.

For several reasons, Asian nations have become more outspoken. First, economic achievement has increased national self-confidence, which is reflected in increased assertiveness towards Western donors. Second, there is a growing perception that the relationships between Western donors and Eastern recipients can be realigned in favor of the latter because of weaknesses discerned in the Western position. These include the lack of consistency with which conditionalities, as well as sanctions in the case of noncompliance, thus far have been applied to Asia by the Western aid donors (compare, for example, the cases of

Myanmar, China, and Indonesia). In the perception of the ASEAN countries, such lack of consistency suggests that the Western donor countries have not quite resolved the issue of a political agenda that is in competition with other—predominantly economic—interests (as the behavior of the United States toward China after Tiananmen Square illustrates). The impression is that the Western camp lacks resolve about the question of compatibility of the political part of the agenda with other parts. This impression is reinforced by the substantially different stands of Western donors and Japan in these matters.

ASEAN countries are determined to defend and further their position in such matters. In a few cases, this determination has been expressed in demonstrative action, i.e., the termination of the aid relationship with donor countries; a prime example is Indonesia's abrupt suspension of Dutch assistance in 1992. There appears to be little prospect, then, for the Western donor countries to accomplish their agenda of political liberalization, democratization, and human rights in ASEAN countries in the near future by directly linking these issues and aid disbursement to government agencies.

## Conclusions

By any standards, East and Southeast Asia have performed remarkably well in pursuing economic growth. Foreign aid often contributed to this success, though not usually as its main component. Nevertheless,  Pacific Asia today offers a tantalizing model for other developing regions to emulate—if the model can be replicated to any significant extent in other regional settings. Such progress was achieved in a part of the world where Japanese aid, with its characteristic focus on producing economic growth, was dominant. This is not to say that Japan's assistance is more successful than that of other donors; but its intimate linkage with investment and trade flows has shown remarkable results. In several countries in the region, strong economic growth, fueled by private resource transfers, has diminished the need of these countries to draw on official aid flows. They are now in a position to be selective and have started to redefine the role assigned to aid flows in development financing.

Presently, foreign aid receipts in many countries seem to have reached a ceiling or are even declining. In some cases this is the logical result of economic success and in others the realization that the concessionary element in yen-denominated soft loans may not always live up to expectations in the era of *en-daka* (high valued yen). More disturbing, however, is the case of the poorest countries of the region, predominantly in South Asia. Countries such as Pakistan and Bangladesh are victims of partial abandonment by some donors following the loss of strategic interests after the end of the Cold War and ensuing "aid fatigue" among donors. Little in the realm of private investment activity, domestic or foreign, would seem to compensate for a decline in bilateral aid in some of the neediest nations of the world. Japan, distant and with relatively small economic interests, does not perform a similarly active donor role in South Asia as it does in East and Southeast Asia. Somewhat exceptional so far is the position of the centrally planned economies of China and the countries of Indochina. They have the benefit of relatively new aid programs, some still expanding. In addition, their economic and resource potential is attractive to foreign donors and investors alike (primarily the Japanese).

In the post–Cold War era, the "new world order" in Pacific Asia is rather different from the pattern that has emerged elsewhere. In Pacific Asia economic harmonization is proceeding successfully, whereas political harmonization is as yet hardly an agenda item. In this sense, the region offers the inverse image of Europe, where socialism in the East has given way to multiparty democracy, accompanied by near collapse of the economy. In Pacific Asia, centrally planned economies such as those of China and Vietnam make effective use of market-oriented economic recipes, without any serious advance toward political liberalization as advocated by the West. This also holds true for the authoritarian market economies in the region, especially countries where the elite seeks to protect its privileges in the face of rapid economic change, such as Indonesia. The exclusion of sociopolitical change is not really an issue for Japan, which traditionally has a politically neutral, economy-focused mode of international cooperation. Thus, the priorities of the region's major donor and recipient countries are a perfect fit.

There is, however, a growing gap between the Asian recipients of aid and Western donors, which are more inclined to stress "new" emancipatory objectives of ecological sustainability, poverty eradication, and democratization. Increasing Western insistence on political reform clashes with a growing Asian assertiveness. In view of the region's economic success and the continuing of high levels of aid from Japanese and other Asian donors, the countries of Southeast and East Asia can afford their newfound confidence in "Asian values."

# Part Four

*Views of Foreign Aid
Donors and Recipients*

# The Future of United States Foreign Assistance

## J. Brian Atwood

FOR YEARS practitioners of foreign policy have undervalued the role of U.S. assistance programs in foreign policy. Foreign aid has been referred to as if it were only food and blankets, humanitarian relief, parceled out in the wake of earthquakes or famines. It has been pigeon-holed as an international charity program, a sop tossed to those who think they can actually do something about the human condition. It has been dismissed as a sideshow, a digression—"a grace note," as one member of Congress put it, "tagged onto the great issues of state."

I have not shared these views, but I have well understood how a security-oriented foreign policy community concerned about the contingencies of the Cold War could develop such perceptions. But this debate is behind us. It is time to address a new set of threats to our interests, a new set of contingencies. I believe that foreign assistance can and must occupy a central role in our foreign policy in the aftermath of the Cold War.

I offer two rationales for why our foreign aid program is more important than ever. First, we need it to deal proactively and effectively with the fundamental threat to American security in the post–Cold War era, the breakdown of international order and the failure of nations. We in the Clinton administration call this *crisis prevention*.

Second, we need it to create markets abroad for our goods and to en-

Brian Atwood's remarks were abstracted with his permission from a speech delivered at the American Enterprise Institute in Washington, D.C., October 17, 1994.

sure the economic well-being of the United States into the next century. We call this *competing in the global economy.*

The end of the Cold War unleashed ethnic, environmental, and political tensions that are still emerging. Disorder tends to emerge gradually, in part because events take time to gestate; this is particularly true of protracted, complex crises, in which natural disasters and political breakdowns combine with refugee movements, lack of infrastructure, and donor fatigue. Chaos builds with growing swiftness as the perception spreads that the kind of adventurism that once would have involved the United States and the Soviet Union may now occur without outside intervention. At a certain point warlordism and aggressive politics become inevitable. The very perception that the international situation is becoming more lawless accelerates change. It drives chaos.

When ethnic groups feel impelled to end peaceful coexistence, when they fear their ethnic rivals are about to do the same thing to them, when people feel they have no other choices, and when opportunists see that political capital can be made by playing the card of ethnic politics and civil war, the attitude becomes infectious. With modern communications, it spreads across borders and throughout the world like a plague. This is one way in which seemingly stable states can begin to fail.

 A diplomacy that focuses only on nations and governments and not on the conditions that impel their behavior will forever be caught short. These conditions include persistent repression, unabating poverty, unsustainable rates of population growth, and environmental damage. We in the United States, even though isolated by oceans, cannot escape their impact. But the crisis prevention approach to foreign policy that the United States Agency for International Development (USAID) in no small part implements is a strategic response to this strategic threat.

This is where American leadership—in the security field, in international economics, in diplomacy, and in the field of development—comes so vitally into play. For just as chaos feeds on itself, so does sustainable development. So does respect for the rule of law. So does the expectation of international order. And most important, so does democratic governance.

The immediate post–Cold War era is not just a time of spreading conflict. It is also a time of democratic experimentation and consolidation. Our emphasis on cooperation, development, and democracy building is consistent both with our national values and with our national security interests. Democracies help each other. They reinforce and support each other. They insist upon respect for the rule of law and thus serve to restrain one another. And they are skilled at pursuing their national interests through peaceful negotiations.

Moreover, the cooperation and transparency of democratic systems expose and inhibit the opportunism that is part and parcel of the new strategic threat. Finally, the consolidation of democracy and the success of policies and programs that prevent crises make economic sense: the price of peace and stability is infinitely less than the cost of reconstructing entire nations.

Our policy of crisis prevention through development emphasizes the role of subnational entities and individual human beings. People will inevitably form small, localized affinity groups that protect their interests, give them a sense of identity, accomplish social tasks, and enable them to act politically. These groups can be clans, militias, mobs, youth gangs, or cells of religious fanatics; or they can be the kind of local nongovernmental organizations (NGOs) that are the building blocks of a true civil society: political parties, cooperatives, labor unions, or women's groups. The development approaches we advocate for our programs and those of other donor governments—approaches that focus on NGOs and individual empowerment—enhance our strategic position and serve our national interest because they address at a local and individual level the alienation and powerlessness that drive the conditions that threaten our interests.

People the world over aspire to the same opportunities—to gain control over their lives. If given the necessary tools and the freedom to use them, they will create opportunities to solve their own problems. They will actively work for their own well-being, but in doing so they will help us achieve peace and stability, two longtime objectives of our foreign policy.

Such an approach is really the key to "sustainable development," the objective of our work. Sustainable development is a process that uses change to improve permanently the ability of societies and their citizens to anticipate problems, to establish the institutions to deal with them, to acquire and transmit the necessary expertise, to find and allocate the needed resources, and, in so doing, to maintain the cohesion of society, whatever the crises that may confront it. This form of development— sustainable development—can become an antidote to chaos.

The second rationale for foreign assistance, mentioned above, is the creation of markets for our goods. Foreign aid creates jobs for U.S.

workers and advances our economic well-being. Much of our development policy today is shaped to encourage capital flows, and our assistance over time can promote these flows.

Trade does not simply materialize. The ground must be prepared
first. That is partly a matter of policy reforms; that is why we are helping
nations liberalize their markets. That is why we have launched initiatives
to remove institutional and legal barriers to trade. That is why we are
fostering trading cultures that are receptive to foreign investment. And
that is why we are supporting programs that create broad-based economic growth in developing countries. All these endeavors help create markets that have the desire and the wherewithal to buy what we have to sell.

That authoritarian regimes have overseen periods of economic
growth is clear, but the link between their repressiveness and their
growth is questionable. If it is ever present, it is not enduring. In the
long run, authoritarianism is a drag on economic efficiency and growth.
Although authoritarian regimes may be able to impose contentious economic reforms and suppress the social backlash they create, the sometimes messy pluralism of democracies allows free societies to embrace
and sustain change and respond to the inevitable unforeseen needs that
arise. As economic growth increases, interest groups and complex problems arise. Authoritarian governments see such developments as a challenge to their power; democracies know they are a source of strength.

Sustainable economic growth requires government with democratic
authority, not authoritarian government. The USAID program is
putting this principle into practice: in the former Soviet Union we have
provided extensive technical support for privatization but in the context
of an effort to help these societies democratize. Millions of citizens in
Russia have acquired a stake in the market economy. And as they have
acquired that stake, they want their elected leaders to help them preserve
it. These twin efforts—privatization and democratization—have set in
motion a psychological revolution, a process that approaches our goal:
irreversible change.

We now are trying to reinforce this change by supporting new legal
codes and by training municipal officials in how a democratic society
functions. In some ways, this is even more revolutionary than privatization, for the hallmark of the former Soviet Union was an arbitrary system of privilege that was inherently lawless. We want to help Russia
become a society of laws, where people can enjoy the fruits of their
labors and where they have the freedom to make the rational economic

and political choices on which a free economy depends. If we succeed, the U.S. economy will benefit from an important new market; and if we succeed, the cost of our investment will be a fraction of what we might spend to defend ourselves once again from a military threat.

Every emerging nation has used foreign aid as a primary means of building markets. And our emphasis on supporting broad institutional change is producing enormous benefits: developing nations now represent the fastest-growing markets for U.S. goods. They are growing ten times as quickly as our traditional markets in Europe and Japan. Developing countries are particularly good customers for our high-value exports: pollution-control equipment, computers, communications equipment, and expert services. Exports to emerging economies in Latin America and Asia are one of the main reasons our unemployment is low and why exports are the fastest-growing sector of our economy.

The end of the Cold War has created an opportunity for the United States to deal directly with the international factors that can advance its political and economic interests or injure them profoundly. We stand now at a turning point. Our decision to use the tools at hand, the appropriate weapons for the strategic needs of our era, will affect the outcome—and, likely, determine it.

# 12

# Japan's Development Assistance after the Cold War

## Hiroyuki Yanagitsubo

T HE END OF THE COLD WAR resulted in new issues being placed on top of the foreign aid agenda. Whereas most of the donor countries have experienced the so-called aid fatigue, Japan's foreign aid has increased tremendously since the mid-1980s and has improved to meet the changing needs of socioeconomic development in developing countries.

Japan's development assistance in 1994 amounted to $13.24 billion, excluding aid to East European countries and to the European Bank for Reconstruction and Development (EBRD). Japanese aid accounted for 22.9 percent of the total aid provided by Development Assistance Committee (DAC) countries, and Japan has been the largest donor in the world for the past four years. The main motivation behind the increase is Japan's recognition that foreign assistance is an important instrument for contributing to peace, stability, and prosperity in the world.

Japan also recognizes that foreign aid is in its own national interest, as its economy is heavily dependent on foreign trade. Nevertheless, Japan's aid programs are organized to provide maximum benefits to the recipients. For example, the fraction of Japan's untied aid in 1992 was 78.8 percent, the sixth highest among DAC countries. In fiscal year 1994, 98.3 percent of its yen loans were general untied aid, and the purchase of goods and services on a contract basis from Japan companies in yen loan projects accounted for only 27 percent of the total amount of loans. These data imply that projects using Japan's official development assistance (ODA) are quite open to all other countries and not for Japan's own commercial purposes. In addition, the amount of grant aid in Japan's ODA in absolute terms is substantial. It amounted to $8.98 billion in 1994, the second-largest among DAC countries.

Most Japanese development aid is provided by the Japanese government and less by private agencies. Public support for foreign aid is strong, although there has been some criticism with regard to the large size of the budget and alleged lack of transparency and effectiveness of the programs. In response to the changing needs of developing countries, a number of nongovernmental and local aid organizations have been established in recent years. These organizations have received strong support and subsidies from the Japanese government.

Japan has provided ODA primarily to Asian countries, because of its close historical, geographical, and economic ties with them. Of thirty-four recipient countries for which Japan was the largest donor in 1993, seventeen were located in Asia, and $5.54 billion, accounting for 57.3 percent of the Japan's total ODA in 1994, was given to this region. By sector, in 1994, 41.2 percent of Japan's ODA went to economic infrastructure, including transportation, communications, and energy; and 23.2 percent went to social infrastructure, including education, health and sanitation, and population. In addition to this bilateral aid, Japan has also made financial contributions to various multilateral organizations amounting to $3.8 billion in 1994, or 28 percent of the total amount of Japan's ODA.

Japan is tackling various new challenges to ODA that have emerged in recent years. The importance of coping with the environmental issue is emphasized in Japan's ODA. At the United Nations Conference on Environment and Development (UNCED) held in Brazil in June 1992, Japan committed to providing 900 billion yen to 1 trillion yen ($7 billion to $7.8 billion at the exchange rate then prevailing) to developing countries to assist in their environment-related projects between 1993 and 1998. Japan has disbursed about 700 billion yen in the first three years of that period.

Because of the significance of overpopulation and AIDS, Japan was an active participant in the United Nations Conference on Population and Development in September 1994 in Cairo and the AIDS Summit Meeting in December 1994 in Paris. In February 1994, Japan announced a "Global Issues Initiative [GII] on Population and AIDS" and committed $3 billion for the coming seven years (fiscal years 1994 to 2000) to help solve the issues of overpopulation and AIDS.

Recognizing the importance of women in development, Japan has implemented a number of projects to promote the participation and benefit sharing of women in development, such as the construction of vocational training centers, health care services for mothers and children, and family planning programs.

Yet another new challenge concerns countries in transition to democracy and market economies. To assist them during these transitions, Japan's ODA has been given to Central and Eastern European countries, Mongolia, Vietnam, Cambodia, Laos, five Central Asian republics, Latin American countries, Palestine, and South Africa.

Finally, to help refugees and disaster victims—27 million people, according to the United Nations High Commission on Refugees (UNHCR)—Japan's ODA has been extended to them through its contributions to the UNHCR and other multilateral organizations.

Recognizing new needs for foreign assistance in the world in the post–Cold War era, the Japanese government adopted the so-called ODA Charter in 1992, which has four guiding principles:

1. Environmental conservation and development should be pursued in tandem.

2. Any use of ODA for military purposes or for aggravation of international conflicts should be avoided.

3. Full attention should be paid to trends in recipient countries' military expenditures, their development and production of mass–destruction weapons and missiles, their export and import of arms, etc., so as to maintain and strengthen international peace and stability, and in order to encourage developing countries to place appropriate priorities in the allocation of their resources on their own economic and social development.

4. Full attention should be paid to efforts for promoting democratization, the introduction of a market–oriented economy, and basic human rights and freedoms in the recipient country.

In the case of a recipient country violating any of these principles, the Japanese government investigates the relevant facts, giving due consideration to the policy and attitude of that country's government and the country's political and economic relationship with Japan, as well as the international situation. The Japanese government then expresses its concerns and continues a dialogue with the country's representatives to enable them to take remedial measures prior to final action, such as a decrease or suspension of aid.

In addition to changes in the size and character of aid programs, the Japanese government has been striving to improve the effectiveness and efficiency, as well as the transparency, of Japan's foreign aid in recent years. Such improvements are achieved through policy dialogues with recipient countries, the supervision of fair procurement procedures, and better project evaluations.

# 13

# Dutch Development Cooperation since the End of the Cold War

## Marnix Krop

I N THE MIDST of the turmoil created by the collapse of the bipolar world, Dutch development cooperation was restructured to bring it in line with the dominant features of the emerging international order. The new policy underlined the importance of poverty reduction as the central task for development cooperation. This was considered to be particularly essential at a time when the gap between haves and have-nots seemed to be growing as a result of the globalization of economic and technological processes.

The reorientation of Dutch foreign aid policy was based on three developments. First, the situation arising from the end of the Cold War seemed to be propitious for the fight against poverty. Old power games and ideological rigidities could give way to a new pattern of international—but also intrastate—relations, characterized by cooperation, openness and reconciliation. Decreased military spending and increased respect for democratic rights could foster a climate in which poor countries and people would find it easier to direct their energies to economic and human development.

Second, the rapidly increasing fragility of the natural environment, under pressure from human activities, called for new ways of making economic progress, in both rich and poor countries. If the earth should in the long run be able to sustain economic development, it would among other things be imperative to redistribute human "ecospace" between rich and poor.

Third, given the great speed with which economic and technological processes globalize, the independence of national states in managing their economies and societies decreased rapidly. Delinking from the world economy was no longer possible or desirable, and countries simply had to adapt to the outside world. Such adaptation seemed to rule out certain development strategies that were practiced by some countries—and supported with foreign aid—in the past.

Thus the stage was set for a range of changes in Dutch development cooperation. On the whole, there was a considerable and conscious shift toward programs of structural poverty alleviation, and increasingly in a multilateral context. Special programs were launched that aimed at strengthening the position of women in development, alleviating urban poverty, and promoting ecologically sustainable development. In addition, increased support was given for human rights initiatives in developing countries, and a "West-East-South" program was initiated with the purpose of forging new links between countries that during the Cold War used to be worlds apart.

The cautious optimism invoked by the revolution of 1989, however, was soon dampened by the outbreak of a large number of armed conflicts. The end of the Cold War thus produced a mixed and paradoxical picture: in one place an old conflict could finally be resolved because of the changed geopolitical context, but in another place these geopolitical changes allowed simmering conflicts to finally erupt. In particular, many parts of Africa and East Europe suddenly imploded with various forms of civil strife. Often contested under the banners of ethnicity or religion, these conflicts amounted to serious cases of the disintegration of regimes and states. It seemed as if people now felt free to question given political structures and withdraw into rediscovered (or recreated and manipulated) traditional identities. Sometimes, a tendency to cling to old or new fundamentalisms surfaced and appeared to point to a deep-seated discontent with the conditions of modern life. Thus globalization in the economy was counteracted by fragmentation in political, social, and spiritual spheres of life. The world was becoming a village, but then again it was not: instead, it was disintegrating into separate villages.

For development cooperation, these new phenomena presented a number of existential challenges. In the course of a few years, between 1989 and 1992, expenditures for emergency and humanitarian assistance—mostly related to armed conflict—more than tripled. Because the increase was of such magnitude that it began to eat away from programs for "structural" development assistance, some serious questions were raised about the relation between development cooperation and conflict-related humanitarian aid. The issue was compounded by the proliferation of peacekeeping operations under the aegis of the UN, to which The Netherlands was a notable contributor (in 1992 it participated simultaneously in ten different operations). The question was whether these efforts should also be funded from the development cooperation budget and, more fundamentally, what the relation was between peacemaking and development cooperation.

The ensuing policy debates resulted in four major conclusions. First, there is indeed an intricate relation between development and conflict or peace. It is therefore legitimate for those concerned with development cooperation to participate in efforts to prevent or solve conflicts that impede development.

Second, most of these conflicts express themselves in terms of struggles for political power and structures, the latter usually being weak to begin with. The reverse is also true in that countries with reasonably well-developed political structures tend to be more successful in development efforts and in avoiding civil strife. Hence, the traditional economic, sociological, and anthropological biases of development cooperation should be amended to make way for an approach that integrates insights from political science. To put it a different way: "good governance" should be high on the development agenda.

Third, a particular problem is posed by countries whose political, economic, and social systems are in a stage of transition. This applies not only to the former communist countries of the Eastern bloc but also to a range of countries in the Third World that are moving from authoritarian rule to representative democracy and free markets. For the purposes of both poverty alleviation and conflict prevention, it is prudent for development cooperation to assist these countries through the transition.

Finally, all things considered, the new problems of conflict and development should not be tackled only on a narrow bilateral basis, nor should assistance be limited to financial support of one kind or another. These problems require a multifaceted approach consisting of diplomatic initiatives, various military peace operations, and a whole range of activities in the sphere of peace building, rehabilitation, support for democratization, and reinforcement of civic organizations. Not only will this way of dealing with such problems reduce any tension between development cooperation and humanitarian aid, but at the same time it will allow for the "decompartmentalization" of various concepts and tools of international policymaking needed in the tackling of unconventional problems that require an integrated approach. Foreign policy, security and defense policies, human rights advocacy, development cooperation and economic support, arms trade and arms control should all be part of a sustained and integrated effort to forge a better, more manageable, and less chaotic world. Indeed, it is the call for a "decompartmentalized" and more integrated policy that best summarizes the new Dutch development cooperation.

In the course of the past few years, this philosophy has begun to be put in practice. To begin with, the list of countries with which The Netherlands maintains intensive relations of development cooperation has been remodeled to allow for the inclusion of a range of countries in "transition" (for instance, Romania, Vietnam, and South Africa) as well as countries in "conflict" or "rehabilitation" (for instance, Cambodia, Eritrea, Rwanda, Sudan, Bosnia, and Palestine). Programs for these countries are geared to specific problems related to their particular conditions. For countries in transition programs involve an emphasis on support for macroeconomic stabilization and institutional reform. For countries in conflict or in rehabilitation, they often involve a mixture of emergency aid and more structural development assistance, including the repair of the physical infrastructure, assistance in the process of demobilization, the removal of mines, and the rebuilding of reliable judiciary and police forces. The resettlement of refugees is an additional concern in all of these countries. Dutch development cooperation increasingly emphasizes humanitarian and peace operations. Much has been done to establish close working relations with the ministry of defense, which is actively restructuring the armed forces for the tasks involved in the new peace operations.

For The Netherlands to assert itself and have a meaningful role in a rapidly changing world, it must bundle its external activities in an integrated and concerted fashion. Among other things, this should be expressed in a reorganized ministry of foreign affairs centered around decompartmentalized regional and country desks. On the basis of integrated "country strategies," it will be easier to conduct a synergized policy vis-à-vis different regions with different problems and potentials. This reorganization will also entail the creation of a special unit for international crisis management and humanitarian assistance under the joint responsibility of the ministers of foreign affairs, defense, and development cooperation.

Since 1989, in the course of less than six years, Dutch development cooperation has undergone a remarkable metamorphosis. It has adapted, both conceptually and operationally, to the changing requirements of poverty alleviation. Overall, greater flexibility has been introduced in dealings with different countries and situations in the developing world. The minister of development cooperation will have more say in the external policies of The Netherlands. The provision of financial and technical assistance is no longer a sufficient way to improve the conditions of developing countries. It is of critical importance to developing countries that the overall policies of aid donors, with regard to aid, trade, foreign investments, peace and security, show greater coherence and consistency.

## 14

# Western Assistance to Transition in Poland

### Krzysztof J. Ners

AFTER THE JUNE 1989 elections, the first postcommunist government was formed in Poland, marking the beginning of the process of economic and political liberalization in Central and Eastern Europe (CEE). As a result of the summit of the Group of Seven (G-7) in July 1989, the West declared itself ready to assist the transition process in the postcommunist countries.

At first, the main aim of assistance was to help Poland implement a stabilization plan—a stable exchange rate of the Polish zloty. To this end, many donor countries contributed (in the form of either loans or grants) to a stabilization fund of $1 billion (fortunately, Poland was not forced to draw on this). In early 1990, to avoid the danger of social unrest caused by "shock treatment," domestic supplies of food and agricultural products were supplemented by aid in kind from the European Union (EU) and other bilateral donors.

The Polish authorities considered the primary goal of Western assistance to be the securing of the continuity of transition until it had successfully fulfilled its aims. Generally, while the recipients of assistance have borne the main responsibility for making the transition succeed, Western support has been crucial to this process. The main long-term aim is to enable the recipients to build viable civil societies and self-sustaining market economies. Effective economic reform underpins the securing of a pluralist democracy and human rights and also acts as a form of security expenditure in helping to achieve stability in Europe. Accordingly the West believed that it should provide aid to CEE countries to ensure that the Cold War division in Europe would not be replaced by a new destabilizing division between rich and poor countries.

The concept of *assistance to transition* has recent origins. As the issue is often exploited politically, donors and recipients must agree on a common understanding of this notion. They should specify the various forms of assistance and exclude commercially driven transfers (long- and short-term commercial loans, private export credits, direct and portfolio foreign investment). The common definition of assistance to transition in postcommunist countries differs from the definition of official development assistance (ODA) in that it usually includes reimbursable official assistance (multilateral and bilateral), official export credits, and investment guarantees. However, an unfortunate assumption in debates on the types of assistance is that assistance to transition is provided on a concessional basis, or even in the form of grants. The issue of debt reorganization arrangements (including debt reduction) is particularly problematic. A clear distinction should be made between the reduction of the old debt and new assistance transfers.

During their July 1989 Paris meeting, the G-7 countries devoted special attention to the transformation that was just beginning to gain impetus in CEE. Since then, programs designed to promote change in the region have been launched. Cumulative commitments of all forms of assistance to the twelve CEE countries by the Group of Twenty-Four (G-24) countries and the international financial institutions for the period 1990–94 totaled $99.3 billion (of which some $13.5 billion involved debt reorganization). As far as cumulative commitments are concerned for the period 1990–94, Poland was allotted $22.2 billion, which brings the Polish share to 26.7 percent of all twelve countries.

These assistance figures should be treated with caution, however. The figures concerning the commitments of assistance represent an upper limit, whereas disbursements are generally spread over several years. It is therefore important not only to look at the announced commitments but also to scrutinize actual disbursement. Although the modernization and restructuring of CEE economies need important injections of new capital, the slow disbursement of assistance to date can be attributed to problems with appropriate intermediaries in lending to the private sector, slower-than-expected progress with privatization, problems in securing co-financing from domestic resources (an especially acute consideration for infrastructure investment), and institutional and policy impediments in absorbing restructuring loans and loans for the restructuring of the social sectors.

The slowing of the disbursement process could also be attributed to a "crowding-out" effect. That is, increasing Western assistance to the newly independent states (NIS), especially Russia and Ukraine, might have a negative impact on assistance to CEE. The Middle East peace process and the democratization of South Africa, as well as a growing awareness of domestic poverty in OECD (Organization for Economic Cooperation and Development) countries, merely compound this problem. In effect, competition for limited assistance resources has grown and continues to grow.

The fear that assistance to transition will divert resources from development aid has been exaggerated. There are no precise figures on aid for transition, because it is impossible to differentiate between CEE or NIS disbursements within the OECD data on official development assistance. The average ratio of assistance disbursement of both CEE and NIS to donors' GNP remains very low: 0.04 percent between 1991 and 1993. According to the OECD, it is very low compared with the same ratio for Third World development aid (0.33 percent in 1992 and 0.30 percent in 1993).

The small proportions of foreign aid to Poland can be illustrated through a comparison with other kinds of aid flows in Europe. The average per capita disbursement from 1990 to 1994 in Poland was around $25 per year, or $59 including debt reduction assistance. A comparison with the EU's internal regional funds disbursed to the relatively poor and declining regions within the EU is revealing. For instance, Ireland received more than $1,310 per person over the period from 1989 to 1993, a yearly average of $262, whereas Portugal received $868 for the same period, or $173 annually (*Financial Times*, Oct. 25, 1994). At the Edinburgh summit in December 1992, regional and structural aid plans totaling over $195 billion from 1994 to 1999 were agreed upon (*Financial Times*, June 21, 1994).

West German official gross transfers to former East Germany are even more impressive: on average, more than $100 billion of German government funds flowed annually to Eastern Germany between 1991 and 1994. In 1992, for example, Germany's disbursements of both reimbursable and nonreimbursable assistance to Eastern Germany amounted to $5,600 per capita, while those to the CEE countries were only $36 per capita.

With assistance transfers leveling off from their peak in 1991, it would seem that the economic recovery in Poland has not been assistance-driven. Assistance has, however, played a role in supporting structural reforms, promoting higher savings rates, and raising levels of efficiency. By removing critical barriers, so that domestic resources can be mobilized and better utilized, assistance can make a difference. Western assistance should pave the way for private investment, both domestic and foreign. As the levels of assistance to CEE have been modest in comparison to the flow of aid to the Third World and to the needs of transition, its value would appear to have been more qualitative than quantitative.

In the sixth year of transition in Poland, even with successful macroeconomic stabilization and rapid economic growth, it is becoming clear that readjustment to the market economy and world economic system is a complicated and lengthy process. Macroeconomic reforms have not been accompanied by fundamental social, political, and institutional changes. There is a danger that retaining structural features from the communist past, including the nonreform of the social sectors, will result in stagnation. Assistance is required even after economic recovery has been attained.

The dialogue with the EU about possible future membership adds urgency to these requirements and increases the importance of the institutional dimension of assistance. It provides further incentives to consolidate structural reforms in the transition to stable democracy and a free-market economy.

## 15

# Foreign Aid to Bangladesh

### Anwarul Karim Chowdhury

BANGLADESH IS A least-developed country (LDC) whose economy is characterized by the so-called low-level equilibrium trap. The country is overpopulated, it has limited resources, and the standard of living is, on the average, very low. The most important assets of the country are land and human power. But the person-to-land and land-to-capital ratios are unfavorable, and the mode of production as well as the existing factors of production are not naturally conducive to economic growth. In addition, recurring natural disasters have hindered attainment of desired economic goals.

In such an economy, domestic savings cannot be significant, and there are insufficient domestic resources for capital investment. This insufficiency, in combination with an adverse export-import gap, necessitates external assistance. Since independence in 1971, international assistance has played a crucial role in the country's development. Bangladesh is one of the largest recipients of external assistance among the LDCs. Up to June 30, 1994, a total amount of $33.5 million of external assistance was committed. Of the total amount, 15.7 percent was food aid, 27.2 percent was commodity aid, and 57.1 percent was project aid. The most important bilateral donors are presently Japan, France, the United States, and Canada. The most important multilateral donors are the International Development Association (IDA) of the World Bank, the UN system, and the Asian Development Bank.

In the period immediately following independence, external economic assistance was designed mainly to support the relief and rehabilitation efforts for the recovery of the war-ravaged economy. With the launching of the first five-year plan in 1973, external economic assistance was needed for the implementation of development projects as well as for imports of food and essential commodities.

Since 1971, the aid package has undergone some significant changes. The share of grants (mostly from bilateral sources) has decreased gradually. As bilateral aid declined, aid from multilateral sources increased. Bilateral aid decreased from 75 percent of total aid in the period from 1971 to 1975, to 47 percent in the period between 1990 and 1994. Conversely, multilateral aid grew from 25 percent to 53 percent over the same period. The result has been a larger proportion of loans in the total aid package.

Further, food and commodity aid declined consistently from a total of 84 percent in the period from 1971 to 1975 to 36 percent in the period 1990 to 1994. Over the same period, project aid increased sharply, from 1 percent to 64 percent. Project aid is extended to finance projects for human resource development; infrastructure building; development of social welfare, health, and family planning; and the education sector.

The government's central development goal is poverty reduction. Its strategy consists of (1) labor-intensive, export-led, private sector growth spurred by structural reforms and efficient investments in physical infrastructure and (2) human resource development to improve the lives of the poor directly and to enable them to participate in the economy. To ensure that the poor benefit from this strategy, special programs are included to enable them to improve their health and skills and access to credit, and thus increase their incomes.

The country has made impressive strides since independence. Growth of the gross domestic product (GDP) has averaged over 4 percent a year. More pertinently, Bangladesh has promoted human development as an important way out of poverty. Although they remain low compared to other Asian countries, social indicators have improved over the past two decades. In the social sectors, there is considerable progress in family planning and in the education of girls. The fertility rate dropped from over seven to under four. Infant mortality declined from 151 per 1,000 live births in 1960 to 91 in 1994. Life expectancy at birth increased from 44 for females and 46 for males in 1970 to 55 for both males and females in 1994. Gross primary school enrollment increased from 54 percent to 77 percent during the same period (the percentage for girls doubled in two decades and stood at 71 percent in 1994). The record of improved social indicators suggests that, with sustained commitment to economic reform and external support, the government can successfully reap the fruits of its poverty-reducing and social development strategy.

Bangladesh has shown itself capable of making tough decisions, as reflected in stabilization at the macroeconomic level in recent years, progress on trade reform, and the value added tax. Compared to those of the 1980s, entrepreneurs today face a more liberal trade and industrial regulatory regime and fewer foreign investment restrictions. Good progress has been made in reducing the nominal level of import tariffs and removing quantitative restrictions. The Industrial Policy of 1991 relaxed investment sanctions, removed impediments to foreign investment, and opened telecommunications, power generation, and domestic air transport to the private sector.

Despite sluggish global economic growth in the early nineties, the economy of Bangladesh performed well, particularly in consolidating macroeconomic stability. Economic growth increased because the government seriously addressed macroeconomic and structural problems. There was a significant increase in the mobilization of domestic resources, a lowering of the inflation rate, and an increase in foreign exchange reserves.

But the longer-term challenges facing Bangladesh remain great. Per capita income is below $250, and half the population still lives below the poverty line. Having doubled since the mid-1960s, the population is now 120 million; at its current 2 percent growth, it will double again in thirty-five to forty years. The 2.5 percent average per capita GDP growth achieved on an annual basis since 1990 compares well with that of many other developing countries, but it is well below what is needed to tackle Bangladesh's extreme poverty. At current economic growth rates, even with a further decline in population growth and a favorable income distribution, the absolute number of poor will continue to grow.

Post–Cold War developments did not significantly change the rationale behind foreign aid to Bangladesh: the bulk of its aid served developmental rather than geostrategic purposes. A number of other recipients were much more affected than Bangladesh was. Nevertheless, there were some important indirect effects. In the nineties, the foreign aid regime underwent some changes with implications for Bangladesh.

First, there was a general tightening of the sources of international assistance, especially with regard to bilateral flows. According to data from the Organization for Economic Cooperation and Development (OECD), total net official development assistance to Bangladesh in 1993 ($1.4 million) was substantially lower than in 1990 ($2.1 million), although it went up again in 1994 ($1.8 million).

Second, foreign aid management, debt servicing, and human and social development have emerged as the key elements of consideration by the foreign aid donors. In other words, donors are increasingly monitoring the quality of management of external assistance by the recipient governments.

Foreign aid has undoubtedly contributed to the development of the economy, but is also leading to growing indebtedness, especially in light of the growing ratio of loans to grants. Bangladesh's large structural trade deficit, savings-investment gaps, slow growth of revenues, and rapid growth of current public expenditures all necessitate external funding, which in turn feeds the increasing public debt. The country's per capita debt increased from $6.59 in 1974 to $133 in 1994.

Dependence on foreign aid mirrors the lack of mobilization of domestic resources. Continuous dependence on foreign aid is not desirable for a self-respecting nation, particularly because its economy will be controlled by the donors. It is evident, however, that in the coming years Bangladesh will have little choice but to rely on foreign assistance to attain desired levels of economic development. At the same time, if foreign aid is used effectively and judiciously, and is aimed at improving the quality of life of all people, it serves as a primary tool to break the cycle of poverty.

Since its birth over a quarter of a century ago, Bangladesh has emerged from the ruins of war to become a symbol of many new positive forms of humanitarian and development cooperation in the relations between rich and poor countries. According to most measures, progress has been slow but nonetheless real. The struggle for meeting basic needs continues for the teeming millions of a country endowed with the soft beauty of nature.

# 16

# The Role of Foreign Aid
# in Bolivian Adjustment Reforms

Marcelo Méndez Ferry

B OLIVIA IS ONE of the Latin American countries that has most benefited from foreign assistance since about 1985. In this period, aid
was instrumental in reestablishing economic stability and in completing
a wide program of structural reforms. For instance, aid facilitated an
agenda of complex reforms and structural adjustment—mainly through
debt relief, balance-of-payments support, and project financing. These
reforms permitted the country to recover international credit-worthi-
ness, to attain a one-digit inflation rate, and to reach growth rates above
4 percent in recent years.

Bolivia has been able to improve many of the economic conditions of
the mid-1980s. In that period Bolivia accumulated a huge external debt,
for which annual service represented more than one-third of its exports
earnings. In addition, the fiscal disequilibrium, the balance-of-payments
deficit, and the lack of appropriate economic policies have together resulted in extreme price instability, with an inflation above 1,000 percent
per annum and a permanent fall in the gross domestic product (GDP).

In those deteriorating circumstances, the government of Bolivia de-
cided to undertake a radical stabilization and structural adjustment program, based primarily on the complete liberalization of prices and
foreign trade, sharp fiscal discipline, and the renegotiation of the external debt.

Foreign assistance programs effectively facilitated the reduction of the commercial foreign debt through several debt buy-back operations, swaps, and other modalities of stock reduction, which enabled Bolivia to become the first country on the continent to eliminate its foreign debt with the international private banks. Similarly, foreign aid played an important and constructive role in policies of bilateral debt reduction that were financially supported by various donor countries themselves. In March 1995, Bolivia was one of the first countries to qualify for a stock reduction of its foreign debt. Bolivia's debt is now under control: the foreign debt service pressure is at tolerable levels for the economy.

Multilateral aid also played a role in reforming the Bolivian debt crisis. The International Monetary Fund (IMF), as well as the World Bank and the Inter-American Development Bank (IDB), offered strong support to the structural adjustment program in the late 1980s, whose objective was the recovery of economic stability and establishment of the foundations for sustained economic growth under market conditions. This external multilateral funding at concessional (i.e., friendly) terms was complemented with bilateral loans and grants to support the balance of payments and the financing of labor-intensive programs.

During the structural adjustment period, significant amounts of aid were raised each year mainly through meetings organized by the World Bank for Bolivia. For instance, global pledges from multilateral organizations and bilateral donor countries exceeded $1 billion in 1994.

The volume of foreign assistance, comprising grants and concessional loans, is significant compared to the size of the Bolivian economy. During the early 1990s official foreign assistance amounted to almost 14 percent of the country's GDP, or the equivalent of total domestic investment. In some years foreign exchange provided from aid compared almost to the value of total exports of goods and services.

It is important to specify that almost half of the amount of aid disbursed each year is in grant terms and mainly from European countries, the United States, and Japan. The other half consists of loans—most of them in concessional terms—given by international development agencies and international development banks and bilateral development loans. Only in exceptional circumstances are loans extended at market conditions from regional or bilateral financial sources.

Foreign assistance has helped support public investment as a main source of financing for priority investment projects in economic and social sectors. In 1994, 57 percent of the Public Investment Program was financed by external resources. Foreign aid has also been a main component in fostering economic growth and employment.

It is estimated that about 50 percent of the official foreign assistance to Bolivia is allocated to investment projects or related activities, such as preinvestment studies. The other half consists mainly of balance-of-payments support, food aid, technical assistance, and emergency aid. The impact of these flows has been very important to attenuate the effects of the deterioration in trade terms due to the fall of Bolivian export commodity prices. The importance of foreign aid to the Bolivian economy can be understood by recognizing that in 1992 the amount of official foreign assistance was higher than the total value of exports of goods and services.

The volume of aid has progressively declined in recent years (an estimated 15 percent decline in 1994 compared to the 1992 record), mainly because of financial restrictions in the donor countries. The biggest reduction in this period is attributed to the decline in U.S. aid from $215 million in 1992 to $12 million in 1994.

The future prospects of foreign aid to Bolivia are quite somber. Because of pressure to reduce the fiscal deficit in the United States, U.S. contributions to the concessional resources of both the World Bank and the IDB will probably be reduced, and hence the access of Bolivia to that type of funding will become more restricted. Furthermore, Bolivia faces domestic macrofinancial problems and persistent side effects of the foreign debt. In addition, its domestic savings capacity is still limited. For this reason, Bolivia is not ready to apply for ordinary capital loans from multilateral banks in amounts that would substitute its previous access to concessional funds.

In addition, Bolivia is engaged in a second generation of reforms to consolidate its economic stability and to ensure dynamic and equitable growth. These reforms, which include capitalization of the main public enterprises, educational reform, and a redistributive process of economic and political power known as Popular Participation, represent a high cost to state finances. It has been estimated that the combined cost of the reforms in 1995 and 1996 would represent 3 percent of the GDP, thus requiring considerable support from external concessional funds. If the international community does not respond with consistent support over the period 1996–99, Bolivia will have difficulties completing its economic and social reforms; paradoxically, these reforms were designed to reduce the very dependency of Bolivia on foreign aid.

In view of the ever-growing restrictions of foreign aid for development, Bolivia is implementing an active resource mobilization policy, optimizing the utilization of traditional sources of funds, and exploring new financial sources and donors, as well as promoting private domestic and foreign investment as a substitute for public investment and foreign aid.

# 17

# Foreign Aid to El Salvador

## Mirna Liévano de Marques

T HE NATURE OF international relations is profoundly affected, at a global scale, by several recent developments. Changes in international relations have major implications for foreign aid, and evidence for this can be found in the Central American region in the last few years. Overall, the evolution of foreign aid in the Central American region reflects the changing global priorities of the major donors, especially the United States.

During the Cold War aid to the Central American region was a response to the presence of a communist threat. Largely due to the region's proximity to the United States and perceived security threats posed by guerrilla movements, Washington considered Central America a strategic interest. Consequently, massive bilateral aid was given to various countries in the region, including El Salvador.

In the 1980s, El Salvador experienced serious internal conflicts accompanied by a chronic economic crisis. The results were impoverishment of the population, destruction of the country's physical infrastructure, large-scale migration from rural to urban areas and displacement of people, and a return to economic productivity levels of the sixties. By 1989 the country faced the worst economic, social, and political crises in its history. Foreign aid did much to reduce the proportions of the crises of the 1980s and to maintain some degree of stability in the country. Without foreign aid, conditions would have been significantly worse. Assistance programs were orientated toward alleviating balance-

of-payments problems and to a variety of social and infrastructural projects. In the 1980s it was largely because of the level of foreign assistance
that the country could function on a day-to-day basis.

From 1990 onward, global geopolitical change occurred, and U.S. aid
began to decline drastically. The fall of the Berlin Wall and the end of
the Cold War brought about new priorities for the international community. The economic transition in former Soviet countries and Eastern
Europe became the focus of attention for foreign aid donors. Multilateral organizations and individual countries turned their financial and technical assistance efforts toward Eastern Europe and the former Soviet
Union. Thus in the 1990s, Latin America finds itself relegated to a lower position in terms of foreign aid. Its place has been taken by former
communist countries that are now in a transition to market economies
and by African countries with critical levels of poverty.

In recent years many Latin American countries began to be seen as
equal and potential economic partners and, in some cases, even as economic competitors. This trend may reflect the confidence that the global
community had in Latin America in the early 1990s, when Latin American countries registered their greatest potential for economic growth.
Proof of this new reality came with the signing of the North American
Free Trade Agreement (NAFTA) by the United States, Canada, and
Mexico, and with the emerging possibility of Chile's inclusion in the future. But such views of Latin America ignore regional differences and
the critical phase of development in which some countries, including El
Salvador, find themselves.

The global changes that caused the redirection of foreign aid flows
coincided with important transformations inside El Salvador. The country went through a transition in the late 1980s. The people's disgust with
twelve years of civil war, in combination with the vanishing ideological
context of the conflict and a government committed to entering a new
era, helped to create the appropriate environment for negotiations that
resulted in the signing of the Peace Accords in 1992. The international
community also played an important role in this process, from fostering
negotiations to providing financial resources for the implementation of
the accords.

There are many signs of moral support by the international community for El Salvador's policies aimed at political, social, and economic
progress. It is ironic, however, that as the country takes off economically,
as a result of austerity and adjustment measures, financial support in the

form of foreign aid has dwindled. Except for some programs tied to the Peace Accords and the Plan for National Reconstruction, the country has not received bilateral grants at the level that might have been expected. The United States has identified new priorities for foreign assistance and has chosen to exercise greater influence in the countries of the region through multilateral organizations in the restructuring of foreign debts. For instance, President Bush's Initiative for the Americas included various mechanisms for debt restructuring.

El Salvador, not unlike East European countries, is a country in transition with a nascent peace and the promise of democratic stability. It still struggles with high levels of poverty, but its economic performance has shown signs of improvement. Clearly, El Salvador has a long way to go, and there are no guarantees of successful development, but its changing and positive economic and political climate merits more foreign aid.

# 18

# Foreign Aid in the New World Order
## *Implications for Egypt*

### Youssef Boutros-Ghali

IN RECENT YEARS a number of developments converged to drive donor countries to reduce their foreign assistance programs in both relative and absolute terms. These developments include the ending of the Cold War, the increased need for fiscal restraint in the donor economies, aid fatigue in donor societies, and the perceived lack of long-term success of aid programs in the recipient countries. From 1990 to 1995, official development assistance (ODA) to all developing countries declined in real terms.

Major cutbacks in foreign aid, or even its complete elimination, would not significantly affect the overall government budgets of donors. Indeed, if all foreign aid were discontinued today, industrial countries would be able to raise their domestic social safety nets by a mere 0.3 percent of their combined GNP. But the discontinuation of aid programs would surely exacerbate backwardness in the South. This in turn would cause disruptions in bilateral and global relations: in a growing world of interdependence and globalization, the economic development of the South—or lack of it—has a direct bearing on prospects of prosperity for the North. This does not mean that the aid regime should not be allowed to change. The persistent failure of the economies of a number of recipients despite a long history of assistance demands that donors and recipients embark on a critical examination of aid programs.

Clearly, massive amounts of external assistance cannot replace essential reforms in the domestic economy. Both donors and beneficiaries must work toward strategies aimed at restructuring aid requirements and at innovating assistance programs in relation to the changing world economy. Necessary reforms include, first, reorienting government to complement the private sector through reprioritizing public spending toward health, education, nutrition, family planning, infrastructure, and environmental protection. Second, the role of the state as predator should be made to evolve into one of arbitrator, regulator, and ultimately partner of economic agents in the system. Third, the legislature and judiciary institutions of governance and the vehicles for technology transfer must be strengthened. Constraining institutional environments such as the civil service and the legal and regulatory frameworks must be reformed. Social services, capital markets, tax administration and fiscal decentralization must all be made more efficient.

Global developments such as regional integration initiatives, world trade liberalization agreements, and acceleration of technological innovation and dissemination all need to be addressed by multilateral institutions through a renewed emphasis on effective assistance, be it technical support, achieving trade competitiveness, or technology transfer.

In addition to reforms of this kind, it is, however, necessary to view foreign assistance in the context of the broader economic relations between donors and recipients. Changes in international trade practices by the developed countries are of fundamental importance. Existing trade barriers imposed by the developed countries render the relationship between the North and South unequal; and losses incurred by developing countries as a result of this inequity have often handicapped ODA contributions. The Organization for Economic Cooperation and Development (OECD) estimates that such damages exceed the value of aid flows to these countries. If industrial countries abolished all their barriers to imports for developing countries, the increase in the latter's exports would be twice what they are given in aid. Similarly, in 1991, OECD subsidies for agriculture reached almost $200 billion dollars. Removing nontariff barriers would yield not only widespread gains for both developing and Eastern European economies but also big savings in the budgets of OECD countries. The complete elimination of all agricultural subsidies in the developed nations would raise the developing economies' export earnings by $50 billion per year.

These figures show that there must be improved opportunities for poor countries to increase their export earnings in order for them to abandon aid as a vehicle for development. Indeed, trade and financial opportunities in international markets are needed more than aid flows. In the "new world order," aid donors have a greater responsibility than before to admit their previous beneficiaries into the world economy. Such admission would prevent them from becoming "shrinking countries" and from becoming an inescapable burden to the world community in the future.

What are the implications of these changes for Egypt? Official development assistance to Egypt amounts to $40.8 per capita per year and consists of official concessional loans and technical cooperation grants, as well as other grants. Most of these grants are provided exclusively by OECD members, with the United States as the largest source. Multilateral agencies provide a relatively small percentage. As a ratio of Egypt's GDP, foreign aid comprises 6.4 percent.

Egypt will be one of few countries that may experience only moderate decline in the short term in ODA, with OECD grants continuing at their current nominal levels of $2.3 to $2.7 billion a year. And if it is classified as eligible for greater financial support from the European Union (EU), the decline in real terms in ODA to Egypt is expected to be slow and gradual by the millennium, with a faster pace of decline afterward.

In the medium term, the current account is expected to show a deficit in the order of 1 to 2 percent of the gross domestic product (GDP), which would need to be covered by aid flows and increased foreign investments. In the longer term, the absence of aid assumed, domestic savings should be increased to fill in the gap to raise the ratio of gross domestic investment to GDP from the current average of 17 percent to more than 23 percent and effect a growth in real output between 4.5 and 5 percent a year.

The anticipated reduction of aid would necessitate moving forward with the liberalization and deregulation of the economy to attract more foreign direct investment and to establish mechanisms through which the private sector will increase its investments and through which international competitiveness is enhanced.

In past years both Egypt and multilateral donors attempted large, all-encompassing, extremely detailed, impressive-looking, and ultimately unimplementable reform schemes. This old format of assistance must be changed to specific, smaller, cost-effective, environmentally sustainable schemes that yield quick systemic results and achieve the required increases in output, savings, and investment that would generate the needed self-reliance for the longer aid-free term.

Experiences with private sector participation in infrastructure projects worldwide could be replicated in Egypt through increasing allocations to projects that initiate the systemic changes that will allow private capital and equity investments in this sector. The injection of private capital can free up resources for loan and investment guarantees and overall assistance for small and microentrepreneurs, which would be a major element in the fight against poverty.

But the ultimate impact of the decline of ODA on Egypt and other developing economies should be assessed also in terms of the wider perspective of the responsibility of the Northern countries toward helping their beneficiaries gradually decrease their reliance on aid through abandoning international anticompetitive trade practices and through helping them in the reassessment of priorities in aid.

These global changes have prompted Egypt to seek a partnership with the EU and the United States that focuses on increasing bilateral trade and investments, technology transfer, human development, environmental protection, and increased collaboration among these countries' private sectors. Egypt is also engaged in regional cooperation within the Middle East and North Africa with the goal of creating mutually beneficial policies and a competitive economic and trading bloc. Furthermore, Egypt is currently negotiating a partnership agreement centering around a free trade area within the EU. All these initiatives require ingenuity in developing assistance formats from the multilateral organizations.

It is the obligation of donor countries and aid institutions to help recipients reorient their development priorities. At the same time, the industrial countries should yield to the importance of the notion that the global economy opens up to the poor. Trade liberalization in combination with pointed foreign assistance programs will generate self-reliance in the longer run. Ultimately, the victor would be not just the donors who have cut aid contributions but also Egypt and other recipients who in the course have started new engines for development.

# Part Five

*Conclusion*

# Foreign Aid at the End of the Century
## *The Emerging Transnational Liberal Order and the Crisis of Modernity*

### Richard Grant and Jan Nijman

AFTER THE SECOND WORLD WAR, a foreign aid regime emerged that formed an integral part of the global order. During most of the postwar period, the purpose and meaning of foreign assistance could be understood in the context of, first, the Cold War order and, second, the prevalence of a modernist paradigm that implied a strong belief in progress, growth, and social engineering. As such, the foreign aid regime was characterized by two coexisting and often competing models of progress.

In so far as the superpower struggle was an ideological one, it represented a quest to re-make the world in the image of the United States or the Soviet Union. Each superpower often legitimized its hegemonic pretenses on the basis of the alleged superiority of its political, social, and economic systems. In so far as foreign aid was supposed to serve developmental purposes, the paths of development were clearly defined. During the early postwar years, the United States and the Soviet Union tried to make West and East Europe into showcases of "development." Later, such efforts were replicated in places around the globe, from Cuba to Egypt and from Ethiopia to the Koreas—all large recipients of foreign assistance.

Accordingly, the prevailing development discourse upon which foreign aid debates were predicated represented a peculiar blend of modernist and geopolitical paradigms (Escobar 1995). Seen from the West,
the Third World was "the world of tradition, culture, religion, irra-
tionality, underdevelopment, overpopulation, political chaos, and so on.
The Second World was modern, technologically sophisticated, rational
to a degree but authoritarian (or totalitarian) and repressive, and ultimately inefficient and impoverished by contamination with ideological
preconceptions and burdened with an ideologically motivated socialist
elite. The First World is purely modern, a haven of science, efficient,
democratic, free—in short, a natural society unfettered by religion or
ideology" (Pletsch 1981, 574).

In practice, development goals were of secondary importance, and
foreign aid was used as an instrument of realpolitik: it served mainly to
keep certain countries within the donor's sphere of influence and out of
the camp of the opposition, helping to justify foreign aid to domestic
constituencies. As a consequence, in many cases it did not really matter
what kinds of development strategies were pursued by the recipient government and how much these deviated from the prototypical development models that were propagated by the superpowers. For example,
Zaire could not be labeled a showcase of a free market, liberal democracy, or development; it was nonetheless a major beneficiary of U.S. aid.
Similarly, Angola received significant aid from the Soviet Union while
paying little more than lip service to socialist or communist ideals (both
Zaire and Angola joined the ranks of Cold War orphans in the 1990s, after their geopolitical significance had evaporated). Furthermore, many
poor governments around the world tried to capitalize on the superpowers' efforts to lure countries into their circle of friends. One of the
most successful examples of this strategy is Egypt, one of the largest aid
recipients.

Of course, not all aid during the Cold War was donated exclusively by
the two superpowers. Other major donors, including European countries and Japan, had their own variants of development that they wished
to promote. For example, French foreign aid policy was aimed at maintaining ties with former French colonies. But large parts of their programs, too, must be understood in the context of the Cold War and the
U.S. hegemonic position in presenting its development philosophy as
the Western model. Western European aid typically coincided with U.S.
programs and their destinations. The exceptions to this pattern were

some programs by social democratic governments of Europe (including neutral Sweden) that were more experimental in design and carried distinct humanitarian and even socialist features. Much of Japan's aid, though not all of it, served the purpose of burden sharing with the United States. Even if the forms of Japanese assistance and the possible impacts on development were quite different, its destination was strongly influenced by Cold War considerations and the alliance with the United States. In a similar way, donations from East European countries were often instigated by Moscow and seemed to function as a proxy for Soviet aid.

The East-West conflict was predicated on a belief in social engineering: economies, polities, and societies could be designed and constructed (or reconstructed). The American and the Soviet model each held the promise of engineered development through "modernization," albeit with different emphases and goals. Foreign aid was an important tool in this endeavor. A striking feature of the old foreign aid regime was that these models of development were continuously put forward to justify the existence of foreign assistance, but aid effectiveness was rarely tested. This lack of attention to the effects of aid was partly related to the priority given to realpolitik over matters of development during the Cold War. It also resulted from superpower arrogance, their unwillingness to admit failure, and their unquestioned belief in modernism.

## The Emerging Transnational Liberal Order

With the demise of the Cold War, the foreign aid regime that accompanied it has disappeared as well. There are no longer competing models of development that are imposed on the Third World (incidentally, a term that has lost its literal meaning in the process) by outside contenders. The socialist model of development has, for all practical purposes, expired, and in today's world its proponents are hard to find among donors or recipients. This is true not just for former socialist states. Several European donors, such as The Netherlands and Sweden, have in the past supported quasi-socialist development strategies (e.g., in Tanzania), but these projects have been abandoned in recent years as they became harder to justify. Tanzania most recently has turned toward the promotion of a regional trading bloc (with Kenya and Uganda) to foster development.

In the "new world order" the spirit of the free market prevails, marking the victory of the West in the Cold War. In the present discourse there is really only one viable development path, and its key feature is liberalization. In theory, a variation of this liberalist development model constituted one of the two prominent competing paradigms during the Cold War, propagated by the United States. But at present, it is much more forcefully implemented than in the past. Loans are highly conditional and largely based on the track record of the recipient state in implementing reforms. International financial institutions and supranational entities—the European Union (EU), the North American Free Trade Agreement (NAFTA), and the Asia Pacific Economic Cooperation (APEC)—have all become advocates of the liberalist development model. That developing countries have all rushed to implement liberalization schemes has contributed to a kind of global policy convergence that never existed before.

During the Cold War it was often more important for the United States to use foreign aid to secure the loyalty of a "client" against the Soviet Union; how effectively those funds were used for development purposes seemed a lesser concern. Today, aid is legitimized primarily on the basis of the alleged impact on the recipient's economic and increasingly political development. Poor countries must meet various criteria to be eligible for aid: above all, they must present themselves as model free market reformers, complete with all the appropriate liberalization schemes and stabilization policies. Ghana is a country that is presently hailed as a role model of this kind. Others, like Kenya, have had aid withheld because of only intermittent commitments to economic reform and slow progress in some sectors (e.g., political freedom and privatization efforts).

Foreign aid is now part of a global order that has been characterized as "transnational liberalism" (Agnew and Corbridge 1995). The new transnational liberal order is different from past geopolitical orders in that it is based not on the hegemony of one particular state but on the hegemony of an ideology: "a new ideology of the market (and of market-access) is being embedded in and reproduced by a powerful constituency of liberal states, international institutions, and what might be called the 'circuits of capital' themselves" (Agnew and Corbridge 1995, 164). This ideology, which adheres to liberal principles and the supremacy of the market over the state, has always been advanced by the leading proponent, the United States, but its very success implied the gradual retreat of the United States as a political hegemon that used to independently impose its will on the global political environment.

The current prevalence of transnational liberalism has important consequences for foreign assistance. (The long-term ideological hegemony is not a given; as we argue later on, the relevance of this ideology around the world tends to be exaggerated.) First, one of the corollaries of the reassertion of the free market is a growing belief that development is better left to the private sector as an engine of growth than to government-run foreign aid programs. This belief has taken a high toll in some regions. The United States, especially, has tightened the purse strings and engages increasingly in rhetoric of "trade not aid." Moreover, this rhetoric has also caught on with some recipients, who have argued that genuine free trade with the West would bring them significant economic benefits. For instance, Youssef Boutros-Ghali, the Egyptian Minister of State for International Cooperation, in the preceding chapter estimated that the total elimination of agricultural subsidies in the developed world would raise export earnings of the poor countries by $50 billion per year. Hence, across-the-board trade liberalization could be an important substitute for foreign aid. Others would rather see alternative instruments highlighted. For example, Hewitt (1994) emphasized the growing importance of foreign direct investments as a more effective way of transferring funds and technical know-how.

Second, the primary condition for a government to receive aid is to pay tribute to this ideology of transnational liberalism. What has not changed, then, is that foreign aid still appears to function as a reward for allegiance to the prevailing policy consensus and its ideology. Foreign aid continues to represent a key political function in international relations: it is a vehicle to allow donors to reproduce their developmental model in the poor world by engaging countries in the global trade economy and in the process reduces the viability of alternative political and economic systems. On the other hand, others (e.g., Campanella 1993) argue that the emerging order may create more opportunities for developing countries to engage developed countries. Under the Cold War order, multilateralism was based on the creation of clublike minimalist arrangements; for example, the Organization for Economic Cooperation and Development (OECD) was restricted to countries at a similar economic level. By contrast, the emerging transnational liberal order offers the potential of embracing a wider range of actors, including recipients and multinational corporations who previously had no formal input in policy formulation. The emphasis on interdependence and transgovernmental relations encourages global coordination and cooperation. Furthermore, the renewed interest in supranational regional institutions (or trading blocs) can be seen as a further indicator that developing countries are committed to liberalization.

## The Renewed Politicization of Foreign Aid

Today's main cleavage in world politics is not between East and West but between the West and the rest. The West pertains to the international community of liberal democratic and capitalistic states. Over the past few years, the foreign policy of the United States has been said to be aimed at enlargement of this worldwide community, ruled by the transnational liberal order. In contrast, the "rest" is viewed as having no inherent order, and perhaps its most important commonality is disorder. Goldgeier and McFaul (1992) spoke of "a tale of two worlds" in which it seems every state's ultimate goal to join the West or, to use their term, the "core."

Foreign aid has become an important instrument in supporting particular states (e.g., Russia and South Africa) in their efforts to join the "West." To qualify for foreign assistance, states must proclaim their intent to join the transnational liberal order, and they must prove serious in the implementation of liberalization measures. In the process, "good  governance" on part of the recipient has become the single most important criterion on the basis of which donors decide to give (sometimes, recipients are held to standards that few donors live up to themselves). Whether it is the United States, Japan, or The Netherlands, all donors increasingly define foreign aid in these political terms, linking economics and politics: development is considered dependent upon good governance and liberal economic practices.

This trend is most vividly expressed in aid to countries "in transition." Initially, this term was reserved for the former communist states of East Europe, but lately it has acquired a much broader meaning, referring to any country trying to shift its form of governance toward one that fits liberal democratic ideals and a free market. Countries such as South Africa and Eritrea, too, are countries in transition. Many other poor states try hard to portray themselves as transitional in hopes of securing assistance (or having it continued). But this is much easier to do when the old system of governance stood out as extremely antidemocratic (apartheid, communism) and has already been dismantled; it is more difficult to make the case for a country with a more moderate past, like Bolivia or El Salvador, even if the intentions of liberalization are sincere.

On the donor side, the foreign aid policy of The Netherlands is an interesting illustration of these shifts in the foreign aid regime. In recent years, old-style structural development assistance has been cut, while more and more aid is given to countries that are in either "transition" or "conflict." Dutch foreign aid policy is now based on the assumption that development and politics cannot be separated. Indeed, economic development is now considered to be so intricately linked to broader political processes that aid policy is to be reintegrated with overall Dutch foreign policy, including the specialized military operations of peacekeeping forces.

Across all donors, there is a reorientation of assistance toward short-term programs aimed at good governance, and long-term economic development programs are slowly disappearing. Apart from the paradigmatic shift emphasizing political economy, this reorientation is also closely related to the growing realization that those long-term programs have failed miserably in the past. In many African countries, such programs led to ubiquitous corruption, a destructive rent mentality, and growing dependence on foreign funds—all with little or no economic growth. The result was widespread aid addiction. The London-based economist Peter Boone (1995) demonstrated that the dismal results in alleviating poverty were not confined to Africa but rather represent a much more general worldwide phenomenon.

This is not good news for countries that have a long history of foreign assistance but are not thought of as countries "in transition." Thus, regardless of the need for assistance based on poverty levels, countries like India, Bangladesh, and Kenya have seen their foreign aid funds diminish in the 1990s, especially bilateral flows.

This is not to suggest that all it takes to receive aid is to be a poor country in transition. Many former Soviet republics have received little support, especially in comparison to the former motherland, Russia. Similarly, Egypt remains one of the largest overall foreign aid recipients in the world without being a showcase of liberal democracy. Realpolitik still plays a part in the motivations of the donors. More than one-half of U.S. bilateral aid continues to go to Israel and Egypt, and two-thirds of Japanese aid continues to go to countries in Asia with which the Japanese maintain vital economic relations. For the two largest bilateral donors, foreign aid policies are built on varying and inconsistent mixes of old and new politics. Because countries are increasingly seeking to emulate the success of the Japanese model, and because there has been a lack of development successes in Africa and Latin America, there is beginning to be friction about what should be emphasized in the transnational liberal model. Geographically, at least, there appears to be a growing differentiation of aid experiences that is a cause of tension in the newly emerging foreign regime.

## Into the Fray: Foreign Aid and the Crisis of Modernity

Development aid is a typical product of the modernist era: its very existence is predicated on the belief that modernization is not only possible but can even be induced and accelerated. Generally, it also assumes a preferred and linear direction of the process of development. In the early days, the economic logic behind foreign assistance was that it provided capital for investment that the recipient country could not garner itself, allowing for industrial development and "takeoff." The idea was that once the recipient's economy had taken off, foreign assistance could be scaled back and terminated. Thus, foreign aid would allow poor countries to move through the successive stages of growth so that they would replicate the experiences and trajectories of the developed countries.

As we near the end of the twentieth century, it has become clear that most poor countries have failed to develop in this modernist sense, despite foreign aid. To many academic observers, this failure seems an inextricable and telling part of the crisis of modernity. Postmodernism implies the ending of the modernist project, of notions of steady trajectories converging at single destinations, of entire concepts of progress and order. Instead, in the postmodern perspective, the term *development* is reduced and returned to designate a process of social change without a blueprint, a predictable path, or even a purpose, and largely beyond the control of governmental or nongovernmental agencies. The current emphasis on postmodernity seems to have caused reflection almost to the point of confusion—something that academicians can better afford than policymakers.

Currently, the declared purposes of Dutch assistance programs are so broad and complex that policymakers have argued for the "decompartmentalization" of foreign aid. This means that aid must be integrated with foreign policy, security and defense policies, human rights advocacy, economic relations, arms control, trade relations, and so on. The irony of the Dutch case is that there seems to be a real possibility that the efforts at decompartmentalization, aiming to make foreign aid more effective, could jeopardize the integrity of the Ministry of Development Cooperation and eventually that of the Dutch foreign assistance program itself.

Even if their pessimism is rarely acknowledged, many donors seem to have lost faith in the future of Africa, and increasingly the continent faces the grim prospect of becoming the "slums of the new world order" (Van der Wusten 1992, 21). Some have pointed to the fundamental disjunction between Africa's traditional societies and models of state organization and liberal democracy that were imposed by the former Western colonial rulers. In equally gloomy terms, Basil Davidson (1993) summarized Africa's predicament as "the curse of the nation-state."

While there has been an across-the-board reassessment of development aid, especially that to African countries, most governmental and nongovernmental donors have pledged similar aid to new recipients such as East Europe or South Africa. But to postmodern observers (and other skeptics), it is a continuation of old-fashioned modernist beliefs: the so-called transitional countries just need a little push to move from the "Second World" (in case of the former communist countries) to become active participants in the global trade economy and members of the "First World." The transition may well prove illusory. Five years of large-scale assistance has done little to secure democracy in Russia, South Africa is in a deepening postapartheid crisis, and many analysts argue that aid to the East European countries must be expanded and prolonged if it is to be successful. Unfortunately, if the experiences of other large-scale aid recipients of the past are illustrative, aid dependence might result and a debt crisis might loom.

Postmodernism is not a very appealing paradigm for policymakers. In policy circles, modernism lives on, even if it has changed appearance. One could argue that, after the failure of development in most of the Third World, the modernist architects found a new category of subjects to keep their project alive: the transforming "Second World." Hence, the failure of development in Africa and other poor countries is attributed to import substitution–oriented strategies of the 1960s and 1970s and to lack of attention to the political dimension of the development process.

The essence of the notion of "transition" befits the modernist paradigm, and in essence it is not very different from the imagined transitory stages of the past, through which countries were supposed to move prior to their "takeoff." In what seems an odd blend of wishful thinking, ethnocentrism, and a desire to invent theories that can be applied without geographical limitations, current modernist thinking proposes that all countries can become liberal democracies, if there is the political will. Applying simple geographic assumptions and making sweeping generalizations about states and peoples' histories has not changed much: during the Cold War, world development was interpreted through the lenses of the East-West opposition, ignoring local and regional developments. Today, countries that are neither already stable liberal democracies nor in transition are considered to be in a state of perennial instability. Such a description of world politics leaves little or no room to alternative ways of societal organization; there is either liberal democracy and capitalism, or there is chaos and disorder. Simplistic geographical assumptions about the world persist, albeit in a different guise.

In opposition to these unsettling uncertainties of the postmodernist perspective, stand those who argue that the modernist paradigm has been vindicated by the West's victory in the Cold War and by the alleged proliferation of liberal democracies around the world. But these new "democracies" have rarely moved beyond the stages of aspiration and intention, and their long-term stability is far from certain. Further, the alleged process of democratization seems heavily influenced by the important symbolic function of a government labeling itself democratic to get on the right side of the division between the West and the rest (if they say they are democratic, we believe them). One of the rewards for such a proclamation is the possibility of foreign assistance.

## One Regime or More?

The transnational liberal order, and the new foreign aid regime that is subsumed within it, do not have the same geographic expression in all the world's regions. This is not so much about individual differences in donor or recipient policies—such differences can and do exist within a single regime. Rather, it is about the basic parameters of foreign aid, a set of rules and codes of conduct that are adhered to by all the players. In essence, the existence of a foreign aid regime is based on the shared meaning of foreign aid, by donors and recipients alike, in the wider international order. Ultimately, the structural stability of a regime rests on the consensus among the players about the rules of the game—i.e., what it takes to receive or give foreign aid and how it is valued.

The most important deviation from this regime is found in East Asia.

Despite the presence in the region of a number of traditional strategic allies of the United States (especially Japan and South Korea), most countries have never fully shared Western liberal democratic values. This deviation is sometimes referred to as the Asian variant of democracy, and it is often said to be based on "Asian values." Thus, among other things, Asian democracy typically deviates from the Western model in terms of widespread political patronage, violations of human rights, the lack of worker organizations and unions, and sometimes the absence of free elections. In addition, the economies of many East Asian countries are quite unlike the laissez-faire approach taken in the West. Instead, they attest to the importance of government guidance and intervention in the marketplace and of arbitrarily created comparative advantage.

Rather than viewing Asian development as a re-creation of the Western example or as a simulacrum of the West, the former prime minister of Singapore Lee Kuan Yu remarked in an interview in *Foreign Affairs* a few years ago that "culture is destiny" (Zakaria 1994). He suggested that Asian culture does not accommodate full-fledged Western liberalism, either politically or economically. He also argued that the existing Asian variant of the Western model forms a reflection of Asian values and is the basis of the impressive regional economic successes.

This is not to say that all governments in this region openly reject transnational liberalism or the corresponding terms of the foreign aid. But the economic successes in the region do seem to contribute to a certain assertiveness vis-à-vis Western donors. The point is that in Asia one can observe two partly overlapping, and uneasily coexisting, foreign aid regimes.

The foreign aid policy of the world's largest donor, Japan, reflects the simultaneous adherence to both regimes. On the one hand, Japan's declaratory policies echo the transnational liberal discourse of the United States and other Western donors on such matters as democratization, free markets, and good governance. On the other hand, Japan is extremely reluctant to press recipient governments to match deeds with words. The only time that Tokyo used foreign aid as a leverage vis-à-vis China was in 1995 when it protested Chinese nuclear tests. This response was motivated more by Japanese security interests than by concerns about Chinese disregard for the rules of transnational liberalism.

Violations of human rights and international patent and trading laws by China are a frequent source of conflict with the United States and other Western states (some of which give aid to China). But the behaviors of the protagonists are not based merely on ideology. Indeed, the United States, especially, has often been criticized for letting realpolitik prevail in its dealings with China at the expense of moral principles. Thus, seen from Beijing, Western protests and ultimatums appear as little more than empty threats, and the proclaimed adherence to transnational liberal principles by the West is viewed as little more than rhetoric or an ideological assault on the Chinese government. Perceptions by Asians of this inconsistency—real or not—on the part of Western aid donors only contributes further to their assertiveness in maintaining the Asian development model.

An interesting example of friction between a Western donor and an East Asian recipient concerns the Dutch-Indonesian relationship. In 1992, Jakarta rejected all further Dutch development aid after the Dutch government linked aid to progress in human rights. At the time, The Netherlands chaired an organization uniting all donors that gave aid to the country, the so-called Intergovernmental Group on Indonesia. In The Hague, this dismissal was felt as a blow to Dutch prestige, especially because Indonesia did not seem to have a problem in attracting other aid donors and was favorably considered by many foreign investors. In 1995 the Dutch government undertook some major efforts to rekindle ties with its former colony, including a visit to Jakarta by the Dutch queen (the first in over twenty years by the Dutch monarch). Significantly, the queen was accompanied by the largest-ever Dutch economic mission abroad, led by the Minister of Economic Affairs and including some sixty senior executives of Dutch corporations, many of whom had been hurt by the suspension of aid to Indonesia.

As we approach the end of this century, the foreign aid regime that prevailed for some forty years since its inception in the late 1940s has all but disappeared. In its place we witness the emergence of a regime that is tightly integrated in the new transnational liberal order. From a historical perspective, the ideological consensus that is at the basis of this new order seems unprecedented and holds a promise of stability and durability. At the same time, however, from a postmodern perspective, there are many reasons to question the revival of the modernist paradigm in a new guise. Not only are there currently geographical limits to the new foreign aid regime, there is also reason for major doubt as to whether newfound forms of transitional aid will deliver on their promises.

Still, one lesson that stands out in our reading of the past is that the survivability of ideology and belief in modernization seem to bear an ambivalent relationship to reality. In the past foreign aid regime, East and West applied their development models for over forty years without clear evidence of success. Yet their ideologies survived for a long time.

There are already many signs that this role of ideology is no different for the new transnationalist liberal order. It is likely that transnational liberalism will constitute the ideological basis for foreign aid for quite some time to come. There is little reason to assume that the economic results of assistance programs will be significantly different from those in the past. Above all, foreign aid will continue to function as an expression of the structure of political relations and hegemony in the international system. The fundamental role of foreign aid in the international order remains; it is the order that has changed.

*Works Cited*
*Index*

# Works Cited

*Africa Research Bulletin (ARB).* 1993–96. Economic, Financial and Technical Series. Exeter.

Agnew, John A., and Stuart Corbridge. 1995. *Mastering Space: Hegemony, Territory, and International Economy.* New York: Routledge.

Arndt, Dorothea. 1992. "Foreign Assistance and Economic Policies in Laos, 1976–1986." *Contemporary Southeast Asia* 14, no. 2: 188–209.

Ash, Timothy G. 1993. *In Europe's Name: Germany and the Divided Continent.* London: Jonathan Cape.

Association for the Promotion of International Cooperation (APIC). 1994. *Japanese ODA Data.* Tokyo: APIC.

Balcerowicz, Leszek. 1994. "Poland." In *The Political Economy of Policy Reform,* edited by John Williamson, 153–77. Washington, D.C.: Institute for International Economics.

Barry, Tom, and Deb Preusch. 1988. *The Soft War: Uses and Abuses of US Economic Aid in Central America.* New York: Grove Press.

Bauer, Peter T. 1971. *Dissent on Development.* Cambridge, Mass.: Harvard Univ. Press.

Biståndet och EG. 1991. Stockholm: Utrikesdepartementet.

Boone, Peter. 1994. *The Impact of Foreign Aid on Savings and Growth.* Center for Economic Performance, Working Paper No. 627. London: London School of Economics.

————. 1995. *Politics and the Effectiveness of Foreign Aid.* Center for Economic Performance, Working Paper No. 678. London: London School of Economics.

Brooke, James. 1994. "U.S. and 33 Hemisphere Nations Agree to Create Free-Trade Zone." *New York Times,* Dec. 11.

Brown, Frederick Z. 1993. "The Economic Development of Vietnam, Laos and Cambodia." *Journal of Northeast Asian Studies* 12, no. 4: 3–21.

Brzezinski, Zbigniew. 1994. "The Premature Partnership." *Foreign Affairs* 73 (Mar./Apr.): 67–82.

*Business America.* 1992. "Recipients of Japan's Untied Foreign Aid Are Able to Use It for Procurement of U.S. Goods and Services." Feb. 10.

Caldwell, John C. 1986. "Routes to Low Mortality in Poor Countries." *Population and Development Review* 12, no. 2: 171–212.

Campanella, M. 1993. "The Effects of Globalization and Turbulence on the Policy-Making Process." *Government and Opposition* 28: 190–205.

Cassen, Robert, and Associates. 1994. *Does Aid Work?* 2d ed. Oxford: Clarendon Press.

Cheng, Chen. 1961. *Land Reform in Taiwan.* Taipei: Chinn Publishing.

Chowaniec, Jan, and David K. Harbinson. 1994. "An Alternative Approach to American Foreign Aid: Regional Partnership in Poland." *East European Quarterly* 28, no. 1: 131–51.

Clad, James C., and Roger D. Stone. 1993. "Foreign Aid for Sustainable Development." *Foreign Affairs* 72 (Jan.): 196–205.

Congressional Research Service. 1986. *Trends in Foreign Aid, 1977–86.* Foreign Affairs and National Defense Division, CRS. Study Prepared for the Select Committee on Hunger, House of Representatives. Washington, D.C., Nov.

Council of the European Communities. 1989. Compilation of texts adopted by the Council of Ministers for Development Co-operation, 1 Jan. 1981–31 Dec. 1988. Brussels.

Crouch, Colin, and David Marquand, eds. 1992. *Towards Greater Europe? A Continent Without an Iron Curtain.* Oxford: Blackwell.

Curry, Robert L., Jr. 1994. "Issues in Official Development Assistance to Vietnam." *Journal of Third World Studies* 11, no. 1: 262–81.

Dahrendorf, Ralf. 1990. *Reflections on the Revolution in Europe: In a Letter Intended to Have Been Sent to a Gentleman in Warsaw 1990.* London: Chatto & Windus.

Davidson, Basil. 1993. *The Search for Africa.* New York: Random House.

DePalma, Anthony. 1994. "U.S. Wife's Resolute Quest Shakes Guatemala." *New York Times,* Nov. 6.

*Development Cooperation: Aid in Transition.* 1993, 1994. Paris: OECD.

Doherty, Carroll J. 1995. "Pared-Back Foreign Aid Bill Heads for the House Floor." *Congressional Quarterly Weekly,* June 17: 1760–63.

Dreze, Jean, and Amartya Sen. 1992. *Hunger and Public Action.* Oxford: Oxford Univ. Press.

Drysdale, Alasdair. 1993. "Syria since 1988: From Crisis to Opportunity." In *The Middle East after Iraq's Invasion of Kuwait,* edited by Robert O. Freedman, 276–96. Gainesville: Univ. Press of Florida.

*EC Courier.* 1981. Brussels: The European Commission.

———. 1993. Brussels. The European Commission.

*The Economist.* 1993. "EC Aid to the East: Good Intentions, Poor Performance." Apr. 10.

———. 1994. "Japan Survey. Death of a Role Model." July 9.

Ek, Rolf, and Hans-Olof Stjernström. 1993. *Det Internationella Biståndet Och Samarbetet Med Central Och steuropa: Med Fokusering På EGs Bistånd.* Stockholm: NUTEK.

Escobar, Arturo. 1995. *Encountering Development: The Making and Unmaking of the Third World.* Princeton: Princeton Univ. Press.

European Bank for Reconstruction and Development (EBRD). 1992. *A Challenging Europe: EBRD 1991 Annual Report.* London: EBRD.

European Commission. 1995. *G-24 Assistance to the Countries of Central and Eastern Europe, 1990–1994.* Brussels: European Commission, Directorate General, G-24 Coordination Unit.

*The Europe-South Dialogue.* 1988. Luxembourg: Office for Official Publications of the European Communities.

Farah, Douglas. 1994. "Salvador's Leader Says Aid Cuts Pose Threat." *Washington Post,* Mar. 11, p. 5.

Ferguson, James. 1990. *The Anti-Politics Machine: Development, Depoliticization and Bureaucratic Power in Lesotho.* London: Cambridge Univ. Press.

*Financial Times.* 1992. "European Bank for Reconstruction and Development," Apr. 15.

———. 1994. "Excess Gives Way to Restraint," Mar. 4.

Freedman, Robert O., ed. 1993. *The Middle East after Iraq's Invasion of Kuwait.* Gainesville: Univ. Press of Florida.

Friedman, Milton. 1958. "Foreign Economic Aid." *Yale Review* 47, no. 4: 500–516.

Fukuyama, Francis. 1992. *The End of History and the Last Man.* London: Hamish Hamilton.

Gellner, Ernest. 1994. *Conditions of Liberty: Civil Society and Its Rivals.* London: Hamish Hamilton.

General Accounting Office (GAO). 1993. *Foreign Assistance: AID Strategic Direction and Continued Management Improvements Needed.* Washington, D.C.: Report to the Congress.

———. 1995a. *Former Soviet Union: U.S. Bilateral Programs Lack Effective Coordination.* Washington, D.C.: Report to Congressional Committees.

———. 1995b. *Poland—Economic Restructuring and Donor Assistance.* Washington, D.C.: Report to Congressional Committees.

Goldgeier, James M., and Michael McFaul. 1992. "A Tale of Two Worlds: Core and Periphery in the Post–Cold War Era." *International Organization* 46 (spring): 467–91.

Greenhouse, Steven. 1995. "U.S., Protesting Rights Abuses, Ends Military Aid to Guatemala." *New York Times,* Mar. 11.

Grieve, Malcolm J. 1993. "International Assistance and Democracy: Assessing Efforts to Assist Post-Communist Development." *Studies in Comparative International Development* 27, no. 4: 80–101.

Havel, Vaclav. 1994. "A Call for Sacrifice." *Foreign Affairs* 73 (spring): 2–7.

Hewitt, Adrian, ed. 1994. *Crisis or Transition in Foreign Aid.* London: Overseas Development Institute.

Holdar, Sven. 1993a. "Helping Others or Yourself? A Political Geography of  Foreign Aid." Ph.D. diss., Univ. of Colorado.

———. 1993b. "The Study of Foreign Aid: Unbroken Ground in Geography." *Progress in Human Geography* 17, no. 4: 453–70.

Hook, Steven. 1995. *National Interest and Foreign Aid.* Boulder, Colo.: Lynne Rienner.

Hyden, Goran. 1983. *No Shortcuts to Progress: African Development Management in Perspective.* Berkeley: Univ. of California Press.

Inoguchi, Takashi. 1993. *Japan's Foreign Policy in an Era of Global Change.* New York: St. Martin's.

*International Economic Insights.* 1994. "What's a BEM?" Mar.–Apr., 12.

International Monetary Fund (IMF). 1994a. "Camdessus Urges Stabilization and Reform." *IMF Survey*, Feb. 7, 42–48.

———. 1994b. *World Economic Outlook, May 1994*. Washington, D.C.: IMF.

———. 1995. *United Germany: The First Five Years, Performance and Policy Issues*. Washington, D.C.: IMF.

———. 1966–96. *Direction of Trade Statistics Yearbook*. Washington, D.C.: IMF.

———. 1966–96. *International Financial Statistics Yearbook*. Washington, D.C.: IMF.

Ishii, Takashi. 1994. "Creating Stability and Growth for Developing Nations." Interview with Akira Nishigaki, President of the Overseas Economic Cooperation Fund. *Japan 21st Century* (Jan.): 12–13.

Islam, Shafiqul. 1993. "Foreign Aid and Burdensharing: Is Japan Free Riding to a Coprosperity Sphere in Pacific Asia?" In *Regionalism and Rivalry: Japan and the United States in Pacific Asia*, edited by Jeffrey Frankel and Miles Kahler, 321–72. Chicago: Univ. of Chicago Press.

*Japan Economic Review*. 1994. "New Boost to the System, Functions of the Japan International Cooperation Agency (JICA)," June 15, 10.

Jepma, Catrinus J. 1991. *The Tying of Aid*. Paris: OECD.

Joffé, E. George H. 1994. "Relations between the Middle East and the West." *Middle East Journal* 48 (spring): 250–67.

Karawan, Ibrahim. 1994. "Arab Dilemmas in the 1990s: Breaking Taboos and Searching for Signposts." *Middle East Journal* 48 (summer): 433–54.

Keddie, Nikki. 1992. "The End of the Cold War and the Middle East." *Diplomatic History* 16 (winter): 95–103.

Kennedy, David, and David E. Webb. 1990. "Integration: Eastern Europe and the European Economic Communities." *Columbia Journal of Transnational Law* 28, no. 3: 635–75.

Kerr, Malcolm. 1971. *The Arab Cold War*. New York: Oxford Univ. Press.

Khouri, Rami G. 1991. "The Post-War Middle East." *The Link* 24, no. 1: 1–11.

Killick, Tony. 1990. *The Developmental Effectiveness of Aid to Africa*. Working Paper (WPS 646). Washington, D.C.: World Bank, International Economics Department.

Kissinger, Henry. 1994. *Diplomacy*. New York: Simon & Schuster.

Klaus, Vadev. 1994. "So Far, So Good." *The Economist*, Sept. 10.

Koppel, Bruce M. 1993. "The Prospects for Democratization in Southeast Asia: Local Perspectives and International Roles." *Journal of Northeast Asian Studies* 12, no. 3: 3–33.

Kramer, Henry. 1993. "The European Community's Response to the 'New Eastern Europe.'" *Journal of Common Market Studies* 31, no. 2: 213–44.

Kuo, Shirley. 1994. "The Taiwanese Economy in the 1990s." In *Taiwan in the Asia-Pacific in the 1990s*, edited by Gary Klintworth, 89–105. St. Leonards: Allen & Unwin.

Langguth, Gerd. 1992. "The Single European Market: Also an Opportunity for Eastern Europe?" *Aussen Politik* 43, no. 2: 107–14.

Lappé, Frances M., Joseph Collins, and David Kinley. 1981. *Aid as Obstacle:*

*Twenty Questions about Our Foreign Aid and Hunger.* San Francisco: Institute for Food First and Development Policy.

Laux, Jean. 1991. *Reform, Reintegration and Regional Security: The Role of Western Assistance in Overcoming Insecurity in Central and Eastern Europe.* Working Paper 37. Ottawa: Canadian Institute for International Peace and Security.

Lebovic, John H. 1988. "National Interests and US Foreign Aid: The Carter and Reagan Years." *Journal of Peace Research* 25, no. 2: 115–35.

Light, M. 1992. "Moscow's Retreat from Africa." *Journal of Communist Studies* 8, no. 2: 21–40.

Lippman, Thomas W. 1995. "Senate Votes 10 Percent Cut in Foreign Aid." *Washington Post,* Sept. 23.

Lofgren, Hans. 1993. "Economic Policy in Egypt: A Breakdown in Reform Resistance." *International Journal of Middle East Studies* 25 (Aug.): 407–21.

Lowenthal, Mark. 1991. "U.S. Foreign Aid in a Changing World: Options for New Priorities." Report for the Committee on Foreign Affairs of the House of Representatives. Washington, D.C.: Congressional Research Service.

Lumsdaine, David H. 1993. *Moral Vision in International Politics: The Foreign Aid Regime, 1949–1989.* Princeton: Princeton Univ. Press.

Malek, Mohammed H. 1991. *Contemporary Issues in European Development Aid.* Aldershot, U.K.: Avebury.

Marquis, Christopher. 1993a. "Nicaragua Still Looking to U.S. for Answers." *Miami Herald,* May 17.

———. 1993b. "U.S. Demands Nicaraguan Reforms as Condition to Aid." *Miami Herald,* Aug. 13.

Mastropasqua, Cristina, and Vakeria Rolli. 1994. "Industrial Countries' Protectionism with Respect to Eastern Europe: The Impact of Association Agreements Concluded with the EC on Exports of Poland, Czechoslovakia and Hungary." *The World Economy* 17, no. 2: 151–69.

Maull, Hans W. 1991. "Germany and Japan: The New Civilian Powers." *Foreign Affairs* 64: 91–106.

———. 1992. "Japan's Global Environmental Policies." In *International Politics of the Environment,* edited by Andrew Hurrell and Benedict Kingsbury, 354–72. Oxford: Clarendon Press.

McCawley, Peter. 1993. "Development Assistance in Asia." *Asian-Pacific Economic Literature* 7, no. 2: 1–13.

McKinlay, Robert D., and R. Little. 1978. "A Foreign Policy Model of the Distribution of British Bilateral Aid: 1960–70." *British Journal of Political Science* 8 (July): 313–22.

Merritt, Giles. 1991. *Eastern Europe and the USSR: The Challenge of Freedom.* Luxembourg and London: Kogan Page.

Mesarovic, Stephan J. 1994. *The Balkanization of the West: The Confluence of Postmodernism and Postcommunism.* London: Routledge.

Meyer, Charles G. 1992. "1992 and the Constitutional Development of Eastern Europe." *Virginia Journal of International Law* 32, no. 2: 431–69.

*The Middle East and North Africa, 1994.* 1994. London: Europa Publications.

*Middle East Review, 1993/94.* 1994. Essex: Saffron Walden.

Ministry of Foreign Affairs (MOFA). 1991. *Japan's ODA. Official Development Assistance Annual Report.* Tokyo: Ministry of Foreign Affairs.

————. 1992. *Japan's ODA. Official Development Assistance Annual Report.* Tokyo: Ministry of Foreign Affairs.

————. 1993. *Japan's ODA. Official Development Assistance Annual Report.* Tokyo: Ministry of Foreign Affairs.

————. 1994. *Japan's ODA. Official Development Assistance Annual Report.* Tokyo: Ministry of Foreign Affairs.

Morrissey, Oliver. 1993. "The Mixing of Aid and Trade Policies." *World Economy* 16 (Jan.): 69–84.

Mosley, Paul. 1991. *Aid and Power: The World Bank and Policy Based Lending.* Vols. 1–2. New York: Routledge.

Muniz, B. 1980. "EEC–Latin America: A Relationship to Be Defined." *Journal of Common Market Studies* 29, no. 1: 55–64.

Mytelka, Lynn, and M. Dolan. 1980. "The EEC and the ACP Countries." In *Integration and Unequal Development: The Experience of the EEC,* edited by Dudley Seers and C. Varitsos, 237–60. London: Macmillan.

Neff, Donald. 1990. "American Aid to Israel: the Facts." *Middle East International,* June 8, 18–19.

Nello, Susan S. 1991. *The New Europe: Changing Economic Relations Between East and West.* London: Harvester-Wheatsheaf.

Ners, Krzysztof. 1992. *Moving Beyond Assistance.* New York: Institute for East/West Studies.

*New York Times.* 1994. "Balanced Budget: What One Would Look Like." Nov. 28.

————. 1995. "Call It Aid or a Bribe, It's the Price of Peace." Mar. 26, E3.

Nijman, Jan. 1993. *The Geopolitics of Power and Conflict: Superpowers in the International System, 1945–1992.* London: Belhaven.

Nowels, Larry Q. 1994. "Foreign Policy Budget Request for FY 1995: A New Framework for the Post–Cold War World." Report for Congress, Feb. 23. Washington, D.C.: Congressional Research Service.

————. 1995. "Foreign Aid Budget and Policy Issues for the 104th Congress." CRS Issue Brief.

Organization for Economic Cooperation and Development (OECD)(a). 1978–96. *Development and Co-operation.* Paris: OECD.

————(b). 1966–1996. *Geographical Distribution of Financial Flows to Developing Countries.* Paris: OECD.

Orr, Robert. M. 1990. "Japanese Foreign Aid in a New Global Era." *SAIS [School of Advanced International Studies] Review* 11 (summer/fall): 135–48.

Østergaard, Clements S. 1993. "Values for Money? Political Conditionality in Aid: The Case of China." *European Journal of Development Research* 5, no. 1: 112–34.

Pack, Howard, and Janet Rothenberg Pack. 1993. "Foreign Aid and the Question of Fungibility." *Review of Economics and Statistics* 75, no. 2: 258–65.

Papanek, Gustav F. 1973. "Aid, Foreign Private Investment, Savings and Growth in Less Developed Countries." *Journal of Political Economy* 81, no. 1: 121–30.

Pelkmans, Jacques, and Alexander Murphy. 1991. "Catapulted into Leadership: The Community's Trade and Aid Policies Vis-à-vis Eastern Europe." *Journal of European Integration* 14, no. 2–3: 125–51.

Pelletreau, Robert H. 1995. "FY 1996 Economic Programs for Promoting Peace in the Middle East." *Dispatch* 6, no. 21: 432–37.

Pitzl, Gerald R. 1995. "The 'Northern Territories' Controversy: A Four-Decade Stalemate between Japan and Russia." Pew Case Study no. 364. Pew Case Studies in International Affairs, Georgetown University.

Pletsch, Carl. 1981. "The Three Worlds, Or the Division of Social Scientific Labor, circa 1950–75." *Comparative Studies in Society and History* 23: 565–90.

Pomian, Krzystof. 1994. "Klopoty Europy." *Polityka* 1917, no. 5 (Jan.).

Pradetto, August. 1992. "Transformation in Eastern Europe, International Cooperation, and the German Position." *Studies in Comparative Communism* 25, no. 1: 23–30.

Preeg, Ernest H. 1993. "The Aid for Trade Debate." *Washington Quarterly* 16 (winter): 99–114.

Rabie, Mohamed. 1988. *The Politics of Foreign Aid: U.S. Foreign Assistance and Aid to Israel.* New York: Praeger.

Radio Free Europe/Radio Liberty (RFE/RL). 1993a. "Chernomyrdin Sees a Western Plot." *RFE/RL Daily Report No. 159,* Aug. 20. Washington, D.C.: RFE/RL Research Institute.

———. 1993b. "Western Aid Said to Be Misdirected." *RFE/RL Daily Report No. 233,* Dec. 7. Washington, D.C.: RFE/RL Research Institute.

———. 1993c. "Yavlinsky Criticizes Yeltsin." *RFE/RL Daily Report No. 216,* Nov. 10. Washington, D.C.: RFE/RL Research Institute.

Richburg, Keith. 1992. "How America Left Somalia Behind: The Country Went from Pivotal Ally to Cold War Orphan." *Washington Post,* National Weekly Edition, Oct. 26.

Riddell, Roger. 1992. "European Aid to Sub-Saharan Africa: Performance in the 1980s and Future Prospects." *European Journal of Development Research* 4, no. 2: 59–80.

Rohter, Larry. 1995. "U.S. Prods Nicaragua on Seized Land." *New York Times,* July 25.

Roskins, Ronald. 1990. "Address by the Administrator of USAID before the Fertilizer Institute, San Francisco, September 17." In *American Foreign Policy Current Documents,* 127–28. Washington, D.C.: Department of State.

Rostow, Walt Whitman. 1990. *The Stages of Economic Growth: A Non-Communist Manifesto.* 3d ed. New York and Melbourne: Cambridge Univ. Press.

Sachs, Jeffrey. 1994. "Russia's Struggle with Stabilization: Conceptual Issues and Evidence." Annual Bank Conference on Development Economics (ABCDE). Unpublished paper. Washington, D.C.: World Bank.

Sachs, Jeffrey, and C. Wyplosz. 1994. "How the West Should Help Russian Reform." *Financial Times,* Jan. 11.

Sadowski, Yahya. 1991. "Arab Economies after the Gulf War." *Middle East Report* 170 (May–June): 4–10.

———. 1992. "Scuds vs. Butter: The Political Economy of Arms Control in the Arab World." *Middle East Report* 177 (July–Aug.): 2–13.

Sarcinelli, Mario. 1992. "Scarcity of Capital and the Reconstruction of Eastern Europe: A Challenge and the Role of the EBRD." *Review of Economic Conditions in Italy* 1: 9–24.

Schöpflin, George. 1993. *Politics in Eastern Europe, 1945–1992*. Oxford: Blackwell.

Schröder, Klaus. 1991. "Western Financial Assistance for Reforms in Eastern Europe: Conditions and Risks." *Aussen Politik* 42, no. 4: 326–35.

Schultz, S. 1991. "Trends and Issues of German Aid Policy." In *Contemporary Issues in European Development Aid*, edited by Mohammed H. Malek, 45–64. Aldershot, U.K.: Avebury.

Semmel, Anthony K. 1984. "Evolving Patterns of US Security Assistance, 1950–1980." In *The Global Agenda: Issues and Perspectives*, edited by Charles W. Kegley and Eugene R. Wittkopf, 114–36. New York: Random House.

Sewell, John W. 1991. "Foreign Aid for a New World Order." *Washington Quarterly* 14 (summer): 181–91.

Shultz, George C. 1984. "Foreign Aid and U.S. Policy Objectives." Statement Before the House Foreign Affairs Committee, Feb. 9, Current Policy No. 548. Washington, D.C.: Department of State, Bureau of Public Affairs.

Stuurgroep. 1991. *Impactstudie Medefinancieringsprogramma: Betekenis van het Medefinancieringsprogramma: een Verkenning*. Utrecht.

Sullivan, Denis J. 1990. "Bureaucracy and Foreign Aid in Egypt: The Primacy of Politics." In *The Political Economy of Contemporary Egypt*, edited by Ibrahim M. Oweiss, 20–36. Washington, D.C.: Center for Contemporary Arab Studies.

Szacki, Jan. 1994. *Liberalizm Po Komunizmie*. Kraków: Znak.

Sztompka, Piotr. 1993. *The Sociology of Social Change*. Oxford: Blackwell.

Tadem, Eduardo C. 1990. "Japan, the US, and Official Development Assistance to the Philippines." *Philippine Development Review* 5, no. 3–4: 127–54.

Tarnoff, Curt, and Larry Q. Nowels. 1993. "Foreign Assistance and Commercial Interests: The Aid for Trade Debate." Report for Congress, May 24. Washington, D.C.: Congressional Research Service.

Treverton, Gregory F. 1992. "The New Europe." *Foreign Affairs* 71, no. 1: 94–112.

United Nations. 1991. *International Trade Statistics*. New York: UN.

———. 1993. *Commodity Trade Statistics, 1992*. Geneva: UN.

United Nations Conference for Trade and Development (UNCTAD). 1992. *International Monetary and Financial Issues for the 1990s: Research Papers for the Group of Twenty-Four*. Vol. 1. New York: UN.

United Nations Economic Commission for Europe (UNECE). 1992. *Economic Survey of Europe in 1991–1992*. Geneva: UN, Economic Commission for Europe.

———. 1993. *Economic Survey of Europe in 1992–1993*. Geneva: UN Economic Commission for Europe.

————. 1994. *Economic Survey of Europe in 1993–1994.* Geneva: UN Economic Commission for Europe.

————. 1995. *Economic Survey of Europe in 1994–1995.* Geneva: UN Economic Commission for Europe.

United States Agency for International Development (USAID). 1994a. *The Peace, Prosperity & Democracy Act (PPDA) of 1994.* Washington, D.C.: Government Printing Office.

————. 1994b. *Strategies for Sustainable Development.* March. Washington, D.C.: USAID.

————. 1996. *FY 1996 U.S. Economic and Military Assistance Request.* Washington, D.C.: USAID.

————. 1966–96. *US Overseas Loans and Grants, and Assistance from International Organizations.* Washington, D.C.: Government Printing Office.

United States Government. 1994. *Fiscal Year 1995 International Affairs Budget Request.* Washington, D.C: Department of State, Bureau of Public Affairs.

Van Brabant, Jozef M. 1992. "Silent Features of the Economic and Political Transformations in the East." *Journal of Development Planning* 23: 5–44.

Van der Wusten, H. 1992. "A New World Order (No Less)." *The Professional Geographer* 44: 19–22.

Van Ham, Piotr. 1993. *The EC, Eastern Europe and European Unity: Discord, Collaboration and Integration since 1947.* London: Pinter.

Vernon, Raymond, and Deborah Sparr. 1989. *Beyond Globalism.* New York: Free Press.

Walesa, Lech. 1991. *The Struggle and the Triumph: An Autobiography.* New York: Arcade Publishing.

Wandycz, P. 1992. *The Price of Freedom: A History of East Central Europe from the Middle Ages to the Present.* London: Routledge.

*Washington Post National Weekly Edition.* 1994. "Helms Aims His Guns at the Foreign Aid Budget." Nov. 28.

Weber, Stephen. 1994. "Origins of the European Bank for Reconstruction and Development." *International Organizations* 48, no. 1: 1–38.

Weinbaum, Marvin G. 1986. "Dependent Development and U.S. Economic Aid to Egypt." *International Journal of Middle East Studies* 19 (May): 119–34.

Weiner, Tim. 1995. "Tale of Evasion of Ban on Aid for Guatemala." *New York Times,* Mar. 30.

Wellard, K., and J. G. Copestake. 1993. *Non-Governmental Organizations and the State in Africa: Rethinking Roles in Sustainable Agricultural Development.* New York: Routledge.

Wenger, Martha. 1990. "The Money Tree: US Aid to Israel." *Middle East Report* 164–65 (May–Aug.): 12–13.

*West Africa.* 1993. "Diminishing Returns." (Jan. 10): 2229.

*Wharton Report.* 1993. "Preventive Diplomacy: Revitalizing A.I.D. and Foreign Assistance for the Post–Cold War Era." Report of the Task Force to Reform A.I.D. and the International Affairs Budget. Washington, D.C.: Government Printing Office.

White, John. 1974. *The Politics of Foreign Aid.* New York: St. Martin's.

White Paper. 1992. *Reinventing Foreign Aid: White Paper on US Development*

*Cooperation in a New Democratic Era.* The Independent Group on the Future of US Development Cooperation. Facilitated and supported by the Overseas Development Council and the Rockefeller Foundation, Dec.

Wilkinson, Tracy. 1993. "A Legacy of Conflict and Confusion." *Los Angeles Times*, Oct. 17.

———. 1994. "Salvadorans Gird for Losses as Special Status in U.S. Ends." *Los Angeles Times*, Dec. 1.

Wilson, Rodney. 1989. "The Islamic Development Bank's Role as an Aid Agency for Moslem Countries." *Journal of International Development* 1, no. 2: 444–66.

Wingborg, Mats. 1993. *EG Och Tredje Världen: Bistånd, Tullar Och Flyktingpolitik.* Stockholm: TCO.

Wood, R. E. 1986. *From Marshall Plan to Debt Crisis: Foreign Aid and Development Choices in the World Economy.* Berkeley and Los Angeles: Univ. of California Press.

World Bank. 1988. *Evaluation Results for 1988: Issues in World Bank Lending Over Two Decades.* Washington, D.C.: World Bank.

———. 1989. *World Development Report 1989.* Washington, D.C.: World Bank.

———. 1992. *World Development Report 1992.* Washington, D.C.: World Bank.

———. 1993. *World Development Report 1993.* Washington, D.C.: World Bank.

———. 1994a. *World Development Report 1994.* Washington, D.C.: World Bank.

———. 1994b. *World Tables.* Washington, D.C.: World Bank.

———. 1995. *Strengthening the Effectiveness of Aid: Lessons for Donors.* Washington, D.C.: World Bank.

Yasutomo, Dennis T. 1993. "The Politicization of Japan's 'Post–Cold War' Multilateral Diplomacy." In *Japan's Foreign Policy after the Cold War: Coping with Change,* edited by Gerald L. Curtis, 323–46. New York: Sharpe.

Zakaria, Fareed. 1994. "Culture Is Destiny." *Foreign Affairs* 73 (spring): 109–26.

Zimmerman, Robert F. 1993. *Dollars, Diplomacy, and Dependency: Dilemmas of U.S. Economic Aid.* Boulder, Colo.: Lynne Rienner.

# Index

*Italic page number denotes illustration.*

Afghanistan: Soviet invasion of, 86; U.S. aid to, 40
Africa: aid and international position of, 95–97; aid donors as having lost faith in, 191; aid patterns changing in, 90–93; annual aid during 1980s, 89; Asian aid to, 92; after Cold War, 90–91, 92–93, 157; colonial trade, 97–98; debt, 96–97; economic development in, 98–101; European aid to, 61, 63, 67, 68; exports, 97–98; failure of long-term aid in, 189; foreign aid to, 89–102; French involvement in, 93; inter-African aid, 92; intra-African trade, 97–98; Japanese aid to, 46, *51*, 52–53; major aid recipients, 1989–90, *90;* nongovernmental aid to, 93–95; official development assistance in 1990, 89; per capita aid in 1990, 89; poverty in, 11; private capital flow, 95–96; regional share of U.S. aid, *39*, 40; rent mentality in governments of, 101–2; structural adjustment programs in, 99–101; trade patterns, 97–98; U.S. aid to, 31, *39, 40*, 93; World Bank projects, 100. *See also* Egypt; North Africa; Sub-Saharan Africa
African Development Bank, 98
Agnew, John A., 186
agriculture: in European community trade policy, 63; Japanese aid for, 55; OECD subsidies for, 177, 187
aid addiction, 4, 89, 189
aid fatigue, 152
"aid for trade," 33
AIDS Summit Meeting (1994), 153
aid tying. *See* tied aid
Ake, Claude, 93
Albania: aid committed to, *119;* in the Balkans, 117; Italian aid to, 119; official aid disbursements, 1991–92, *121*
Algeria: aid increase, 1983–89, 91; aid increase, 1989–91, 91; aid increase, 1989–93, 92; debt, 96; European trade agreements

with, 64; French trade with, 98; negative capital flow, 96; official development assistance receipts, 1993, *79*
Alliance for Progress, 103
Angola: aid, 1983–89, 91; civil war in, 92; as Cold War orphan, 184; elite rampaging in, 102; South African development aid to, 92; Soviet aid to, 184
APEC (Asia Pacific Economic Cooperation), 186
Arab Cold War, 84–85
Argentina: dams, 25; in U.S. "Big Emerging Markets Strategy," 38
Armenia: official aid disbursements, 1991–92, *121;* U.S. aid to, 119
Arndt, Dorothea, 140
ASEAN (Association of South East Asian Nations), 64–65, 130, 131, 142–43
Ash, Timothy G., 127
Asia. *See* Asia-Pacific Rim
Asian Development Bank, 165
Asian development model, 8, 193
Asia Pacific Economic Cooperation (APEC), 186
Asia-Pacific Rim: adjusting to new aid regime, 8; authoritarian market economies in, 144; emerging economies as U.S. markets, 151; European aid to, 63, 64; foreign aid to, 130–44; as growth region, 130; Japanese aid for penetrating markets of, 46; Japanese aid to, 50–51, *51,* 53, 54, 58, 143, 153, 189; in New World Order, 144; nongovernmental aid to, 132; ODA and development in, 137–40; official development assistance disbursement in, 131–37; political change and aid in, 140–43; poverty in, 11; public infrastructure investment returns, *20;* regional share of U.S. aid, *39, 40;* values of, 142, 193. *See also* Central Asia; East Asia; South Asia; Southeast Asia
assistance to transition, 162

## 224 Index

Uzbekistan: Japanese aid to, 52; official aid disbursements, 1991–92, *121;* Turkish aid to, 120

Van Brabant, Jozef M., 124
Van der Wusten, H., 191
Van Ham, Piotr, 114
Vernon, Raymond, 30
Vietnam: Dutch relations with, 159; Japanese aid to, 58, 154; Japanese war reparations, 46; market-oriented economy without political liberalization, 144; ODA and development in, 139, 140; official development assistance to, 136; percentage change of net ODA receipts, 1978–93, *133;* political change and aid in, 141; share in ODA disbursements, 1987–93, *135;* Western culture in, 139
Vietnam War, 31, 38
Visegrad Four: actual aid disbursed, 120; aid committed to, 118; as Eastern European area, 117; European Union and NATO membership sought in, 127; in German orbit, 127; market reform in, 124; official aid disbursements, 1991–92, 121; regional aid as concentrated in, 125, 127. *See also* Czech Republic; Hungary; Poland; Slovakia

Walesa, Lech, 116
Wandycz, P., 126
Webb, David E., 127
Weinbaum, Marvin G., 83
Wellard, K., 95
Wenger, Martha, 82
West Bank, U.S. aid to, 81
"West-East-South" program (The Netherlands), 157
Western Africa: Chad, 99–100; Niger, 99; public infrastructure investment returns, *20;* Togo, 99. *See also* Benin; Burkina Faso; Cameroon; Ghana; Guinea; Ivory Coast; Liberia; Mali; Nigeria; Senegal; Sierra Leone
Western Europe: regional share of U.S. aid, *39. See also* European Union
*Wharton Report* (1993), 34, 35
White, John, 62
Wilson, Rodney, 78
Wingborg, Mats, 64, 68
women: in Dutch aid policy, 157; education

of girls in Bangladesh, 166–67; Japan's "women in development" policy, 55, 59, 154
Wood, R. E., 63
World Bank (International Bank for Reconstruction and Development; IBRD): African projects, 100; Bangladesh aid, 165; Bolivian aid, 170; conditional aid programs, 23–24; conditions on aid to Eastern Europe, 124; in Eastern European transition, 116–17, 118; elite economic and political ideology of, 5; on health program effectiveness, 19; Japanese loans, 45; Japan's role in, 60; Keynes's view of poverty in creation of, 12; loan commitments to Africa, 93; as multilateral assistance agency, 4; public infrastructure investment, 19–20, *20;* Russian criticism of, 125; senior creditor clause, 20; size reduction for, 26; social fund channeled through NGOs, 94; structural adjustment loans, 99
Wyplosz, C., 72

Yaoundé treaties, 62, 63
Yasutomo, Dennis T., 59
Yavlinsky, Grigorii, 125
Yeltsin, Boris, 116
Yemen: official development assistance receipts, 1993, *79;* Soviet aid suspension, 78; U.S. aid to, 81
Yom Kippur War, 33
Yugoslavia (former): aid committed to, *119;* in the Balkans, 117; Croatia, 119; economic performance in, 125; European aid to, 68; European Union mediation efforts in, 73; U.S. aid to, 119. *See also* Bosnia-Herzegovina; Macedonia; Slovenia

Zaire: aid decrease, 1989–91, 91; aid to, 1980–89, *90;* as Cold War orphan, 184; European aid to, 65; Japanese aid policy regarding, 58; per capita GNP, 1980–90, 99; taxes compared with aid in, 102; as U.S. security aid recipient, 34, 42, 184
Zambia: aid increase, 1989–91, 91; aid increase, 1989–93, 92
Zimbabwe: aid increase, 1989–93, 92; South Africa development aid to, 92
Zimmerman, Robert F., 34, 84

*The Global Crisis in Foreign Aid* was composed in 10.5/13 Ehrhardt MT in QuarkXpress 4.0 on a Macintosh by Kachergis Book Design; printed by sheet-fed offset on 50-pound, acid-free Natural Smooth, and Smyth-sewn and bound over binder's boards in Arrestox B-grade cloth with dust jackets printed in 2 colors and laminated by Braun-Brumfield; designed by Kachergis Book Design of Pittsboro, North Carolina; published by Syracuse University Press, Syracuse, New York 13244-5160.